FEELING

Psychologically Treated,

AND

PROLEGOMENA TO PSYCHOLOGY.

BY

DENTON J. SNIDER

ISBN: 979-8-89096-268-3

All Rights reserved. No part of this book maybe reproduced without written permission from the publishers, except by a reviewer who may quote brief passages in a review to be printed in a newspaper or magazine.

Printed: 2023

Published and Distributed By:
Lushena Books
607 Country Club Drive, Unit E
Bensenville, IL 60106
www.lushenabks.com

ISBN: 979-8-89096-268-3

CONTENTS.

	PAGE.
PROLEGOMENA TO PSYCHOLOGY	i
A PHENOMENOLOGY	iv
THE EGO	x
THE UNIVERSAL SCIENCE	xiii
THE PSYCHOSIS	xix
THE TRIAD	xxvii
FEELING, WILLING, AND KNOWING	xliii
PRIMACY IN GENERAL	l
PRIMACY OF THE WILL	lvii
METHOD OF PSYCHOLOGY	lxviii
PROBLEM OF SENSATION	lxxvii
DOCTRINE OF PARALLELISM	lxxxvi
THOUGHT IN PSYCHOLOGY	xcvi
CONSCIOUSNESS	cv
PSYCHOLOGICAL NORM	cxi
DIVISIONS	cxxv
PEDAGOGICAL	cxxvii

CONTENTS.

	PAGE.
FEELING	
INTRODUCTION	5
PART FIRST.—ELEMENTAL FEELING	20
SECT. I. SELF-FEELING	24
SIMPLE FEELING	30
DOUBLE FEELING	36
TOTAL FEELING	57
SECT. II. WORLD-FEELING	67
COSMICAL	72
SOMATIC	87
REPRODUCTIVE	102
SECT. III. ALL-FEELING	113
THE ENDOWED SELF: PRECONSCIOUS	120
THE CONSCIOUS SELF	132
THE FREE SELF	212
PART SECOND.—FINITE FEELING	218
SECT. I. IMPRESSION	224
SECT. II. EMOTION	244
SECT. III. SYMPATHY	271
PART THIRD.—ABSOLUTE FEELING	294
SECT. I. RELIGIOUS SENTIMENT	309
SECT. II. PRACTICAL SENTIMENT	336
SECT. III. THEORETIC SENTIMENT	363

Prolegomena to Psychology.

Ours is an age of specialization. The details of knowledge lie scattered about us in enormous and ever-increasing heaps, with as yet little organization. No science, since the decline if not dethronement of Philosophy, has been able to vindicate itself as the ordering principle of our chaotic piles of experience. Still the prayers for some such science have become loud, and endeavors have been made to point it out in an uncertain, temporizing manner. But when an attempt to formulate it is made, we behold little else than a hasty retreat to some bygone philosophical system. In such an emergency all are turning to a new science, or rather to an old science rejuvenating itself with a new spirit and aspiration.

Psychology has declared itself, as the American colonies once did upon a memorable occasion, free and independent. If we glance through the introductions of recent books on this subject, we find them striking a more or less triumphant note of the grand liberation. No longer an enslaved science, subject to Metaphysics on the one side and to Natural Science on the other: let us celebrate the glorious victory. Thus in general a happy undertone is heard singing through the work of many a psychologist in these days, rising sometimes into a kind of Fourth-of-July jubilation.

Of the fact indicated there is no doubt. Nothing can be more evident than the movement away from Philosophy into Psychology, which is now studied almost universally in our higher institutions of education and is coming to be regarded, even if vaguely and presentimentally, as the central discipline of thought. Moreover Physical Science is perceptibly retiring from the foreground which it occupied not many years ago, no longer dominating the psychical domain, but rather being dominated by it. Even experimental Psychology, whose disciples have certainly not been deficient in self-assertion, is beginning to see its own limits, and to get a little modest, at least in some of its propagators who recognize that their science has had and still has a good deal to give the world in the realm of Feeling and Sensation, much less in that of Representation, and little or nothing in that of Thought and Reason. And yet Thought and Reason belong to the *Psyche* and its science, which must, therefore, make a new delimitation of itself.

Let us all, then, rejoice with the rejoicers that Psychology, having gone through its long discipline of servitude to alien masters, and gotten the training thereof, has attained self-mastery and freedom.

And now comes the new problem, for the movement cannot stop at this point or at any other for that matter. What will Psychology do with her freedom? Such is the looming question, enough to run a few sober lines of deliberation, if not of anxiety, through our jubilating faces. Will she keep it all to herself, completely satisfied to have a good thing for her own private use, and merely remaining one individual science among many others, without further ambition? That, in our opinion, would be the best way to lose and to deserve to lose her deeply cherished, newly won boon. On the other hand will she become imperious and autocratic in her power, seeking to force her terms upon other sciences *from the outside?* We may recollect, in our readings of the past, that when Philosophy more than ever became the absolutist, and proceeded with an external might through its army of serried categories to subject the world in a kind of Napoleonic conquest, her seeming triumph rushed rapidly into an eclipse which has by no means yet lifted. Thus Psychology would relapse to Philosophy with its absolutism, to transcend which surely lies in her destiny.

If she is prepared to enter upon her heritage as the universal science, Psychology must be ready and eager to impart her freedom to other sciences, and organize such impartation. If she presents a general scheme or method which they are to adopt, it must be their own, and receive from them the seal of confirmation. If Psychology evidences them as her own, they must with equal force evidence her as their own. If she furnishes the law which they obey in their freedom, they must make her the law-maker. Each science, being self-legislative, must unite with the other sciences on that basis, and thereby form the one great Republic of Science with its own organic law. Thus we shall see that each science in legislating for itself or in determining its own method, has therein a common principle with all the rest, which common principle is also to have its formulation as science.

I.

Psychology has had a considerable history, which we may read in books. This means that it has gone through a long evolution with repeated changes in its conception. The prevailing conception of it at present is that it has simply to deal with the phenomena of Mind or Consciousness. To use a special term for this view, it is a PHENOMENOLOGY, a word employed in German Philosophy, though generally with a somewhat different purport. Moreover such a conception with its term shows its derivation from Kant, whose grand dualism between Phenomenon and Thing-in-itself lurks in the very definition of Psychology as at present conceived, even if this fact be unknown to most psychologists. Thus the thought (and we may add, the limitation) of the philosopher of Königsberg determines, more or less secretly to be sure, the definition and the procedure of our science to-day.

But for the sake of the future, we may try to look a little more deeply into this word. Psychology implies by its constituents that there is a *Logos* of the *Psyche*, which gives the ultimate processes of the Mind, Soul, Ego as they are in themselves, in their true reality, and not simply as they appear. Such a view intimates, even if from afar, that there is another and profounder side to Psychology than the merely phenomenal — a side which is not to be put down by being branded as metaphysical (as is usually done). Thus our science is to be, when fully unfolded, not another special science, but a kind of Logic (truly sprung from the *Logos*) of the Spirit which runs through and orders all sciences as products of Mind. This kind of Logic is indeed not the old Aristotelian one, nor the modern Hegelian one, but their complement and final evolution, which goes back to these and shows them to be earlier forms of itself in this line of development. Such an outlook comes to us when we peer into the depths of meaning which lie in the *Logos* of the *Psyche*, foreshadowing the approach of a new universal science.

Taken in its literal simplicity, Psychology signifies the science of the Soul, or of the Mind. Even such a definition gives to it a broad sweep which has been narrowed in various ways by different writers, who have in them the prevalent bent toward specialization. On the whole, however, Psychology shows a tendency to break over artificial restriction, and to persist in being the science of the Ego, which means the Self in the largest sense, including the human and rising to the divine Self.

At the present time, as already stated, the most common view of Psychology holds it to be the science of the phenomena of the mind, such as perception, sensation, memory, which this science finds and picks up (so to speak), and then proceeds to describe and to put into some kind of order. As there are phenomena of Nature with which physical science deals, so there are phenomena of Mind with which psychological science deals. As there are classes of flowers, so there are classes of mental activities; as there are strata of the earth in geology, so there are strata of mind in psychology. Thus both kinds of science, psychical and physical, treat of the phenomena, the facts as they appear, or are made to appear by experiment, and their common procedure is to describe and to order these facts.

Next we may note the difference in the two kinds. The geologist perceives the stratum and arranges it according to his scheme; but if he perceives himself perceiving the stratum, he no longer geologizes but psychologizes. The moment his mind passes from regarding the outer object to regarding its own activity he changes to a new field which has its distinct science. A wholly different set of phenomena rises to view, whose science is Psychology.

The preceding view of Psychology takes it to be one among many sciences, separate, independent. It is not Natural Science, not Philosophy, not Ethics, not Sociology, each of which has its own sphere seemingly quite as separate and independent. Once indeed Psychology was subject to Philosophy, and received its method and its position from some metaphysical system; but that time has passed except for a few antediluvians. On the other hand it was subject quite recently to Natural

Science, particularly to Physiology; but this servitude of it has receded, if not vanished. Psychology, as above said, at present proclaims itself free and independent as a science, and places itself on an equality with other sciences.

It is to be noted that the foregoing conception of Science as a whole regards it as broken up into a galaxy of disjointed and disparate Sciences without any unity. There is no central commanding Science which can hold together these centrifugal units; each is a republic in itself distinct from, yea jealous of its sister republics, and ready to do battle against any one of them which may be getting too prominent. To continue the political metaphor, there is no federation of the Sciences with its supreme Constitution governing and uniting the scattered members, after granting them and even securing to them inner autonomy. They resemble the political system of Europe with its cluster of separated and antagonistic sovereignties instead of the United States, which combines a central government with the freedom of its members. In other words Science at present is European and is stamped with the impress of the institutional life of Europe. In this form it has been brought to America and is cultivated here. Must not it too be made to bear the visage of our own institutional world, so different from the European? If so, there is to be again a central Science, as there is a central Government, not dominating imperially its subject provinces, but composed of equal and autonomous commonwealths which both create and are created by their union. Art, Science and Institutions are the work of the nation's spirit, and must ultimately wear the likeness of the people which produce them.

Once there was a central Science; Philosophy bore that proud title, being called the *scientia scientiarum*. But it has been deposed from its imperial position and reduced to the level of the other sciences, if not degraded to a still lower rank. Philosophy, the supreme European Discipline from ancient Greece till the last century, has been delimited, if not dethroned in its very home, in Europe itself. Hardly can it be reinstated in its former sphere of honor and authority. What is to take its place? Or is the present separative, disorganized, chaotic condition to continue?

From the drift of the foregoing remarks the vigilant reader will observe that a successor to Philosophy has begun to rise into vision, and show its outlines to watchmen on the tower, and also that its name is Psychology. This, however, must be something more than "the science of the phenomena of mind," though it be that too; the phenomenological conception is not to be thrown away but is to be evolved into something higher, and thus taken along.

II.

A little attention to the conception of Psychology just set forth will show the science composed of two elements: mind and its phenomena (or activities), as if the first might be something different from the latter, and indeed quite unknown or unknowable in itself. But a little further attention to the same subject will reveal a third element secretly working in the above definition, namely mind. That is, the very thing (or Thing-in-itself) whose phenomena are to be described and classified, is the describer and classifier; the hidden demiurge whose mysteries are to be revealed in our science is just the revealer, and evidently he is a very important person in this whole business. In fact, so important is he that we intend to call him by a name of his own; this name is EGO. Mind is a word somewhat vague and general, very useful in its place, quite indispensable. But it lacks the red blood of life circulating through the Ego which is so personal in its activity, so direct in its appeal to me, the learner of Psychology. For after all, I am the one who has to know the phenomena of myself knowing.

It is evident, then, that the Ego is the beginning and end of the psychological process. Its activity is to see and order its own phenomena, which constitute just its activity seeing and ordering. I, this personal particular Ego, must be an explicit element of the science of the Ego in general. The facts of universal mind are not facts for the individual mind till the latter makes them anew and thus becomes a creative part of the total psychical movement. I cannot truly learn Psychology without constructing myself at the same time; I am not simply to commit to memory some phenomena of mind and perchance internally or externally verify them; thus I leave myself out, though I am the subject-matter of this science. While building it, I am building myself; the play of Hamlet, according to the adage, cannot well omit Hamlet himself. What I am, I must re-create, and be perpetually re-creating, and this personal Egoistic activity of mine must have its place in the completely formulated process. Verily the worth of the individual is dawning, and his true position in the Universe is at last to be fully revealed and organized by Psychology.

Taking up once more the ordinary conception of our science, we said that it showed the Kantian dualism. This is undoubtedly true, especially as regards its definition. Yet more deeply still, it shows the dualism in all philosophy, particularly from Plato down. For the Platonic dualism formulates the Phenomenon and its Substance and therein divides the All in twain. But Philosophy itself in its entire sweep, is seeking for the Essence of Being (the *ousia* of the *on*), and thus presupposes the dualism of the universe into Essence and Being. Now this dualistic view of the world is, we hold, an inherent and necessary stage of man's development, yet the time is coming when it must be transcended. Philosophy has been a grand Discipline for our race, the supreme one of Europe, in our judgment. Still there must be a return out of its dualism, a mediation of its innate self-antagonism, which has made it the seething cauldron of this earth, if not of the whole universe. This third stage of mediation and restoration is, if we mistake not, the mission and the message of Psychology, of course in its transfigured norm, which elevates it into a new world-discipline succeeding Philosophy.

To the foregoing "science of the phenomena of mind" must now be joined that Ego making the science, which science becomes thus truly its own. I, the individual, make the universal which makes me, I determine that which determines me, or in the political sphere I on my part must make the law which governs me. The science of the Self, which is our Psychology, must be self-determined; thus it becomes the free science, indeed just the science of freedom, being a kind of archetype of all self-government, personal, political, and universal.

III.

The thoughts contained in the previous section are fundamental, though perhaps somewhat recondite, at least for the beginner. They introduce the Ego as the central moving principle of the science of Psychology, without omitting "the phenomena of mind" as an element of this science. The subject being difficult, we may be permitted to add a few illustrations as well as further developments, at the risk of repeating some matters which have been already mentioned.

If we take Psychology to be simply the science of the facts of mind (or of the Ego), we conceive it primarily as a mass of materials which are to be arranged and put into scientific form by some power outside of themselves, as is the case with physical science. What is this power? becomes the fundamental question of Psychology, and indeed of all other sciences, which are likewise arranged by it and reduced to their order. We have alluded to Geology, which has the same power lying back of it and making it a science. Who or what is it investigating the strata of the earth and throwing them into the scheme of their succession in time and place? There seems to be a secret demiurge (already noted) working behind the phenomena of both mind and matter, and impressing upon them its own order, which transforms them into science.

This secret demiurge knows the object, then it turns upon itself knowing the object and beholds itself in such act of knowing the object. It may make a mistake in describing or classifying this knowledge, but it corrects its own mistake; if not, there is no power in the universe which can make the correction. Some recent psychologists have said that their science has nothing to do with the nature of the object, being concerned only about its appearance in the mind. But Psychology must come to *think* the object, and to think the object is to get at its very truth and genesis. Undoubtedly there may be delusion; but what is to know delusion except mind (or the Ego)? We hear likewise much about the errors of introspection, and they are real; but who detects them and provides against them? Let us grant that the Ego is the source of all deception, but it is, too, the source of all overcoming of deception. Some declare that Psychology does not trouble itself about the truth of the objective world, but only deals with its presentation through the senses, as if there was no such thing as Thought in our science, whose very end and outcome is to know what is true. Hence one of the psychological needs of the time is to vindicate a place for Thought in what is truly the science of Thought.

There must be, in treating of Intellect, not only Sense-perception (Sensation, Perception, etc), not only Representation (Memory, Imagination, etc.), but also Thought as a psychical activity, yea as the supreme psychical activity, which makes Psychology itself a Science. We have to think Sensation, for instance, before it becomes scientific, for it cannot think and order itself as Thought can, the latter being the highest point of the reflexive, self-returning, self-defining Ego. To sense the object may be psychical, but it is not yet psychological. The Ego perceives the outer world, but this Perception has to pass through the alembic of Thought, and therein be defined and ordered ere it can be a part of the science of Psychology. But this science cannot omit the very activity of the Psyche which makes it.

With this statement we have reached down to the peculiar fact of the Ego; it is the observing and the observed in one, the investigating and the investigated, the ordering principle and what is ordered, self-defining and thereby all-defining. From this point of view we may regard it as the image of the All, of the Universe, since the All must define itself, if it be defined, there being nothing outside of it to define it. The Ego, indeed, as consciousness we shall hereafter discover to be the child of the Universe, bearing its impress and hence capable of becoming universal through Thought. The Ego is, accordingly, self-defined, not defined through anything else but itself — a gift possessed by nothing besides in the Universe but the Universe. Every definition in every science must ultimately reach back to self-definition as its very ground and generating source. How could there be any definition of anything unless there was a self-definer to give it? If science rests upon right definition, it must go back to the self-defining Ego for the fulfillment of its purpose. Certainly this looks as if Psychology, when it gets to be truly the science of the self-defining Ego, would be the universal Discipline, the science of all sciences and no longer simply one among many sciences.

Let the student not forget that he is an integral part of this psychological movement, he must create it, or rather recreate it in order to possess it. Not merely is he to test each fact of the Ego from the outside, but he testing is also one with the fact tested, the getter of the fact is also the fact gotten. There is a peculiar intimacy between this science and the one working in it. When the Ego of the student defines itself to be the self-definer, it is in that very act what it defines itself to be. Very different is the case in other sciences. In Ethics a man may define virtue without being virtuous; in Aesthetics he may define beauty without being beautiful, and without his definition being very beautiful; in Philosophy he may define the Universe without becoming universal himself. But in Psychology at its best, he must be what he defines himself to be, he thinking cannot help being his own thought of himself. In the self-defining Ego is the point and the only point where Thinking and Being are one. Thus the Ego as part or individual, rounds itself out into its own total process; it defines that which defines it and therein completes its own inner cycle; and its future psychological character will be to determine that which determines it, to make the law which governs it, in fine to create anew the Universe which created it.

Moreover we may now see that the Ego must always participate in its own complete process; it, though a part, an atom, must have in it the movement of the whole of which it is a part, otherwise it cannot be a part of its own whole. In Metaphysics the Ego projects its own activities outside of itself, beyond its own horizon, so to speak, holding itself aloof from them as if they were something alien, and thus making them mere abstractions. Still these abstractions of Philosophy are not to be thrown away, but they are to be filled afresh with the red life of the Ego whence they originally sprang. This Ego, hitherto the secret demiurge making Philosophy and all science, must now be brought out of its lair to sunlight and must become the open participator in its own process, being determined not simply after the manner of some abstract definition which seems picked up anyhow or anywhere, but being formulated as self-definer, who always is going forth and defining that which is always coming back and defining it. If the Ego formulates any science, that science must also reveal and even formulate the Ego as the formulator of itself (the said science). Moreover this Ego as self-formulator has its own science of self-formulation, which science is Psychology proper.

Accordingly we are brought face to face with the question: How shall this Ego, so long ensconced in its workshop, be brought forth and made to take its place in the process of its own organization? This does not mean that it is merely to show itself and let itself be described, measured, classified in its forms as some outer thing — all this has been often done already, even to superfluity. But how shall the Ego be manifested, formulated, categorized as making the made which makes it, as doing the work which reveals it, as producing the process which produces it? There must be something which explicitly interlinks the Ego with all its activities, and all its activities with it, so that every separate stage of it is not only seen but also expressed as the whole of it, and all of these separate stages thereby connected together. This connecting link uniting each activity or faculty of the Ego, even the most minute, with the whole of it or with it as a whole, we call the Psychosis whose character and function must next be specially set forth.

IV.

We are seeking just now in our investigation the means, the spiritual instrument by which the hitherto implicit, secretly working Ego may be made explicit in its own science, and may become an open, formulated factor in its own complete process. Such an instrument (so we designate it for the nonce) is the PSYCHOSIS. This is the primordial, elemental process of the Ego, which therein formulates its own inherent nature as self-movement. The Psychosis not only suggests but orders the ever-present activity of mind in all the works of the Ego human and divine, and thus makes itself the unifying principle of the Universe both in its totality and in its parts.

Such is the fundamental fact or germinal principle of Psychology as here conceived, the Psychosis, which is not to be grasped as some fixed metaphysical substance but as the primal psychical process of the Ego itself beholding and formulating itself. The word is derived from the Greek *psyche* (soul or Ego), and is thus cognate etymologically with Psychology. The

Greek termination *sis* expresses activity; in the present case it suggests the *psyche* as active, as process. The word has been not a little perverted by recent psychologists from its original meaning, being applied as the psychical counterpart to *neurosis*, in the doctrine of parallelism between soul and body. Likewise it has sunk down to a purely pathological usage, as may be seen by the example cited in the Century Dictionary. From these modern impurities we hope to assist in freeing the word and to restore it to its pure Hellenic fountain-head of meaning.

In the Psychosis, the Ego within itself unfolds and formulates its elemental process, which remains through all its activities and binds them together. The Psychosis is, accordingly, the Ego's primordial act of self-definition, which act it has to go through in defining everything else. That is, every activity, every object, every science completely grasped and expressed by the Ego, must take the form of the Psychosis. You have no other means or implement for getting things mentally except through the process of your Ego, and that is the Psychosis. Thus it is the mould through which all has to pass in order to be known. It is the impress which the Ego stamps upon the world, or rather finds already stamped upon it, for we shall hereafter see that the Universe itself is a Psychosis, being the very process of the All-Ego, or of the Divine

Self. The Ego psychologizing is the Psychosis detecting itself and unfolding itself in all its own activities, and then in all the works of Nature and Man.

At the beginning, therefore, it is necessary to comprehend this process of the Ego, which has three stages.

1. The Ego, in the first stage of the Psychosis, is implicit, undeveloped, undivided within itself, and hence unconscious. We may also call this its immediate or potential stage, not yet realized, full of its own possibilities. The child is the potential man, but the man too has in him a world of potentialities.

But the Ego within itself has the breach, the division, the separation of itself from itself. Hence the following.

2. The second stage of the Psychosis is the divided, the different, the separative, in which the Ego separates itself and makes itself its own object. From the simple or one-fold it becomes the dual or two-fold, which fact is expressed in the two terms, subject and object. The Ego can now become self-knowing, self-conscious; at this stage introspection can begin and hold up the Ego before itself.

Still the Ego in its self-separation is also one and must assert its oneness, which is no longer the first immediate unity, but is mediated through the separation.

3. The third stage of the Psychosis is the self-returning one, the Ego returns out of separation into unity with itself. This new concrete unity of the Ego has, therefore, separation behind it, present but overcome; it completes the Psychosis, and thus reveals the total Psychosis, which is now seen to move in a cycle, in a going forth (separation) and a coming back (return).

It would be well for the student, who is not in too great a hurry, to find some illustrations or trace some analogies of this movement of the Psychosis. It shows the restoration after the fall, the recovery after the lapse, the atonement (at-one-ment) after the sin. It is the inner pulse of all Bibles, religious and literary. It underlies the total sweep of History, from Orient through Europe, to Occident. It hints the grand harmony of existence attained through the resolution of all the discords of life. Finally the Psychosis must be seen to be God's as well as Man's.

Especial notice is to be taken of the fact that the foregoing germinal process of the Ego is threefold, or rather triune, three-in-one. If this be so, it follows that every act of the Ego, as well as every object which it grasps, will ultimately assume the triune form. Any other way can only represent some stage of incompleteness. (For a fuller account of the Psychosis, see our *Psychology and Psychosis*, 12–24.)

It will be observed that in the above account of the Psychosis, we have had to employ abstract or metaphysical terms for describing its stages. When we call its first stage *immediate* or *potential*, its second stage *separative* or *subject and object*, its third stage the *return* or the *restoration*, we are using designations which have long been known in the History of Thought, and which Philosophy had already elaborated far back in ancient Greece. But these terms when employed by Philosophy are taken to express the essence of Being (the *ousia* of *on* in Aristotle's phrase), and not to express the process of the Ego. There is explicitly no Psychosis in Greek Philosophy, or in any Philosophy, though implicitly it is at work all the time, since Philosophy likewise is made by the Ego and bears its stamp from beginning to end. But in the acknowledged, explicit Psychosis, Philosophy is seen passing over into Psychology, and metaphysical terms are transformed into psychological, being brought to describe the very process of the Ego, which has now become the true essence of Being, the concrete fact of it and of all the abstractions generated by Metaphysics for explaining it.

In these statements we are to recognize the great service rendered by Philosophy to man's culture. It has elaborated the language of Thought, and trained the human mind to thinking by means of the same. But its abstractions thrown out from their source in the Ego and held long in a state of separation (we might almost say, alienation), must in the new time and in the new world be brought back to their psychical fountain-head and thus be restored to their original birth-right and even birth-place. Psychology, when it gets to its true significance, can only mean an era of restoration in the widest sense, for the Ego, Man himself, is to return out of his long period of dualism and self-estrangement (very necessary, let it here said), which has found its chief expression in Philosophy. Herein we begin to see that Psychology in its new form belongs itself to a vast World-Psychosis of which it is the third stage, the Return, and of which Philosophy is the second stage, showing the grand breach and separation of the Ego, or Man in his self-alienated condition.

Such is, then, the first attempt to draw the outline of the Psychosis, which winds through our whole science in its vastest sweeps and in its smallest detours, binding them all together into one complete interconnected Totality. It is a simple but very subtle thing, easy enough to see at the start, but difficult to track through all its mazes and meanderings and multitudinous transformations in the universe of mind. Moreover, we may note again in the very terms used to describe it the transition from Philosophy into

Psychology, the bridge from the metaphysical into the psychical realm.

A warning may here be interpolated. The Psychosis has its formal aspect, and it may degenerate into a mechanical *abacadabra*. It may be externally clapped on anything without being made to reach the inner psychical movement of the subject-matter. Every formulation of thought, particularly Philosophy, runs the same danger; yea language itself, being composed of universals in the form of words, easily loses its concreteness in unskillful hands. Yet the Psychosis by its very nature is the bringing back of all abstract forms to their original creative source in the Ego, which is the most concrete thing in the Universe. Into the knowing of every object it seeks to put the genetic process. Least of all formulations has it the tendency to lapse into a mere machine grinding out categories. Still it may be thus perverted, since it cannot do without words, yea abstract words, even if these abstract words it always tries to fill with its own vitalizing movement. Though it seeks to save every organism and every science from being reduced to a heap of dry bones, in certain minds it cannot save itself from such fate. Undoubtedly it is a system, but it is peculiarly that which makes its own and all other systems, and whose system must always be making itself. It does not merely apply to the large divisions of science, but to the small and the smallest, since it is universal. It cannot fetter the spirit by its prescribed movement, since this very prescription prescribes separation from all prescription. For the Psychosis makes separation an integral part of its process, even the separation of itself from itself. Thus freedom in every possible shape can be made organic in the Psychosis, being taken up and put inside its process, and so not left outside where it turns itself and everything else into anarchy. The Psychosis is always free to separate from its own forms, even from its own system, yet it must always return out of such separation, or whiz madly into chaos.

And now it lies directly on our path to take a somewhat detailed survey of this mechanical side of the Psychosis or its quantitative expression, which is very necessary to its appearance in the world, and yet can hardly be deemed its inner governing principle. The outer mechanism of the Psychosis is a Three, a Triplicity, a Triad, as we see from its form already given. Still we are not to forget that this mechanism and all mechanism, yea quantity itself in its farthest mathematical ramifications, is likewise the work of the Ego and the Psychosis. Above all, let us recollect that the number Three does not make the Psychosis, but is made primordially by it, and hence is the basic number as representing the basic process quantitatively.

V.

From the nature of the Psychosis, the inference must be drawn that the movement of the present science in all its varied development will be threefold, triune, triadal. Hence it comes that Psychology will call up and apply to all its details the principle of THE TRIAD as the form of its ultimate, active, psychical germ, of its genetic process.

Equally certain is it that such a procedure will evoke strong objection. Especially at the present time the system of Triads is in disfavor, as something methodical, over-formulated, long since transcended. Our age is scientific, investigative, turning to the particular rather than to the general; even our universities in spite of their name, are distinguished for not being universal. Specialization is the watch-word with its deeply-rooted prejudice against system, which indeed its one-sided devotees become impotent to produce or even to grasp when produced. Moreover, any such system is supposed to retard if not to prevent evolution, though it requires no great knowledge to discover that the evolution of Mind or Spirit has mainly, if not always, proceeded through systems. Darwin himself has his system of evolution.

Here is not the place to give anything like a full account of the history of the Triad as the form of expressing what is deepest and most lasting in Man, Nature, God. In fact just these three — Man, Nature, God — make the exhaustive Triad of the Universe, and hence are the theme of every universal Discipline, such as Religion, Philosophy, and finally Psychology. And we may note here in advance that these three Disciplines constitute a Psychosis — a fact which will be unfolded later.

At present, however, we wish to set forth briefly the Evolution of the Triad, since it illustrates the fundamental psychical activity of man. Three stages we shall find it passing through — the religious, the philosophical, and the psychological. Their history shows that mind has always taken this form, especially in its deeper searchings. We are quite entitled to say from the evidence given in all ages, by all races, in all parts of the world, through the three chief Disciplines of human intelligence — Religion, Philosophy and Psychology — that man's thought both of himself and the Universe precipitates itself ultimately into Triads. This fact we shall now look at.

1. The conception of God has a tendency to take some form of the *religious Triad*, which is composed of divine persons. Asia may be deemed the home of Religions, even if the

savage man everywhere has some kind of worship. In the great Asiatic River-Valleys civilization dawned, and we there get the first peep of the early religion which has unfolded into our own. This first peep shows already some kind of a trinity. In a recent book on Babylon the statement is made that "its great Triad of Gods, Anu, Bel, and Ea" can be traced back "to the very beginning of History." And in the valley of the Nile Egypt was full of divine trinities, each city showing the tendency to have one of its own. Eleven Triads have been counted by one author, and the list is probably not exhaustive. But Egypt had also its one great Triad known as Osiris (father), Isis (mother), and Horus (son). The polytheism of the Greeks often drops into Triadism. The divine dualism of Persia evolves into triplicity (Ormuzd, Ahriman, and finally Mithras). Even in the strong Monotheism of the Hebrews an implicit underlying Trinity has been shown with its Mediator. Of course the culmination is the Christian Trinity, the heart of European religion and civilization, which may well be regarded as the final evolution of the religious Triad, which, however, is still evolving.

The religious Triad has many forms, and its composition varies much. At times it seems hardly more than three separate Gods grouped together. Then it is indicated that these three are somehow one, as we infer from many three-headed idols with one body. In some cases all are males; then a female is one of the members, and even two females are suggested in Homer — Zeus with Hera and Athena. More common and more significant is the trinity of the Family divinized — Father, Mother, Son. Thus the primal institution of man is elevated into the upper world of the Gods, and its creative process is put at the center of all creation. Possibly the institutional changes in the evolution of the Family — Matriarchate, Polygyny, Monogamy (see our *Social Institutions*, pp. 137-154) may have found its reflection in the different relations of women in the religious Triads of tribes and nations — her presence, her exclusion, her restoration. But the fact now to be emphasized is that throughout all this diversity divine triplicity is the rule, with certain exceptions.

In the mind of every thinking man the question now rises — and it rose long ago: Why just the number three in this matter? Why a trinity of Gods or a tri-une God? Why a religious Triad, and not a religious Dyad or even Hebdomad? The Persian religion was indeed dyadal, for a time at least, and we know that the Hebrews regarded the number seven as sacred. Still these two cases, Persian and Hebrew, as we have already seen, are but seeming or temporary exceptions. It explains nothing to say that the number three was regarded by early peoples as sacred, for the point is to ascertain why it was sacred. Man, the human Ego, the individual Psychosis, could grasp the Creator of the Universe only as Ego, as a Psychosis with its threefold process which is expressed in the manifold forms of the Trinity, these showing a gradual evolution toward a more complete conception and formulation. Lurking in the religious Triad of all kinds, and creating it is the Psychosis, which can know God only as the All-Psychosis (Pampsychosis), or as the threefold psychical process of the All. Such is the underlying genetic fact of the race's religious Trinities, both ethnic and Christian.

Here we may inject another word on the number three, about which there is much deep-rooted misconception. It does not determine the Trinity, rather the Trinity determines it — three does not make God but God makes three, making himself three and all things. Or we can say that the Psychosis produces the Triad as its own quantitative expression, and not the reverse.

The attempt of the religious Triad to make each of its stages a personal God and yet to hold them in a unity, is an extremely suggestive psychical fact which will find striking analogies in other spheres beside that of religion. St. Augustine seems to have been the first who had some glimpse of the relation between the tripartite activity of the human mind and the Trinity, since he compares the two in his work on this subject.

2. After Religion, which is essentially Oriental in origin, we pass to Philosophy which is essentially European. The fact comes to light that Philosophy is quite as triadal as Religion, sometimes openly and consciously, sometimes secretly and unconsciously. Hence we must take a glance at the *philosophical* or *metaphysical Triad*, which is not composed of persons (as the religious Triad) but of thoughts, principles, abstractions.

The Orient has philosophical Triads also, though Philosophy has not been its fundamental Discipline. One of the oldest must be that attributed to the Chinaman Lao-tsze, five centuries before the Christian era, who speaks of " the three inscrutables combined into one," which three are categorized as ultimate principles in the following way: " *Yin* the positive, *Yang* the negative, and *Chi* the harmonizer." These seem to be abstract thoughts brought into a triune process, though it is possible that a personal substrate is not wholly eliminated.

But Philosophy as a creative and persistent World-Discipline arose in ancient Greece. And it arose as a reaction against Religion, specially that of the Orient, with its divinely capricious Will as the creator of all things. At Miletus in the sixth century B. C., the old Greek began to grope after and to formulate the abiding Cause, Law, Principle of the Universe. These are all abstract Thoughts, not Persons. (For a more detailed account of this great change see our *Ancient European Philosophy*, pp. 16–22, 79–82.)

At present we wish to emphasize the fact that these abstract metaphysical principles began to take a triadal form in the early Greek philosophers. Very pronounced does this become in Plato, especially in his *Republic*, in which he unfolds the principles or activities of the Soul. But the more significant matter is that Plato uses this Triad of the Soul as the ordering principle of the Virtues and of the Classes in his State, that is, of his moral and institutional worlds. Such is his dim prophecy of the Psychosis as the world-orderer.

Of course it cannot be shown that Plato in all his Dialogues arranged his thought triadally. Nor did Aristotle put his system into Triads, though he has passages which show his insight into the threefold order of things. In fact his whole Works easily fall into Metaphysics, Physics, and Ethics, the triple Norm of all Philosophy, though Aristotle himself seems to have made no such division, since it appears first with distinctness in one of his disciples. This

Norm remains the central pivot on which the philosophical movement of every age has turned.

Passing to Neo-Platonism, we find that its greatest names, Plotinus, Iamblichus, and Proclus cultivated the triadal procedure. Especially should we note Proclus in this connection. In him the metaphysical Triad as the essence of all things is explicitly set forth and formulated in categories. He declares that the fundamental process of the world has three stages which he calls the Stay (*Mone*) the Going-forth (*Proodos*) and the Turning-back (*Epistrophe*). Very similar is this to the Psychosis with its implicit, separative, and returning stages, as already described. Still this Triad of Proclus is not the Psychosis, since it is never brought back to the Ego, but it remains metaphysical, giving the abstract formulation of the essence of Being. Nevertheless it is a most significant fact that Greek Philosophy in its last great exponent, this Proclus, winds itself up by laying bare its metaphysical Triad which has lurked in it from the beginning. (See account of Proclus in *Ancient European Philosophy*.)

The medieval Philosophers, dominated by the thought of the Trinity, are of course very fully represented in the present field. In modern Philosophy also Triadism takes up a good piece of history. Kant grew into it, rather unconsciously to be sure, after the period of his

Critique of Pure Reason, which work is essentially dyadal rather than triadal. But the greatest modern expounder and promoter of philosophical Triadism is Hegel. It appears in all his works, and is particularly employed and vindicated in his *Logic*, whose tripartite divisions are Being, Essence, and Conception. Philosophical Triadism reaches its culmination in Hegel, and at times shows the tendency to push beyond itself and enter the domain of Psychology. That is, the threefold process of the Ego (the Psychosis) repeatedly breaks through the Hegelian metaphysical Triads, and asserts itself as the coming new procedure, particularly in his doctrine of Conception. (See the essay on Hegel in *Modern European Philosophy*, pp. 727 *et seq.*)

We have, therefore, the right to infer that Philosophy, during the whole course of its history, has shown an inherent tendency to be triadal. It is true that other forms, as the Monad and Dyad and even the Decad, have appeared and have been claimed as fundamental in this sphere. But such cases are sporadic and are often seen on a deeper view to vanish into the Triad. Again one asks, why? Philosophy as well as Religion is an attempt on the part of a human Ego (a Psychosis) to grasp and to formulate the All, which is likewise an Ego (the Pampsychosis). Thus we have a triune process of the

Universe in abstract terms or categories. This gives the philosophical or metaphysical Triad.

3. Secretly lurking and working in the entire movement of Philosophy down the ages is the *psychological Triad*, the threefold process of the Ego, which has been already designated as the Psychosis. This has shown itself the source and inner genetic principle of the preceding philosophical Triad, which is now to be brought back to its first source and made to take up the Ego that created it, into its process, this Ego being formulated as a stage or element of the same. Thus the creative center is no longer the abstraction separated from, yet projected by the Ego, but the latter's own process, the *Psyche* itself in its triune movement — the concrete self, not an abstract projection of it.

Let us illustrate. The above-mentioned philosophic Triad of Proclus is declared to be the Cause, Principle, generative Energy of all things, yet it is the philosopher's Ego which projects this Triad out of itself and impresses upon the same its threefold form. Is all this to be left out of the formulated process? A modern illustration is Hegel, whose creative Conception (*Begriff*) has the three stages, Universality, Particularity and Individuality, which may be deemed Hegel's fundamental Triad, which he makes the organizing principle of all science. But Hegel's Ego is really that secret demiurge first constructing, then working his philosophical machine, causing it to produce all its wonderful results. But is that demiurgic Self of his to be left wholly out of the account, or recognized merely as "looking on" at its own world-making? So Hegel says repeatedly, and in his treatment of logical Conception (*Begriff*), he explicitly eliminates the psychological element, or that of the Ego. Still it is his Ego which is doing all this, and cannot be put down. In like manner ancient Aristotle posits his Thought-thinking-Thought (noēsis noēseōs), as the essence of Being, which has nothing directly to do with the Ego, even if it be the Thought which thinks itself. In other words Aristotle is persistently metaphysical, and Hegel as European philosopher consciously turns away from Psychology to his philosophical Triad. And yet both these greatest philosophers (being Egos) have the psychological Triad fermenting underneath and secretly determining their entire formulation.

It is to be observed in these three vast sweeps, religious, philosophical, and psychological, that the triadal character of human thinking persists, though subject to great variations. The Orient and Europe, through their fundamental disciplines, Religion and Philosophy, manifest in their deepest struggles for self-utterance, a threefold process, which can only be referred to the Ego itself, which we have already seen describing itself as a Psychosis in abstract or metaphysical terms, and identifying the philosophic Triad as really its own.

But now the Ego must begin to look at itself by its own light and describe its process in its own nomenclature, which is, therefore, psychological. When I say that I feel and will and know, I have started to formulate my *Psyche*, even if unconsciously, in its own speech. To be sure, this had its origin far back, but like many another old thing and thought, it is just coming to its full validity.

VI.

An observation may be made at this point in regard to the *religious aspect* of Psychology in its new form. Evidently it is in the profoundest sense trinitarian, and requires its student to behold the creative process of the Trinity in all things, which indeed are unable to be known or even sensed by the individual Ego without reproducing in its own activity the triune process of the Universe. Thus Psychology brings man to God in the large and in the small. That Psychosis of his re-enacts the divinely creative act in its form at least, and Psychology is the becoming conscious of the Psychosis within the Ego and outside of it in the world and finally in the All. Through this science we dwell in the eternal presence of the universal Self in whom we now consciously "live and move and have our being." The omnipresent deity is still a feeling, but no longer a mere feeling, having come to be a participant in our very self-consciousness; we cannot know without the divine factor, and know that we cannot know. Thus Religion begins to be secularized in the right sense, not being divorced from our daily life but perpetually re-created in our occupation with the affairs of this world.

Some such ideal has indeed always hovered before the Christian Church. Its greatest theologian, Thomas Aquinas, bears witness to its spirit in the following sentence: *Creare est commune toti Trinitati.* The triune process of Godhood is creative, and is common to its three members — Father, Son, and Holy Ghost. Drawing out the thought we may say: the total Trinity (or Divine Psychosis) imparts its triune movement to its members, each of whom must have within himself the divinely creative process of the Whole, in order to be a member of that Whole. Later on we shall discuss more fully the psychological nature of this fact. At present, however, it is enough to say that the Psychosis has three stages forming its process, yet each of these stages must show the same triune process in order to be a stage of that totality from which it is derived. The Christian Trinity in its way maintains the genetic principle of the Universe as personal and also as triune, as an Ego with a three-fold process within itself, each of whose members is also an Ego. And if this is what creates all things both great and small, surely we are to find in them just this process in order to know them in their truth, that is, creatively. Hence from this religious point of view we may catch a glimpse of the far-reaching significance of the Psychosis.

We shall also put some stress upon the point (already hinted) that through Psychology thus conceived, all our secular existence is to be religionized. The old distinction between religious and secular life is certainly to be transcended, though perchance not obliterated. It is European, sprung of Europe's needs, particularly in the propagation of Early Christianity; moreover it manifests the dualism inherent in European spirit from old Greece down to the present.

The next great step in Religion must make the triune God universal in His creativity, which can only mean that His divine process must be seen in the least thing in order to know it truly, as it is in itself. The Trinity thus may become again an active vital fountain of Faith, yea of Knowledge. Surely it is not to be hidden away in the church, made an object of devotion on Sunday, and then to lapse from thought and life for the rest of the week. Psychology is to restore Religion, to unify it and universalize it out of its European dualistic stage. In the State America feels and knows that it has evolved out of Europe; but in the Church it is the merest copyist of European forms, often with the tendency to revert to still earlier stages, even Asiatic. That same spirit which has revealed and realized itself in our political institution, must get into our religious organizations, and make them over into an institutional counterpart of our State and our Social Order.

If the Ego in knowing has the triune process, will not everything known by it have to be also passed through such a triune process, which must be, therefore, the very form of knowledge? Science, fashioned and formulated by the Ego, cannot help being psychical in its order, which must show the Psychosis working through all its details. You have no other instrument except your Ego for cognizing the world, and for recognizing it when made into science. And the creative principle of the Universe, God, must be taken as Ego, and hence his creation has to be likewise triune, having within it the genetic movement of the Maker, which can be nothing else but the Psychosis. The destiny of science is that it be psychologized and thereby be brought into harmony with a divinely creative Ego, from which it has been so deeply estranged, especially in recent times.

VII.

Having obtained the primordial Triad of the Ego (the Psychosis), the immediate or *psychical* one, which cannot yet describe itself in its own speech, we come to the more developed *psychological* Triad, in which the Ego begins to unfold itself in its special categories. This Triad is FEELING, WILLING, and KNOWING, which terms always imply a self-reference of the Ego to itself. In them the mind has begun to formulate its activities, and thus to cognize itself. Hence the science of Psychology proper opens its organization with Feeling, Will, and Intellect which are its primal divisions, in their due order.

Looking back at the genesis of this last triadal process, we can observe its movement through the following stages — the metaphysical, the psychical (Psychosis), and the psychological (Feeling, Will, and Intellect). Taking up the metaphysical Triad in its three phases (the Potential, the Separative, and the Returning) we have seen them brought back to their source, the Ego, and employed to describe the process of the same, which we have designated as the Psychosis. Let us here emphasize that the abstract nomenclature of the world is the work of Philosophy, which is still the language of thinking and must remain so. But this abstract metaphysical speech is to be filled with that which created it, namely the Ego's genetic activity, and thereby become psychological in matter, if not in form. To express its primal psychical process, the Psychosis, the Ego has to borrow its tongue from the antecedent discipline, Philosophy, for it has as yet no formulation of its own. In the Psychosis, therefore, we see the philosophical Triad transformed into the psychological Triad. Moreover the former is many, appearing different in each kind of Philosophy; but the latter is one fundamentally, being the one process of the Self which we shall find to be the product and the image of the All.

But now this Psychosis, being born and started on its career, begins to talk its own language, to formulate its process in its own terms. When the Ego starts to appropriate the world or the non-Ego and to be determined to certain states and activities by the same, it describes these states and activities of itself in its own terminology. My mind getting the object, is likewise influenced by it, acts and is acted upon in the same energy or faculty. To these energies or faculties of itself it begins to give names peculiar to itself, and thus there rises a psychological nomenclature, which, in part at least, supplants the metaphysical. When I speak of the stages or divisions of mind as Feeling, Will, and Intellect, the terms are psychical and are applied to the Ego purely, and with them the science of Psychology proper has opened. But as long as I was defining the Ego as Psychosis in metaphysical terms (Potentiality, Separation, Return) I was constructing out of Philosophy into Psychology a bridge, which by the by must be perpetually reconstructed in thought.

It is not intended to affirm that psychical speech *originates* after philisophical; on the contrary they originate together. In the Greek philosophers we find psychical terms mingled with their Metaphysics. But what can be stated with truth is that the completed Psychology with its own completed expression *develops* after Philosophy, and out of Philosophy into a new World-Discipline.

Thus we have reached the primal psychological process (as distinguished from the psychical) in Feeling, Will, and Intellect. They all together form a Psychosis or psychical Trinity, and each is likewise a Psychosis in its own separate field. Each is the total process through which each interlinks with each, and thus every part or stage is connected with the rest in and through the Whole. Such is our first glimpse of the method of Psychology, which method is to be applied to every activity and to every division of the Ego large and small, whereby they are all united internally, that is psychically, into a great seientific Totality.

The Ego, let us repeat, seeking to take up and to make its own the objective world or the All, develops within itself three primordial energies or forms of such appropriation — namely Feeling, Will, and Intellect, which are, accordingly, the fundamental triune process of the Self as psychological. Here starts the question, Why does the Ego thus seek to make its own the All? Let us first think that the All is really what has created the Ego, and that this must return and reproduce its creator. The Ego is the child of the All, and it as a true child must inherit the creativity of the parent, and so be likewise creative, reproducing what produced it, namely the All, the Universe. This act of reproduction shows itself in manifold stages, but specially in the already named Feeling, Will, and Intellect, these being distinct from the elemental Psychosis, which is the Ego immediately turning back upon itself and describing itself abstractly.

The deepest necessity of man, the Ego as individual, is that he may feel, will, and know (or appropriate mentally) that which is not himself, the world, and through this mental appropriation rise to the All-Ego, to God. By means of Feeling, Will, and Intellect he makes himself a link in the total cycle of creation, and participates in the process of the Universe. He starts with the world, the external object, and finds in it the Psychosis as the essential principle of its being.

From the world he mounts up to the genetic source of it and of himself, to the All-Ego, which he has to re-create in its very creativity, making it his own through Feeling, Will, and Intellect. The science of Psychology may be said, therefore, to bring man back to God. But it does this in its own way, through interlinking the feeling, willing and knowing Ego into the round of the Universe which is made up of God, World and Man, or Ego. This Ego is thus the pivot on which the created centrifugal world turns back to the center whence it came to the creative All-Ego. Yet this creative All-Ego is not simply the center, but also the circumference, and yet not the circumference, but the Universe, of which center and circumference can only be imperfect metaphors.

It is evident, therefore, that Feeling, Willing, and Knowing, with which our science makes its beginning, have a great destiny before them. It must do something more than pick up and arrange, in external fashion, some phenomena of mind. Such a view of Psychology gets rather pitiful after the preceding outlook which glances up a new highway to the all-creating All. And yet in a sense this highway is old, very old, as old as the Ego itself, which started on its pivotal career with the dawn of human consciousness far back in some pre-historic age.

The foregoing tripartite division of mind,

however, has its history. It is not a recent discovery, if we take into account the suggestions of it in ancient writers. Homer explicitly designates the two classes of men — the one of action (Will) and the other of wisdom and deliberation (Intellect), nor does he fail to present the man of emotion and passion (Feeling). Plato formulates three psychical activities in his *Republic* which have some analogy to Feeling, Will, and Intellect though their complete identification is doubtful. In modern Philosophy all three can be distinctly traced, though under different names. Some recent psychologists have sought to invalidate this division, which, however, may be regarded as the Mind's own view of itself through many ages. The Ego of the race as expressed in its best thinkers has separated itself into Feeling, Willing, and Knowing, and we shall obey this very distinct behest of Evolution, this consensus of the best minds thinking upon mind.

If there is a substantial unanimity in regard to the preceding divisions, there is considerable diversity of opinion as to their order. Which ought to come first in the triadal movement, Feeling, Will, or Intellect? Each has been given the priority, though most psychologists have been inclined to place Intellect at the beginning. In one sense this is correct. Psychology is science and must know; scientific knowledge comes through the Intellect which knows itself and then can know other things. Feeling does not know itself, nor does Will; neither is able, therefore, to make a science of itself which is the work of Intellect. But Feeling must exist in order that Intellect may know it; in this sense it is prior, and furnishes the primordial psychical material upon which Intellect works, out of which in fact Intellect develops. Feeling has no complete self-return; though it has the process of the Ego, this is as yet essentially implicit and undeveloped. In our terms, Feeling has self-reference but is not yet self-conscious. (See following pp. 60–1.)

So we affirm the priority of Feeling in the ordering of Psychology. We may here remark in advance that this priority of a mental activity is a different thing from its primacy, which pertains more to its supremacy. Feeling comes first in order, it is the potentiality of the second stage which is Will. We may imagine the Ego as a quiet unruffled lake, till it be stirred to its process purely within itself by some outward blow or determinant. The wind smites this lake of the Ego, and starts it to rolling within, wave upon wave, each echoing each responsively. But when the waters strike the land or the boat, then we see the power sweeping outward in correspondence to the Will, which is the Ego externalizing itself in the object. These waves remain successive; if each could return upon itself and identify itself, it would be Intellect, which has this reflective, self-returning power within itself, and self-identification or self-awareness. Such, then, is the psychological order of these three primal activities of the mind.

Still we must be careful not to get lodged in their separation. These three activities are one and a process, wherein all are in each. When I feel, I have also to act and to know, even if in a subordinate way. My Feeling may dominate my Ego, nevertheless Will and Intellect are not absent from it, else it would not be Ego. We may state here, though the subject will come up later for fuller treatment, that Feeling, Will, and Intellect have each self-division and self-return; each is the total process (the Psychosis) which all are, otherwise there could be no such total process. To use other terms, each has in it self-reference, which is common to the Ego feeling itself (as in Pain and Pleasure) or willing itself (as in self-activity) or knowing itself (as in self-consciousness). The process is the great thing in Psychology, not the single faculty or activity, which taken alone is abstract and always runs the danger of lapsing into something like a metaphysical subtrate, though it be predicated of the Ego.

Finally we are to grasp the fundamental reason of the foregoing psychological order of Feeling, Will, and Intellect: it is that of the Psychosis, whose three stages have been already described as the potential, the separative, the returning. The Psychosis bears the impress of the creative All, and is the fundamental ordering principle of every science, especially that of Psychology. Feeling, Will, and Intellect, therefore, form a Psychosis, and this we may deem the ultimate ground of their order in science, though this order reaches back through the Psychosis to the All-Ego (Pampsychosis), which is the source of it and of everything else.

VIII.

In the foregoing account we have discussed the question of priority in the elemental stages of the mind. We have placed Feeling first in order, then Will, then Intellect, all three constituting the primal process of the Ego out of which is organized the science of Psychology. But a very different proposition is that of the PRIMACY among these same stages. Which comes first in authority and in genetic power, irrespective of their order? The Primacy of Feeling, for instance, must be regarded as quite distinct from that of its Priority. One can hold to the Priority of Feeling in the psychological process of the Ego without maintaining its Primacy in the same, though these two characteristics are usually confused by psychologists.

The question, then, comes to the front: Does

any one of these constituent faculties have authority over the others? Is there a ruler, monarch, autocrat in the domain of the Ego? Very common is it at present to make such an assertion, or at least to imply it; also a claim of this sort has been often made in the past. The situation we may briefly outline by characterizing its three leading stages, which we shall call Emotionalism, Voluntarism and Intellectualism.

1. A certain precedence of our emotional nature not only in the order of the Psychosis but in rank and supremacy has been often maintained and still is upheld. This we may call the Primacy of Feeling (Emotionalism). Particularly Feeling is declared superior to Intellect, a doctrine frequently enounced in the statement that the heart is always to be put above the head. Instinct is said to be higher, more unerring in decision than the Understanding, especially in the case of women. Instinct, which is Feeling, is, moreover, far wider than Intellect, which animals do not possess in any high degree. And the lower grades of men, and man in his lower grades have to be ruled by Instinct as they have no other ruler.

Religion tends to assert the Primacy of Feeling from Paul to Schleiermacher. The supremacy of Love is doctrinal as well as the rule of Faith. And yet the man of Intellect usually sways the man of Feeling, unless Intellect can somehow descend and take possession of Feeling, whereby is attained what is known as the culture of the heart. But Feeling feels itself incomplete without passing over into action or Will.

The unconscious Ego with its vast reservoir of Feeling, the untold stores of our antecedent life through all the stages of our evolution, has also been endowed with the Primacy over the conscious Ego.

2. The favorite doctrine, however, in this field at the present time is the Primacy of the Will or Voluntarism, which can be traced through the ancient and medieval periods, but which gets its preponderance to-day from Kant (who derived it from Hume) and from Schopenhauer and Wundt. From these philosophers it has permeated German thinking, and from Germany it has gone forth to the rest of the world, particularly to America, on whose shores echoes of it are heard on many sides. In the form which it now takes it is peculiarly a German doctrine, and springs from the German institutional situation. We see the Primacy of Will absolute and originative, and hence arbitrary, in the German emperor, in the German army, in the German social and political system. Long ago it was said that the function of Philosophy was to express the spirit of its people and its age in the pure forms of thought. The German thinker is, therefore, right in asserting the supremacy of

Will, Strength, Power, for that is the present spirit, and probably the present mission of himself and his nation. But why should such a doctrine be transferred to the United States, where Social Institutions, and the Ego have put down such an arbitrary Primacy of the Will and are deeply antagonistic to it? For it means autocracy both in the individual and in the State.

The arguments which are usually brought forward to support this doctrine, do not prove it, at least not in any universal sense. It is claimed that the beginning of life is wholly impulse; "the nurseling is all Will." Yet the nurseling must have sensation (which is a form of Intellect) and it must feel what is agreeable or disagreeable to it, which is Feeling. Thus in the young of animals we recognize all three, Feeling, Will, and Intellect, all of them to be sure in a very incipient condition. But the point is that they belong together and form a process even in their least developed condition. For the worm or the polyp as animated must sense, must feel, must will. The Primacy of the Will, as the original primordial function of mind, from which Feeling and Intellect are derived as secondary, never has been and cannot be shown to be a universal mental fact, though the Will appears at particular times in the life of the individual and of the nation as the dominating activity.

3. In the history of thought the Primacy of the Intellect or Intellectualism has been very generally accepted, even when not explicitly formulated. It is an old belief that intelligence rules the world, and there is much to be said in favor of the doctrine. We must recollect that the whole gamut of Intellect runs from Sensation up to Reason, deemed often the godlike faculty.

Let it be said, however, that Intellect cannot possibly do without Will, or without Feeling. When the voluntarist says that the Intellect is the mere instrument of the Will, important but subordinate, the intellectualist replies that the Will is the mere instrument of the Intellect. Both these one-sided advocates are right and also wrong; each of these activities of the Ego is the means as well as the end of the other. Intellect employs Will, and Will employs Intellect, and both employ Feeling, and Feeling employs them and all three form the process of the Ego together, in which process each is for and through the rest.

Such is the outcome of the three Primacies of Feeling, Will, and Intellect, which have played and are still playing a great part in the theory of mind. Our view maintains that there is no such Primacy of any of them, no original, monarchic, autocratic faculty which is supreme in rank, authority and generative power. Feeling, Will, and Intellect are socially equals, of the same right and supremacy; they form not a monarchy in the Ego, but a democracy. It is curious and significant that monarchical Europe has held to a monarchical Primacy in the mind, which fact accords with the institutional world there. Now the truer doctrine (we maintain) is that any one of these constituents can hold the Primacy for a time and for a given emergency, But there is no born Primacy (or Primogeniture), no aristocracy in the realm of the psychological Trinity. Each member of the process can become Primate (or President) and possess authority in the Republic of the Self.

Another fact to be noted here is that each of these three Primacies, Feeling, Will, and Intellect is essentially psychological, assuming a stage or function of the Ego as the essence of it, and indeed of all Being. Voluntarism, for instance, asserts Will to be the fundamental principle of the Universe. We see in this statement that the form is philosophical, though the content is psychological; the philosophical problem receives a psychological answer. The essence of Being is still asked for; the response, however, is not the Atom, the Good, the One, Substance, the Monad, or any other abstract metaphysical entity, but is the Will, a concrete psychical fact. Here the domination of the one principle remains, so that we have still an autocracy, though it be psychological and not philosophical, having gotten one foot out of Metaphysics, while the other still sticks fast. But how can the European mind, where these Primacies originated, free itself from its fundamental Discipline which is Philosophy, necessarily aristocratic or autocratic? Now the democratic Primacy includes all as equals, and their process; in the present case this is the process of the Ego itself within, which thus can make an outer institutional world in correspondence with its own inner nature.

We must, accordingly, see that if the Will be put as the primal, authoritative, genetic essence of the Ego or Soul, it is used as a kind of fixed psychological substance instead of that of Metaphysics. This may be regarded as a step in advance, though there is as yet no psychological process. The essence of Being must be grasped as the psychical process of the Ego, as the Psychosis, then Philosophy has passed into Psychology. The process must not be a metaphysical Triad, like that of Proclus or Hegel for instance, nor must the principle be a psychological faculty-unit, such as we see in all kinds of Primacy, be it of Will, Intellect, or Feeling.

The essence of Being (the philosophical problem) is not now Cause, Law, Atom, but the process of the Ego formulating such a universal essence, which process I have had with me all the while I was seeking it through Philosophy.

Nor are we to put instead of this process of the Ego one of its constituent members as possessing the absolute Primacy to the exclusion of the rest. Thus we are half in Psychology and half in Philosophy. Between these two Disciplines we made the transition when treating of the Psychosis. And yet this halfness has its period, yea its fervent disciples.

IX.

Perhaps enough has been said on the preceding subject, still we are tempted to add some paragraphs especially on the PRIMACY OF THE WILL which is having so much currency in recent Psychology as well as in Philosophy. For it in a manner belongs to both, having one foot in the one and the other foot in the other, and manifesting, therefore, a straddle, a spiritual straddle characteristic of the time.

It has been already stated that this doctrine is not new. Leaving out the ancient moralists, we come to Christian Origen who felt the need of strongly emphasizing the eternally creative Will. In the theological development of the Western Church there is a kind of running fight between the two Primacies of Will and Intellect, culminating in the struggle between the Scotists and the Thomists. In modern German Philosophy the same conflict starts anew with Kant who substantially destroys the validity of Intellect in one *Critique* (that of *Pure Reason*), and affirms strongly the positive nature of the Will in his second *Critique* (that of the *Practical Reason*). The influence of Kant has brought about many variations of this conflict, notably those of Schopenhauer and the neo-Kantians.

But the man who above all others has been the means of scattering over the civilized world of to-day the doctrine of the Primacy of the Will is Professor Wundt of Leipzig. He may be regarded as the psychologist-philosopher of the present era, for he is both, not exclusively the one or the other. He is very great, probably the greatest psychologist among philosophers, and the greatest philosopher among psychologists. His phenomenal career represents better than anything else the transitional stage from Philosophy into Psychology, with its ups and downs, its forwards and backwards repeated many times. For Wundt after making himself the most prominent figure in a new department of Psychology (the physiological), and declaring that Philosophy was a dead duck floating on the morass of past thought, took the back track and wrote a *System of Philosophy* himself, which a little investigation shows to be built on the same old lines of the philosophic Norm of the ages. This step, which we hold to be not only natural but necessary, is said to have brought amazement to opponents and consternation to friends.

It reflects, however, the mental situation and shows Wundt as the true thinker of Europe since he both in his life and thought has given expression to the character, institutional and intellectual, not only of the German but also of the European world, whose spirit has never been able to get rid of a deep inner separation and dualism, whereof the best expression has always been found in its Philosophy. Wundt's career as well as his doctrines show the conflict between Psychology and Philosophy, which also gave trouble to Kant, and may be shown to underlie the various conflicts expressed in his Paralogisms and Antinomies.

But also in Wundt's conception of Voluntarism there lurks a contradictory movement. The two sides may be studied separately.

1st. Wundt, recalling Kant, declares that "there is nothing in man which is his own except his Will" (*System der Phil.* s. 379) — which is certainly a strong statement not only of the Will's Primacy but of its absoluteness. "The activity of the will penetrates all the single states of consciousness, and *mediates their connection*." In this italicized sentence we see that Wundt has before him the ideal of an interconnected Psychology down to its most minute states of consciousness. This is certainly a most important thought. But when he takes for the single mediating element the Will, necessarily arbitrary, we have to protest in the interest of that very experience to which Wundt appeals. Again, "the occurrences of the Will have a *typical* significance which gives the standard for comprehending all psychical activities" (*Grundriss*, s. 17). This is no longer so absolute as the preceding citations, but it still asserts the Will to have the criterion or measure by which we understand mind. Though Wundt protests, he nevertheless here metaphysicizes the Will making it a kind of substance which determines the other activities of mind. Or we may say that he has begun to psychologize Metaphysics, putting the Will in place of Cause, Essence, Law or other abstract principle.

2nd. Now we shall glance at the other side. Wundt denies that "the activity of Willing is a single, really existent form of psychical activity" in a separate state; on the contrary he affirms that "the Feeling and Concepts (Intellect) are closely joined with it, and form inseparable constituents of psychological experience." (*Grundriss*, s. 17). In our translation we have brought to the surface what we think lurks somewhat obscurely in Wundt's statements. Will is indeed first, then Feeling and Conception (*Vorstellung*) he puts together with it, not exactly into a process, but into "a psychological experience." He holds that they are not "separate energies" but are united "in a psychical act." He sharply assails "the attempt to deduce special activities of the mind, from other ones;" which declaration would seem to jeopard his Primacy of the Will, to which, however, he clings after hedging it about with a number of explanations and limitations, evidently made to meet objections.

The two preceding paragraphs must be regarded as containing contradictory statements and doctrines. The supremacy of the Will, even its absoluteness, is affirmed in the one, but decidedly modified in the other. If a man has nothing but Will as his own, then Will is his All, his total Ego. And yet Wundt in other passages is not far from recognizing the process of Will, Feeling, and Intellect, as the three equal constituents of the Ego. He does indeed affirm the process of the Will taken by itself, for he insists upon its being "an occurrence not an object." But he does not explicitly reach the fundamental psychological process, otherwise he would have made use of it in his organization of the science. And yet this process is fermenting within him, and at times sporadically breaks up to the surface. Wundt as European cannot abandon Philosophy as the supreme World-Discipline. Moreover as a German he cannot reject an the chief intellectual heritage of his people, which is certainly Philosophy. Hence Wundt returns to Metaphysics from Psychology, and cannot help metaphysicizing even his Psychology. All of which is, to our mind, deeply characteristic not only of the man, but also of his nation and his age, revealing that old European rent in its most modern form. The Primacy of the Will is still absolutistic as affirmed by Wundt, but he also voices the protest against absolutism, at least in the realm of thought. He is inherently dualistic and cannot help himself; if he were not so, he would not be the typical thinker of his period.

There is another expression above cited which ought to be expanded a little. Wundt conceives of a mental activity which "penetrates all the single states of conciousness and mediates their connection." Evidently such a mental activity would be the organizing principle of the total science of Psychology, penetrating every mental state, even the most minute, and mediating the connection of them all, large and little. Now Wundt makes the Will such an organizing and interconnecting principle. So we look through his Psycholgy in order to find the Will performing this function. But it does not appear fulfilling any such task unless incidentally and implicitly. After enouncing an explicit mediating activity of mind for his science, he never uses it, but drops back into his mere unmediated experimentalism, asserting Psychology to be "the science of immediate experience." The result is that he has only an external, quite arbitrary order in his work, whereby he may affirm the Primacy of his own subjective Will in organizing his science, though this Will of his works and must work capriciously, so that the principle of his scientific edifice cannot be other than his own caprice.

Out of Wundt's performance we come back to that striking aspiration of his for a fundamental psychical activity which will penetrate all the stages of mind and interlink them into a united and completely co-ordinated science. Our attentive reader has probably identified such a fundamental psychical activity reaching through and ordering all other psychical activities as the Psychosis. Of course Wundt has no Psychosis; though he calls for it, his call remains unanswered in his case.

Wundt starts with an attack on the Intellectualism of Herbart, approving however the latter's opposition to the old idea of faculties in psychology, and his unification of mind. But the principle of such unity lies for him not in the Intellect, but in the Will. Thus Wundt seeks to shift Herbart's Primacy to his own, and lays himself open to the chief objection which can be urged against Intellectualism. Mark that both these eminent psychologists cannot help being philosophers too, though each has his own way in the matter.

Moreover in educational science there has been a similar movement from Intellectualism to Voluntarism, from Herbart to Wundt. And there was need of the corrective: Will belongs to the complete Ego as well as Intellect, and both are to receive due training. But the result has been, particularly in America, a one-sided craze for the so-called motor education, imported of course directly from Germany out of whose needs and character it doubtless sprang. For the German child is reported phlegmatic and demands greater motor stimulation than the nervous American child, whose activity often needs the check more than the spur. At any rate the total Ego is to be educated, not merely the Will, or Intellect, or Feeling, no single one of which by itself is to have the Primacy in Education or in Psychology. Let us study German pedagogy by all means, but let us acquire its true lesson not by servile imitation but by adjusting it to our institutions and character.

Primacy is, therefore, to be cast out of Psychology, as elevating unduly some psychical element of the total man at the cost of the rest. It is the autocracy of Philosophy which insists upon the one ultimate authority without the process of the other members. Primacy, therefore, properly belongs to Philosophy, out of which it has been transferred into Psychology by our philosopher-psychologists. Really it is the whole process — Feeling, Will, and Intellect — which has the psychological Primacy, the whole man, not some part of him over-riding the other parts. At the same time we may see that there can be and have been philosophical Primacies, as many indeed as there have been Philosophies past and present. On the contrary there is but one psychological Primacy (if such we may call it) namely the above mentioned process, which is as enduring as the Ego itself. Thus Psychology has a unitary basis which Philosophy never had, and cannot have, and unfolds itself from its center into the cycle of the sciences through its own inner evolution.

Such is the typical order of these mental activities. At the same time there is no denying that one of them may and often must temporarily dominate the rest. Feeling may rule, Will may rule, Intellect may rule the kingdom of mind for a while legitimately, though we also know that each may lapse into excess, into tyranny, which can deeply violate the right mental order. Properly the Ego is an inner Republic in which each psychical member may be endowed with supremacy over the Whole through the Whole, but this supremacy must be laid down at the end of its term of office. Such an Ego with its inner Republic can construct and administer a corresponding outer Republic, which is thus not only an image but a realization of this Ego. Let the reader ponder the fact that the Constitution of the United States has three co-ordinate Primacies whose process makes the Government, one not being allowed to dominate the rest permanently, even if temporarily in an emergency.

And now springs up the question: How shall we organize this inner Republic, giving to it also its rightly formulated Constitution? In other words, how shall this Ego, Soul, Mind, Spirit find and state that general activity of itself which penetrates all the special activities and "mediates their connection" (*vermittelt ihren Zusammenhang*), thus fulfilling the aspiration of Wundt, our epoch-making and epoch-representing philosopher-psychologist? Surely we cannot take as final his conception of Psychology as "the science of immediate experience" (*unmittelbare*), when he demands in the preceding statement that it be mediated (*vermittelt*) through and through, and thereby interconnected by means of one all-prevailing activity of mind. With such an organizing principle as permanent and penetrating, our science cannot be turned over to the ever-varying caprices of the subjective Will, or of immediate experience.

Better it would be to define Psychology as the science not of immediate, but of self-mediated experience. Let us consider the process of Perception. When I perceive the object, it is an immediate psychical act, an immediate experience. But when I turn back and grasp and formulate that Perception, I have decidedly mediated the experience, mediated it with myself, my Ego. Still it is my Ego doing all of this work of mediation. In Psychology, therefore, my Ego mediates its own activities with itself, it is self-mediated (and also self-mediating), and our science is the science of this self-mediation formulated and ordered according to its own fundamental process.

This thought can be further developed. It is an old observation that the total mind is present in every special act of it. When I perceive something, my entire Ego with its process (the Psychosis) is present in this special act of Perception. Now when I turn back to grasp and formulate this act of Perception, my entire Ego with its process (the Psychosis) is what grasps itself (the Psychosis) perceiving. That is, I as process (Psychosis) identify myself as process (Psychosis) in the special mental activity — which movement is to be brought out explicitly and formulated in Psychology. In this way we see the complete self-mediation of mind; every special activity is connected with the whole through the whole and with the parts through the whole. Or we may say somewhat formally: the Psychosis recognizes the Psychosis in every particular faculty and carries it back to the Psychosis, thus mediating it with the total mind yet keeping it particular in such mediation.

Have we not now caught a glimpse of the Method which runs through all the details of Psychology and holds them together in a scientific organism of never-ceasing mental processes, great and small? Such a Method will give a science of experience not merely immediate, but self-mediated through and through, actively inter-relating itself in every part as well as in its grand totality.

X.

If the preceding view be correct, Psychology must show and formulate each activity of the mind, inter-connecting with all its other activities and with itself as a whole. And this is not all: it reaches out and includes the source of the mind, or Ego, or Consciousness, such source being the All-Ego, the Universe itself. But this loftier outlook we must defer at present and develop more fully the question of METHOD in Psychology. For if this science is the universal science, as it has begun claiming to be, its Method cannot lag behind, but must also be the universal Method of Science.

Psychology is, then, to reveal and formulate its Method, ere this can be carried over into other Sciences. In a profound sense, Psychology is its own Method, its own self-legislative process, what is methodized is just the Method. We may deem it a Methodology which first methodizes itself and then everything else, even the Universe

Let us start the discussion of the subject with a glance at the procedure existing at present in Psychology. There is a full recognition that the mind is one in all its activities. Yet this very term *activities* takes for granted that the mind is many. Thus the Ego is unity in one breath, but in the next it is multiplicity. Here we come upon the deep distracting contradiction which tears the science asunder and renders it impossible to be the unitary order of other sciences. Unless it can heal this rent in its own heart, it can never be the means for unifying other disciplines.

In order to emphasize oneness of mind, some psychologists pour out the vials of their wrath (in Herbartian fashion) upon the faculties so-called, implying or declaring that these do not exist; yet we find the same psychologists (with Herbart himself) speaking of sensation, memory, judgment and other faculties, even if a different name be used. Most text-books, however, after affirming the mind's unity, quietly proceed to give an account of the various mental powers one after the other, with little or no inner connection or evolution. The result is the

Mind lies scattered about in pieces, and there is no unity and a very uncertain arrangement.

Now the purpose of Method is to grapple with the foregoing difficulty and reconcile its dualism, seeking thus to bring a consistent order out of the psychological chaos. In some way unity and multiplicity must be made harmonious, nay, must be seen to be parts or elements of the same underlying mental process. Such a result, we have already indicated in the Psychosis with its three stages which show unity as implicit, then separation, then the return to unity. The Ego in and of itself is primordially self-separating and then self-unifying out of its first potential protoplasmic condition. Thus the Ego, here taken as mind, has in it from the start the manifold as well as the one — the one both as beginning and end, or the immediate and mediated. The Psychosis is accordingly the process which unifies in the mind all multiplicity. Moreover it formulates both many and one, both multiplicity and unity in its process.

In the *Parmenides* Plato shows the dialectical play of the Many and the One, which, however, are only two stages of the Ego's process (Psychosis) held asunder and thereby set in opposition to each other. Both are really members of one process which can be expressed metaphysically, as we shall soon see, but whose ultimate expression must be psychological, going back to the Ego itself, which is the original of its own and all other formulations.

The first manifestation of the Psychosis in dividing and unifying Psychology we have already witnessed in the case of Feeling, Will, and Intellect — each a separate stage yet all one process, a Psychosis. But each of these stages as Ego and total Ego divides within itself and returns to itself. For instance, Intellect has the well-known threefold division into Sense-perception, Representation, and Thought, which is also a Psychosis, indicating that the whole Ego is present and active in the special faculty. Still further, Sense-perception has likewise its three forms, Sensation, Perception, and Apperception, constituting a Psychosis, which not only unifies them into the one process of Sense-perception, but interlinks them with the process of Intellect, yea with the original psychological process of the Ego, Feeling, Will, and Intellect. Thus each special activity as process is mediated with the total Ego as process.

It will now be seen that we have a Method which binds together in an explicit formulation all the faculties of the mind from the largest and most comprehensive to the smallest and least obtrusive. The Psychosis has in its separative power the infinite divisibility of mind, but also the return out of such a stage, which power the physical world has not and hence remains in its state divided and divisible. How far shall we carry these mental divisions in Psychology? That depends upon the occasion and the man; science claims for itself a never-ending specialization. But however minute this specialization, the total Ego is there with its Psychosis, which inter-connects and organizes every psychical act, even the humblest into the entire structure of Psychology.

At this point it is worth while to note that Philosophy has long known these cyclical processes in their abstract, metaphysical form. Proclus holds that there is one greatest cycle of the All, which divides into greater and lesser cycles. The rest of the Neo-Platonists express a similar conception. Hegel in his *History of Philosophy* (I, 40) has the following passage: The development of philosophic Thought produces "a row of Evolutions which must not be conceived as a straight line running out to infinity, but as a circle which turns back into itself, which great circle has as its periphery a vast multitude of lesser circles whose entirety is a grand succession of Evolutions bending around into itself." Thus both the Greek and German philosophers conceive the process of the Universe as one supreme cyclical Triad unfolding into a succession of smaller cyclical Triads each of which again shows a triadal development, and so on to infinity.

Now Proclus and Hegel, the one representing the outcome of ancient and the other the outcome of modern Philosophy — each may well be deemed the *ultimus philosphorum* of his epoch — have both caught the fundamental procedure of Mind, but have given to it such an abstract metaphysical expression, that it seems unreal, purely schematic and fanciful, a shadowy reproduction of Shadows. It is no wonder that many a modern reader takes the whole thing as a sport of imagination, a kind of a philosophical romance. And the confession must be made that the end of such metaphysical construction has come. Still it would be a great mistake to consider the foregoing work of Proclus and Hegel to be mere fiction, as is sometimes said. It expresses the process of the Self, human and divine, yet in such an alien, abstract way that the Self cannot recognize itself in its own formulation, which must be now transformed from its philosophical to its psychological stage. This means not merely a change of words, but of thought, of viewpoint, yea a decided evolution in self-consciousness. It means a new Discipline, not special, but universal as Philosophy ever claimed to be

But not alone in the inner world of the Ego do we observe this cyclical movement; it is seen in the remotest outer world, in the sun, stars and planets, whose visible ever-returning cycles may well be deemed among the earliest awakeners of man's inner self. (See following pp. 79-86.)

Accordingly we shall unfold the cylical movement of the inner world or Ego, beholding and formulating its one fundamental process, the Psychosis, in all its divisions. Such is the most direct result of introspection, of our own Self's experience with itself. Over and over again we shall have to repeat that in each part or division is the process of the Whole, which is just what makes it a part of the Whole. Any organ of the Body in order to be such an organ shares in the total corporeal process, must have in it the Whole, otherwise it is not part of the Whole. Cut off the hand, and though it has all its physical constituents, it is dead, it has no longer within itself the process of the organic Whole called Life. Spinoza has noted the element which is equally in the part and in the Whole (*æque in parte ac in toto*) as the unifying element between the All and its particulars, or between Substance and Mode (see *Modern European Philosophy*, p. 221). This metaphysical viewpoint (one among many in the History of Philosophy), becomes psychological when we turn it back into the process of the Ego whence it originally sprang.

In the remotest, most external manifestation of the Universe we may note this cyclical movement. The earth moves on its own axis in a perpetual self-returning revolution every day; at the same time it is revolving around the central sun in an orbit which returns into itself every year; the satellite of the earth, a stage or part of it probably, has the same general character. And we may add that the total Solar System with all its revolving planets in their axial and orbital cycles is moving in still a vaster cycle which is yet to be passed through in the future æons. Such is the complete outer appearance of the All-Ego in the physical Universe, which we have to regard as the visible counterpart of the inner psychical Universe, and which must ultimately itself be psychologized and thus be made fully scientific. For the physical Universe also is to have its special processes interlinked each with each and with the All by the Psychosis.

In the teacher who reads this book, the suggestion has probably been roused that the Psychosis has a very particular and intimate application to pedagogical science. Long ago the old Greeks conceived education to be cyclical, and the word *encyclopedia* in Greek means cyclical education. When instruction follows the process of mind itself in seeking to inform and develop the mind, there will be a new educational epoch. But as the word *encyclopedia* has been degraded into expressing a mere external arrangement of knowledge according to the letters of the alphabet (which undoubtedly is useful in a dictionary), so the educative process has lost its cyclical order, not to speak of its inner psychical movement. Pedagogy cannot rest till it shall pass out of its present abstract formal condition, and be concretely psychologized through the Psychosis.

And yet we must emphasize again that it is possible to make the Psychosis formal, mechanical, quite meaningless in its repetitions. Its formulation must be special for each special activity, as well as general for the universal process. It is not enough to say, "that is a Psychosis," for everything is a Psychosis. The general form must indeed be stated in the definition, but also the specific character, which character is true of nothing else but the given activity. You can make the Psychosis a machine, just as you can make your own Ego a machine, though such is not the true nature of either. Psychology is indeed a system and must employ words which have to be re-thought, re-created as it were anew every time they are used. Otherwise they become hollow, jingling a little with their own meaningless echoes.

Still we must beware of being misled into the notion, very common in these days, that because a system of thought can be perverted and mechanized, therefore all system is to be rejected. If Psychology is ever to fulfill its function, it must be systematized through and through in the largest and smallest divisions. Yet it must not be conceived as a dead passive system, but as the active, creative, universal systematizer systematizing not only itself but all other sciences, indeed the very All. The horror, or rather hate of anything like system, method, or even order is very common among modern psychologists, who write Chaos in their book and teach it to their classes at the University. Really a new chair ought to be established and given to the gentleman who has distinguished himself most in this line, and who deserves the title of Head Professor of Chaotics in the University of Disorder.

Undoubtedly there should be a dislike of formulation when it is felt to be wrong or merely mechanical in the realm of the spirit. The person who cannot make his skeleton live, had better die, in fact he is already dead. Verily¦he cannot be much of an organism without a skeleton, which in the human sphere becomes very intricate and marvelously interconnected. Much psychology in these days has a parallel in the jelly-fish which has not a bone in its body, but is "water slightly organized in a gelatinous mass."

XI.

Having recognized the fact that in Psychology we must employ a Method of procedure, which is universal in its application, and that our result must be an organized System, we shall proceed to point out some of the more difficult problems connected with the Science. At the very threshold lies SENSATION, from which the two opposing world-views, materialism and idealism, take their start, dividing philosophers into two hostile camps quite from the beginning. It is evidently a psychological question, involving Ego and object and their primal conjunction. Here lies the first act of cognition, the forerunner and the type of all other such acts, which, being once made intelligible, opens up the whole field of intellection.

The most persistently difficult problem of Psychology, then, is to bridge over the grand separation between mind and the world, or Ego and non-Ego, not only through knowledge but through knowing knowledge. This is specially the function of the Intellect, and the trouble begins with its first activity, which is to sense the object. Thus Sensation becomes a thorny theme for the psychologist.

When we say that we perceive something, an outer stimulus starts into action the peripheral nerve-ends of the body. This begins a movement in the nerve toward the brain-center, which movement is generally represented as wave-like, proceeding toward its goal in successive undulations and hence measurable. Now these neural waves going forward, soon reach a center at which the movement completely changes and sweeps outward to the object whence it started. This object is thereby *sensed*, having been taken up through one of the senses.

Thus we have the cycle of Sensation in its simplest form. That turning-point or rather pivotal act through which the undulatory movement of the nerve wheels about and returns to its beginning is the Ego, Soul — not a place, but an activity, a process. It is not material, else it would stop the waves as an obstacle, or simply continue their undulating motion. But this is received and turned backward to its starting-point; no wave could ever do that.

We may conceive that there are many thousands of such cycles of Sensation going round and round in the same organism. From the periphery of the whole body they come, everything that touches it produces a cycle faint or strong, unconscious or conscious, painful or pleasant. From the distant outer world they pour in, through Sight and Hearing. They concentrate in one Ego from which they radiate outward in every direction, and form an encompassing invisible sense-world always moving about with the man and always changing and whirling within itself. All externality seems to be hurrying toward an Ego, wafted thither as it were, in order to be passed through the cycle of

Sensation which somehow returns what was sent forth.

But the pith of the difficulty still remains. How does the Ego produce this pivotal turn? How can it, the immaterial and unextended, take up the material and extended? All matter, the world is in a state of separation in itself; the undulations indicate a continual active separation. Now the Ego has also this side, the separative stage as a part of its process; still it has also the opposite, the overcoming of the separation and the return to unity. But let us grasp the salient thought: the Ego as separative is one with the external, material world and hence can and does respond to and take up the latter's undulations; but it also as complete Ego must overcome this separative condition of itself and of the world in itself, annulling all extension yet preserving and restoring it. Thus the Ego has to reproduce the external object in Sensation.

For instance, I see yonder flower. From it proceeds a movement of light-waves one after the other in successive separation till they strike my eye, where another set of wave-movements, the neural, starts for the brain-center. The delicate workings of that center no vision has yet witnessed, but so much can be said from the results: I (my Ego) am stimulated by the incoming influence and receive it, have to receive it in order to get the object. But this object as spatial and extended is annulled — for if it ever got into my brain with its material extension, that would be the end of my sensing it or anything else. I annul it as material, passing it through the zero-point of my Ego; but then I at once reproduce it and see it as a real object before me.

The Ego, grasping undulation or vibration, must be more than the line of waves, which can never turn back and grasp itself; this is just what the Ego is and does. The undulatory succession has to be reversed, else it would go on, wave after wave forever. Such a reversion is the inhibition of matter, immaterializing the material world, and thereby making it sensible. That is, the extended material object is properly a stage of mind, a constituent of its total process as All-Ego, which stage is often called Nature, the external world, the material Universe. This is what stimulates the individual Ego in Sensation, causing it to vibrate in response, since it too has a corresponding stage (the second of the Psychosis). But its final stage is the overcoming of the undulatory movement, and therein the sensing of the object.

The cycle of Sensation may be conceived with two halves or arcs: the first is the sweep from the outer object to the inner Ego, and appears in the external world as if belonging to the realm of matter. Hence it is measureable, subject to quantity, though we must not forget that this act of measuring, yea quantity itself is the work of the Ego turning back upon a phase of itself. But the second half or arc is the sweep back from the Ego to the object, and inhibits the material succession of the first arc, and so is non-material, ideal. The first arc is a progression in Space and a succession in Time; but the second arc is instantaneous, cancelling both Space and Time in the return to the object. Thus the Ego on the one hand responds to Space and Time, and so may be deemed both spatial and temporal; yet on the other hand it negates both and so is above both and determines both.

Hence comes the difficulty about localizing Ego, Mind, Soul. Is it in the brain, body, or elsewhere? It is in one sense localized as responding to Space; yet it is the inhibition of all localization as transcending Space. It is in the brain, yet at once outside of it, where the object is. We may regard the external world flowing in wavelets to the universal sea of the Ego, where all the special forms of Space, Time, and Matter are swallowed up for a moment and then thrown out again into externality as reproduced in Sensation by that Ego.

Undoubtedly there are many points in this process which are inexplicable. The very first fact is a mystery: How can that object ride on the light-waves to my retina, and then stimulate an image of itself? Then that image conveyed by the nervous fluid (as is supposed) to the brain-center — in what way, tell us? Science can yet occupy itself with such details for a million of years, more or less, and still leave something for the future. Meanwhile we too have the right to know somewhat; we can in a general way comprehend its total process, as above given, though an infinity of details remain and always will remain.

In addition to the psychical or immaterial arc producing the return to the object and hence knowledge, there is a second material arc returning through the nerves to the surface of the organism and producing action — the so-called motor energy, a primal manifestation of Will. Thus the outgoing movement may be conceived to have had two arcs, a psychical one to the object, which, however, makes the whole cycle, and a physical one to the corporeal periphery; while the incoming is physical. It is this Sensation with its Feeling (Pain and Pleasure), which bifurcates into Will and Intellect (Knowing), in the outward sweep. That is, in every Sensation I *feel* the object to be agreeable to my organism or the reverse, then I *will* it in some way through my motor organs, finally I *know* the object as sensed.

The outgoing psychical arc turning about and transforming the incoming physical arc makes itself the whole round of Sensation from object to Ego and back again. As this psychical return is the annulment of Time and Place, it cannot well be measured in its velocity. But the outgoing motor movement being physical (like the incoming) may be measurable. Some experimental psychologists seem to have confused these two outgoing arcs since they claim to have measured the time of the psychical return, which is just the annulment of time and must be instantaneous. It is a contradiction to say that psychical movements occur in time. Thought has been also declared to be " a form of motion." Yet it is that which conceives, creates motion; the latter has never yet been able to think itself and formulate what it is, having no self-returning and self-identifying power.

It is well to realize fully the fact that even to sense the world we have to make it over. The Ego is not only where the object is, but recreates it in form at least, and puts it there where God made it and put it. It is the Soul doing this, being not confined to the Body, but going forth and reproducing the objective world. When I see yonder house, I stay with myself here, but I also go out of myself to it and reproduce it and bring it back. Yet all this movement of mine is not in space, for I remain in one spot making the space which I pass through. My body has to penetrate real space in order to reach this object, but not my Ego, which is three things in one process: space-receiving, space-negating and space-positing.

From the foregoing account the doctrine results that the sensing Ego can take up the object and reproduce it formally, its outward form, color, etc., through the process of the Psychosis. But Sensation is not complete reproduction; the creative principle of the object, its essential inner nature, I cannot sense. For Sensation the object is something given, already existent. But cannot I (or Ego) get behind it to its creative source, or get into it and know that which makes it what it is as a whole, namely, object? Later an answer will be given to this question; at present we can only say that Sensation can furnish no such knowledge. Hence in the sense-world the physical and psychical elements are not fully harmonized, both sides in their inner creative essence remain apart, and the dualism persists. The object still defies the Ego from this last inner fortress to which it has betaken itself, and in which Kant says it can never be captured. Hence spring a number of doctrines which recognize both belligerents (Ego and Object) and seek to formulate a kind of peace or compromise, so that there may be a *modus vivendi* between the two sides. The best known of these compromises may be next considered — the doctrine of Parallelism.

XII.

Ever since the philosopher of Königsberg delivered his famous utterance that man cannot know things as they are in themselves, but only their appearance, the European philosophical world has been much troubled, particularly the German portion thereof. It is true that the same problem lurks in all Modern Philosophy from the Seventeenth Century down, as we shall soon note. The herculean labor of mind has been, and is yet to fill up somehow the yawning chasm between man and the world, or at least to build some sort of bridge or even rickety gangway from this side (Ego) to that (Object). Just now the crowd seems to be making a considerable lurch for a passage through what is known as PARALLELISM, an old scheme in a new suit of clothes.

The cycle of Sensation with its two arcs, physical and psychical, is what doubtless called into existence this doctrine of Parallelism, which is at present having such a revival. In its simplest form it runs thus: (1) No physical process, specially that of the brain, can produce directly a psychical process, that of the mind; (2) no psychical process can produce directly a physical process; (3) still between the two there is a correspondence, a parallelism, though there be no interaction.

Such a view implies that there are not two arcs of Sensation material and ideal (physical and psychical) but two cycles thereof, each a complete round in itself, a closed circuit in which the activities and processes are connected causally. In the one there is no member or link of the chain which is not physical; in the other there is no member or link of the chain which is not psychical. Each is a world in itself between which there are no openings for intercommunication. Like the Leibnizian Monad, each has no windows. Each of these worlds is the subject of investigation; the scientist works in the one, the psychologist in the other, each having its own phenomena and laws. The body is an automaton, driving its own machinery (as Descartes long ago held); the mind is also an automaton, though of a very different sort. Let the physiologist dig for his treasures in the one realm, and the psychologist dig in the other, each of these men advancing thereby his own special science.

And still the physical and psychical movements go together in Sensation. When I see a flower, there is a psychical outgoing which follows and seems to respond to the physical incoming. What causes the former state of consciousness? Nothing of its own psychical sort, as far as we are aware, yet the twain move together, though they cannot supposedly interact in a causal way as Body cannot reach Soul, nor Soul reach Body. Still they are parallel, each is the inseparable companion of the other. Nothing psychical without the concomitant physical, nothing physical without the concomitant psychical. No body without the shadow and no shadow without the body, yet both are absolutely separate in their mutual concurrence. Such is a glimpse of the theory usually called Universal Parallelism, which seeks to get the opposites, Nature and Spirit, together, and yet to keep them apart.

To be sure, some will at once begin to search for the common principle, since even the scientist and the naturalist are inclined to say that Spirit and Nature, Mind and Matter are at bottom the same. But the metaphysician particularly is in pursuit of this common principle, which is his *ousia* of the *on* or the essence of Being. It may be said that modern Philosophy has the foregoing problem as its own distinctive theme: How can this psychical Ego get at yonder physical object, sensing it and knowing it? Unquestionably the doctrine of Parallelism between Body and Soul suggests Descartes, who directly asserts that the physical organism of man is an automaton, a self-moving machine. Yet it is connected with the Soul which has its bodily seat in the pineal gland. (See his treatment in *Passions of the Soul*, art. 30, etc.

Also briefly stated in *Modern European Philosophy*, p. 97, etc.)

But it is the second great philosopher of the Seventeenth Century, Spinoza, who has brought to the surface and in his way solved the problem of Parallelism. "Body does not determine Mind to think, nor does the Mind determine the Body to move" (Ethica Bk. II, Pr. 2). Thus anything like mutual causation is eliminated. Still "the order of ideas is the same as the order of things" (Ethica Bk. I, Pr. 7). Such is the decisive statement of Parallelism: *ordo idearum est idem ac ordo rerum.* Thus there are two great streams of Being, which Being is the One, or in Spinozan nomenclature is Substance or sometimes God (*Deus sive Substantia*). In this way he gives the unitary source or cause of his Parallelism, which in its recent form has the tendency to remain dualistic. Nor must we omit in this connection the third great philosopher of the Seventeenth Century, Leibniz, who also wrestles with the same problem fundamentally and answers it with his doctrine of Monads, which are the primodial units or individuals constituting the Universe. Each Monad is independent, "has no windows," either for receiving or giving out, a self-contained atom. Now these Monads, both physical and psychical, have to be ordered, which supreme principle of order Leibniz calls Pre-established Harmony. For instance Soul and Body are compared by Leibniz to two watches, which run wholly independent of each other, yet run together, keeping the same time through the perfect pre-established ordering of their mechanisms by their maker. It is God, however, who establishes this pre-established Harmony, making Soul and Body move in parallel fashion, though they are entirely outside of each other. Thus Leibniz unfolds the idea of Parallelism, though with the Monads below and God above.

From the foregoing account it is evident that Parallelism was peculiarly the problem of the philosophy of the Seventeenth Century. Descartes, Spinoza and Leibniz all have it, and they all assign to God the task of uniting its dualism, though in different ways. The fact is significant that so many philosophers and also psychologists of the latter part of the Nineteenth Century, show the tendency to revert in this manner to the doctrines of the Seventeenth Century, even if with considerable changes. It looks as if Modern Philosophy was completing its cycle by going back to its beginning and thus rounding itself out to its fullness, perchance in preparation for taking some great new step. Of course the modern parallelist is inclined to leave out God entirely, or to supply his place with some "working hypothesis."

Let us now see what underlies this movement,

going back to its source in the great philosophers of the Seventeenth Century. In Spinoza (an Ego) Substance determines Thought as Attribute, and still further down the scale, determines the Ego as Mode. Yet what can be plainer than the fact that Spinoza's Thought is defining, ordering and re-creating Substance? Thus Substance or God is said to determine the philosopher's Ego as Mode at the bottom of the scale, and yet this philosopher's Ego is what is secretly determining Substance or God, who determines him. Without such an Ego to return to it and think it, Substance could not be; Spinoza's Ego is the hidden unmentioned pivot of his whole scheme. And it is his underlying Ego, lurking creatively in Substance, which constructs the parallel between *ordo idearum* and *ordo rerum*, and unconsciously links them together.

Next is to hear Leibniz state his Parallelism in one form: "in this system the Body acts as if there were no Soul, and the Soul acts as if there were no Body; yet both act as if one influenced the other" (*Monadology*, 81.) This last concurrence is the result of Pre-established Harmony between all the Monads of the Universe which are mutually exclusive, impenetrable, unknowable to each other, "having no windows." Still the Ego of Leibniz which is a Monad, knows all these things about unknowable

Monads, and really is the Pre-established Harmony ordering them from top to bottom.

In the case of both Spinoza and Leibniz the philosopher's Ego is again the secret demiurge creating the Universe which creates it, making or at least re-making the God who makes it, implicitly placing itself at the turning-point of the process of the All. Now Psychology is to grasp and to formulate this pivotal position of the Ego, and explicitly to constitute it an essential member of the process of the All. Our recent philosophers, with their doctrines of Parallelism and of psychical Primacy of various sorts, are evidently moving out of Philosophy and into Psychology as the universal science, without, however, reaching fully the goal. Pampsychism was certainly suggested by the fertile genius of Leibniz (see *Modern European Philosophy*, p. 333). Even the cell of Biology has been recently endowed with a soul.

In general the psychological Norm lies back of all these doctrines of Parallelism, but cannot make itself explicit. The Ego cannot yet formulate itself as a part of the process of thinking and of formulating the Universe, though it is doing this work in Philosophy. But in the latter part of the Nineteenth Century the transition begins, showing, as already noted, a psychological content in a philosophical form.

There is a recent and growing phase of this theory which is especially worthy of notice. A view is extensively held that the physical processes of the organism have in them a psychical element which belongs to all life and even to every cell. Fechner has set forth that the plant-world has its psychical, yea that the earth and stars and inorganic matter are sharers in the same principle. So we hear the word *pampsychism* uttered as a category which expresses the essence of all Being, and affirms "soul-life" to be universal, or the principle of the universe.

It must be granted that this is a great step toward a psychological view of the world. The universal soul-life is not conceived as a fixed substance but an active, yea self-active entity. Still it is in form metaphysical, it posits dogmatically an absolute principle, even though this be psychical. Nor is it fully conceived as the process of the Ego, the Psychosis, which reveals itself as the universal inter-connecting process of the All and of all things both physical and psychical. Fechner likewise belongs to the transition from Philosophy to Psychology, partaking of both; he is a psychologist-philosopher, a class to which Wundt also has been assigned, being in a number of things a pupil of Fechner, though he has surpassed his master.

The time has shown that any philosophy resting in Sensation (or Sense-perception), ends in

Parallelism, which cannot help being the foregoing species of dualism. The Ego and the Object can touch only in some outer relations or properties. The Kantian dualism between the two sides, mind and thing-in-itself, is really that of Sense-perception, and unless intelligence has some higher, more creative activity than mere sensuous Presentation, Kant's doctrine must hold in one form or other.

We find, however, that there is such an activity as Representation, in which both Ego and Object (as image) are psychical. But when I think the object which I sense, I have to penetrate and take up its inner creative principle, and not simply rest content with getting its outer form or its appearance. Thus I reach beyond and behind the realm of Sense-perception (to which Sensation belongs), and have begun to recreate the object which was given to me as something fixed, already existent, presupposed when I sensed it. Mark the result. When I start to thinking the object, I make it over, appropriate it, identify it with myself as creative. Its inner essence I find to be mine, so that the dualism between it and me begins to move into unity. What now has become of the independent Parallelism of the physical and psychical? The two arcs which seemed so distinct in Sensation, have found a common creative center, from which both are derived, though the outer sensuous appearance still remains. and is to be accounted for.

So we have attained to another mental activity, Thought, which quite reverses the situation as it came to light in Sensation. For in the sense-world the Ego could only get or seem to get the appearance of the Object, and not the essence; while in the thought-world the Ego gets and identifies with itself the essence of the Object, but not its appearance, which lies beyond it and cannot be re-created by it. Thus another creative principle than my Ego must bring forth the manifestation of the Object. That is, the individual Ego (Psychosis) has reached its limit and calls for the creative All-Ego (Pampsychosis).

One cannot truly *think*, and hold to the doctrine of Parallelism, since this vanishes in the presence of Thought. We have seen how the Thought of Sensation unites into one process the Ego and the Object sensed. Spinoza, upon whom Parallelism is mainly fathered, is not strictly parallelistic or concurrent, but consubstantial, since his parallels, Thought and Extension (psychical and physical) are united in the same Substance, which is the One above both. And if Fechner holds consistently to the universal Soul-Life as the principle of Nature and

Mind, what becomes of the Parallelism of the two sides as wholly separate?

Undoubtedly the psychological task of the preseet time is or has been to investigate Sense-perception, or specially Sensation, whose parallelistic suggestion is so strong. But behind and beyond Sensation, explaining it, unifying it, psychologizing it, has appeared Thought which has a good right to be cursorily considered in the present introductory outline.

XIII.

We have already had our look at Feeling, Will, and Intellect as the basic division of Psychology. Intellect in its turn, when formally divided, has its triune process of three stages which we name Sense-perception, Representation, and Thought. It is not our intention here to give a full and duly ordered exposition of these activities. But the course of our argument in this preliminary discussion has brought us to a place where we must unfold briefly the meaning of THOUGHT in Psychology. (For a fuller exposition of it the reader is referred to our *Psychology and Psychosis*, p. 425 *et seqq.*)

It has been already said that when I think the Object, my Ego penetrates to the creative essence of it and identifies the same with itself, Through Thought I am creatively what the Object is, and the Object is what I am; the process of my Ego finds itself to be the process of the Object, that is, the essential, creative process. When I think yonder house, I seek for its meaning, purpose, creative essence, which I try to state in my definition of it. What makes it a house? is the query of my Thought. It was built by an Ego, and I must in some way get hold of the creative design of the Ego in building it. Thus I re-build the house in and by my Thought; that is just my thinking it in the strict sense of the term. When I view the house, I obtain merely its outer form and some other externals; when I image the house, I recall or re-make that form in its absence. But when I think the house, I must get back of both percept and image; I must enter into the creative idea of its maker, and see that at work, beholding not merely the outer result. My Ego must penetrate to his Ego as manifested in its product, commune with him, and win the secret of his creating the present Object. The creativity of Thought is, then, the element which should be emphasized in defining it.

The reader will be apt to interrogate at this point: What about the natural object? We know that a man made the house, and hence we easily pre-suppose his Ego building it after some design or pattern. But how is it with a tree, for instance? The same general answer must be given. When I truly think the tree, it is not a percept, not an image, neither an external nor an internal copy; I must get its Thought, its Idea, which created it; my conception of it must be genetic. The tree belongs to Nature, and Nature in all her forms is a creative manifestation of the Divine Ego, which you have to recognize in and through your Thought. Natural Science, when we reach down to the bottom of it, will be found to be psychologic also, and its development will reveal the Psychosis, which is the inner working principle of Nature as well as of Mind. The architect of the house and the architect of the world are both Egos, and have ultimately the same archetypal pattern after which and indeed with which they build their structures.

Going back to the illustration of the house, let the reader ask himself: If I had some cunning instrument, some peculiar pair of tweezers, by means of which I could catch hold of the Thought of this house where I am now sitting, and jerk it out, what would become of the house and perchance of me? His answer to himself will be: I had better be getting out of it, for it will tumble to ruin. Thought is that which has constructed this ceiling overhead and holds it there; the floor which I tread on is a product of thinking. I take for granted that yonder door will open and shut, letting me in and out, for that is what created it, and put it into its place. Such indeed is its meaning, purpose, Thought, which we at once identify as an activity of the Ego creating all these parts of the House, each being a Thought which I have to recognize or re-think ere I can employ it. Before raising the window I have to re-think the Thought which made it; even this Thought gets to acting quite unconsciously and automatically.

And now the confession has to be made that this fundamentally creative character of Thought is hardly found with any degree of explicitness in English Psychology. And yet Psychology itself as a science is the product of Thought. Sensation by itself is not Psychology; you have to think Sensation, define, order it, before it becomes scientific. Thought is the third stage of Intellect which returns upon its first stage (Sensation) and then tells what the latter is. Yet this Thought creating Psychology is usually left hazy or left out of its own science. We hold that one of the chief needs of psychological science is to restore Thought. We call it a restoration, for the creative nature of Thought has long been recognized, being specially promulgated during the great Hellenic Period whose three illustrious names are Socrates, Plato, and Aristotle, each of whom represents a stage in the evolution of Thought.

So important do we deem this subject that we shall unfold it further. Socrates was the first philosopher who emphatically declared that the essence of Being (which it is the great purpose of Philosophy to find and formulate) is Thought. Before him indeed there was philosophizing and a good deal of it, but it never reached the point of seeing and asserting that its principle, content, purpose, was Thought. This means that the philosopher must get and express the creative Thought of the Object. If he merely utters this or that opinion about it without coming to its genetic center, he is not thinking. Socrates by his so-called dialectic endeavored to lead men out of opinion into Thought. Thus he makes the greatest epoch in all Philosophy; Plato and Aristotle in this regard simply continued and developed his work. That the essence of all things must be formed in the creative Thought of them, is the world's rich inheritance from Socrates. A consequence is that the essence of Psychology is the Thought of the Ego, which has to go back and think Feeling, Will and Intellect, formulating them into science. Finally the Ego as Thought must think itself thinking, wherein we reach the famous Aristotelian formula which declares that Thought-thinking-Thought is the supreme principle of the universe.

The Socratic view of Thought never fully lapsed from Philosophy, though it suffered obscurations. At the Revival of Learning, the great philosophers of the Seventeenth Century had it and employed it, often quite unconsciously;

we feel it lurking in that marvelously pregnant sentence of Descartes: " I think therefore I am." Now comes a most weighty fact in Modern Philosophy: the negative, skeptical Eighteenth Century abjured the Socratic heritage, declaring that the Ego as thinking cannot get the essence or truth of the Object, cannot know the Thing-in-itself. Locke, Hume, and Kant will all echo this doctrine in their various ways. Now it is the influence of Locke specially which has driven Thought out of Anglo-Saxon Thinking, which seldom if ever conceives of Thought genetically, as the creative essence of the Object.

If we look into the vast mass of works on Psychology produced to-day throughout Anglo-Saxondom, we find that usually there is a chapter on Thought set apart by itself, giving as its two chief characteristics Abstraction (of attributes or properties of the Object) and Generalization, which unites these special attributes into a general notion or idea. This general idea finds expression in language, in such words as *man*, *color*, etc., which are then concepts, the products of Conception. Without denying that these processes do take place, it is evident that they all lie outside of the essence of the Object which thus cannot indeed be known. Thought, it is assumed, is not able to reach that essence, but deals with its appearances, its phenomena, analyzing, synthesizing and classing them according to their external characteristics.

Now it is one purpose of the present work on Psychology to restore the creative nature of Thought, to recall it from its banishment which took place in the Eighteenth Century by the decree of John Locke, the most influential philosopher that the English race has produced. Moreover we hope to promote it from its former place in Philosophy, which it lost through the weakness of its philosophic support, to a new position and a new influence in Psychology, bringing it back to the creative energy of the Ego and endowing it with the latter's process in the Psychosis. In fact the science of Psychology is the product of creative Thought; all its formulated activities beginning with Feeling are Thoughts re-creating in essence and categorizing each stage of mentation. Now is Psychology, the science of Mind, to leave out the very activity of Mind which creates it? Can it be complete without finding and formulating that process of itself which reproduces and formulates all the other process of itself?

All men think, but they rarely know themselves thinking. See a man examining a new machine; he seeks to think it, to find what makes it, what is its creative principle. But he hardly thinks himself thinking, unless he be a psychologist. Yet the psychologists generally have not grasped themselves thinking Thought creatively; though they think and define what is Sensation, Apperception, or Representation, thus recreating in Thought what these really are, they rarely think Thought itself which is the creative energy behind the foregoing mental activities when psychologized. They making their science leave out the maker.

To the influence of Locke, then, we ascribe the fact that there is so little Psychology of Thought at present in the English language. Over and over again he affirms that we have " no knowledge of the internal construction of things, being destitute of the faculties to attain it;" that we have "but some few superficial ideas of things" given by Sensation and Reflection. (See especially Book II of the *Human Understanding*.) All of which means that we cannot truly *think* the object. Locke deeply influenced French Philosophy also, and we may find numerous traces of him to-day in German Wundt who can define Thought simply "as a relating or comparing activity."

At the same time there is something in the Object which the Ego does not and cannot recreate. I cannot make the tree, though I can think what makes it. Also I can sense the tree as Object, which, however, is a thing already created, existent in its own right. Hence we rise to the question: What creates the Object, or in general the World? Still further, whence comes the Ego with its peculiar power—what creates the Ego creative? As Thought previously reached back of the sensuous appearance to the generative principle of the Object, so now it must reach back to the generative principle of the Ego, which has been likewise hitherto taken for granted. Thus behind and beyond the individual Ego begins to loom up an All-Ego, out of and above the Psychosis towers the Pampsychosis.

If Kant had said that we cannot *sense* the Thing-in-itself, we would have to accept his statement; but when he implies that we cannot *think* the Thing-in-itself, we draw the line against him. Knowledge is of two kinds, sensing and thinking; the one knows the Object in its external presence as given or created, the other knows the Object in its inner creative essence. Kant's dictum has, therefore, an ambiguity; we may well ask him, which kind of knowledge do you mean, that furnished by Sensation or by Thought? By the former we cannot know the Thing-in-itself, by the latter we can. Yet how about this Ego knowing, thinking, re-creating the Thing or the Object? Hitherto it has been assumed as our starting-point, with its marvelous gift of self-knowing and world-knowing in one. But Thought, the creative, must at last insist upon getting back to its own creation in order to be true to its own nature. Herewith we impinge upon a new domain.

XIV.

In the foregoing sections we have taken the Ego for granted and in a manner let it unfold itself from its own center according to its inner power. Thus it has shown its peculiar nature in the Psychosis and in various special activities. But now we are to regard this same Ego as derived, created, endowed with the gift of its own process. From such a view-point it is conscious, and its activity we call CONSCIOUSNESS. This is the word which we adopt in order to suggest that the Ego must now be seen not simply as original but also as originated, as having its source in the All-Ego or the Universe.

Such an employment of the term is not usual. Consciousness on the whole has been conceived as the background of the mind behind which it is quite impossible to penetrate. Still the Ego as self-knowing cannot well be excluded from knowing its own origin. Perhaps more desperately than with any other of its concepts Psychology at present is struggling with Consciousness. It seems to lurk in every mental activity, to be the presupposition of the Ego itself. It works largely in the dark, though it can be made to throw its search-light back upon itself. That is, the action of Consciousness is mainly unconscious — a contradiction both in speech and conception till it be solved. The unconscious means the possibility of Consciousness; we hardly speak of a stone as unconscious, but the Ego is or may be. The sweep of Consciousness involves the unconscious (as potential), the conscious (as subject and object), and the self-conscious (the self-returning, self-knowing). Then we also speak of the sub-conscious and the supra-conscious. All these different meanings lurk in Consciousness, which is thus seen to be capable of developing into many separate stages, which will be put into their order later under Elemental Feeling.

Very numerous have been the views concerning Consciousness. For Hamilton it is the primal material "out of which all Philosophy is evolved" (*Lect. Met.*, p. 198). Wundt takes it to be the interconnecting medium "which unites all psychical activities" (*Grundriss*, s. 238). Lewes holds that each nervous center, each arc has its own Consciousness; thus we have millions and millions of Consciousnesses located everywhere in our body; our ordinary Consciousness is but one though the highest one for us, which, however, in its turn is probably integrated with still higher forms. Thus Consciousness seems to be the unitary principle of most if not of all things.

These statements are interesting as they seem

to show glimpses, yet only glimpses of what Consciousness truly is, the Psychosis in its primordial given or created condition. Another point often insisted upon is the absolute veracity and finality of Consciousness in matters of mind; if its report is false, then all philosophy and science are delusions. We can indeed be conscious of lying, but the claim is that just therein Consciousness is telling the truth when it calls us liars. But if it is conceived as telling an untruth, it becomes inherently contradictory and self-negative, for thus Consciousness is made to declare the truth of its untruth, and I am conscious of my Consciousness being false. The integrity, that is, the wholeness or allness of Consciousness (as the impress of the All in me) is asserted in its so-called veracity.

Yet there is a doubleness (as well as oneness) in Consciousness which lurks even in the etymology of the word. I know with Knowledge, (*con, scio*), but also I feel with Feeling. Thus Consciousness divides in itself, and therein goes with itself; it is its own concomitant. What does this mean? We see that Consciousness is a continual self-separating, and self-uniting; it splits itself in twain to be one with itself. This is the process of the Psychosis, of which Consciousness is the original elemental manifestation in the Ego, imaging and springing from the All-Ego. So we affirm that Consciousness is the Psychosis in its primordial protoplasmic form, with the suggestion of its origin, which goes back to the universal Self, bearing the very impress of the same in the threefold process of the Psychosis. Thus Consciousness is the Ego as self-creating and therein imaging the Universe as self-creating. For the Universe (or All-Ego) cannot be completely itself, that is, completely creative, till it creates an Ego like itself, capable of creating anew the Universe, which is itself.

Consciousness is thus the ever-present process of the Whole in each stage or activity of the Ego. The entire mind at work is really the entire Universe in each part or individual, who has, accordingly, Consciousness. The All in each is first shown fully in Consciousness which thereby interlinks each mind with the Universe.

Or we may say that God makes man as Ego, Consciousness, Psychosis, which, though created, must return to its source and re-create what created it — the World, the All. So the Ego as conscious starts with the non-Ego and develops Feeling, Will, and Intellect, as different ways or stages of getting the world.

Now we must especially note the word for this All-Ego which connects with Consciousness — which word is Pampsychosis, the psychical act of the All, or the Universe as psychical process. In this sense we say technically that the Pampsychosis produces the Psychosis, or human Consciousness, whose special trait as Consciousness is to return and reproduce the Pampsychosis. This is just the pure activity of the Ego as conscious: it reproduces the Pampsychosis, or the All-Ego with its process. Such, then, we may deem in Psychology the two extremes: Psychosis and Pampsychosis, or Man and God, between whom lies Nature or the Cosmos, which three and their process form the content of the three world-disciplines — Religion, Philosophy, and Psychology.

At present, however, we wish to emphasize the thought of Consciousness, in its origin and process, both of which spring from the All, which is therefore eternally present in every Ego. Pantheism says that this Ego goes back at death to its source in the All, and vanishes as independent. But the doctrine of immortality affirms the persistence of the Ego, which must be as enduring as the All-Ego, which makes it and is made by it. In fact, the individual Ego must be perpetually recreating the All-Ego, else it would not exist. God's and Man's immortality is one; God cannot endure in His completeness unless Man makes Him endure, and Man must be incessantly winning immortality by re-creating God in and through Consciousness.

In our technical speech we may, therefore, say that Consciousness is the manifestation of the

Pampsychosis in the Psychosis. The two belong together creatively, not merely along side of each other in a divine and human parallelism. Herein we reach down to the deepest suggestion in the word Consciousness. *Conscio*—I (the Psychosis) know with and feel with the Pampsychosis. My Ego cannot work, cannot have its process without the active impress and indeed co-operation of the All-Ego. I cannot know the object without being conscious, without knowing it with the Universe. In like manner I not only feel, but am conscious that I feel; in order to have any special Feeling, I must feel with the All at the same time, and the process of the All must be in me.

The question has been much discussed whether Consciousness is a special faculty, one among many other faculties. According to our view it should be classified as Feeling, yet in the right way. It is primarily a Psychosis, having within itself implicitly Feeling, Will, and Intellect. Still its dominating character puts it into the vast realm of Feeling as elemental. Consciousness taken by itself, is the immediate impress of the Universe in the Ego, or the Feeling of the All. It is not a specialized, finite Feeling such as love, and hate, not an emotion but rather the antecedent condition of all emotions. Consciousness in its simple abstraction is the Ego feeling the Universe as self-creating, or the process of the All-Ego in the individual Ego. (Here we shall drop the subject as we have developed it quite fully under the head of Elemental Feeling whose third stage is this All-Feeling in the Ego, or Consciousness. (See in the present book, pp. 113–217.)

Our next step must be to make explicit what is implied in the nature of Consciousness as just set forth, this being the product and the elemental process of the Universe in the Ego, which Ego we have seen rising to the conception of the Universe through its psychical activities. Thus a vast cycle begins to hover before the mind, the outlines of which we shall try to make more definite in the following section.

XV.

From the preceding account it is evident that Consciousness as the created process of the All-Ego in the individual Ego, which is thus creating and indeed self-creating, calls up for fresh formulation the total round of Being, the Norm of the Universe, which has now become psychological, starting with the Ego whose supreme function is to create anew the All which created it. Hence at present we have to give some considertion to the PSYCHOLOGICAL NORM or the new construction of the Universe through Psychology, which thereby becomes a new World-Discipline not supplanting but taking its place alongside of Religion and Philosophy.

In our ordinary psychical life we begin with two given factors, the Ego on the one side and the World (or the Object, or non-Ego) on the other. Now this Ego, who is Man himself, has a primordial elemental Feeling (which we may here simply assume) compelling him to take up and appropriate the World, or the Object outside of him, the realm of the non-Ego. Herewith rises into activity the original process of his Ego, the Psychosis, which grapples with the non-Ego or objective World, endeavoring to make the same its own through Feeling, Will, and Intellect, which three in this work still further divide into many forms or faculties so-called. These psychical activities of the Ego, seeking to appropriate the Object, constitute the first theme of Psychology, which has as its primary function to formulate and to order them into a science.

But what is the end, scope, design of our Psychology thus conceived? Whither is it bound? Evidently it is trying to think and to re-create in itself the World, to find in the same the creative principle of its Creator, to whom we are necessarily brought in this psychological journey through creation. Psychology may be deemed, therefore, in its primal function to be the return of the individual Ego to God, not through Feeling alone, or Intellect alone, but through the very process of Feeling, Will, and Intellect, which brings my Ego and yours into a psychical communion with the All-Ego, which likewise has in itself the universal process of Feeling, Will, and Intellect, or that of the Universe.

In this way the Ego has made an ascent (so we may conceive it) through Psychology to the source of its own and of all Being. It has mounted through the World reacting upon it and producing its activities, which we may image as a ladder of Feeling, Will, and Intellect, each with an infinite number of gradations, till it attains the all-creating Ego, which it must likewise recreate in order to win. Thus we come to the psychological insight that man has to reproduce that which produces him, he has to make anew not only the World but even his and its Creator. For man is the true child of God only by possessing the gift of his Father, namely, creativity, and possessing it to a similar excellence.

What is now the outlook? Through Feeling, Will, and Intellect, the Ego has risen to the creative fountain head of all things including itself, and has thereby interlinked itself into the process of the Universe which is constituted of God, World, and Man. The Ego through Psychology has made or rather re-made its place in the grand cycle of the All. It is the pivot through which the created World returns to its Creator, this pivotal Ego re-creating all the stages from the lowest to the highest. When I sense, represent or think the object, I have to recreate it in essence as God created it, formulating and putting it into its order through the Psychosis, which is both in me and in it, though of different degrees. Psychology thus is the science of the Psyche returning through the World to its Creator, the soul's return to its divine source.

But Psychology does not, cannot stop with this ascent from below; it must also grasp and formulate the descent from above, down through the created world till it comes back to itself as created, for it has to know itself both as created and creating, the derived on the one hand and the self-unfolding (evolutionary) on the other. Thus Psychology is seen to embrace the round of all Being — God, World, and Man — in its own peculiar Norm, which has the Ego as its turning-point from the created world back to its Creator. I, re-creating the objective world through Feeling, Willing and Knowing, mount up to the creative All-Ego who has created me creative, yea self-creative in Consciousness like unto it. Such is, we repeat, the psychological Norm whose content is God, World, and Man, or the process of the Universe (Pampsychosis).

We may now see that the Object or the World has a created, given, phenomenal side, which the Ego can sense but cannot directly create, since it is already just the created element. Strictly this is what all matter is, which the Ego cannot create but can transform. The Ego cannot, then, create the World, for this is already created, but it can re-create it, can think its creative Thought along with its Creator.

On the other hand the Ego has likewise a side of createdness. It is God-made, yet also Self-made; in fact its self-creative power is just its gift from the All-Ego, which is itself this self-creative power in its universality or as the Universe. The Ego is the created like Nature, and evolves its own self-creative Consciousness, which is nevertheless God-given. I am made by the Universe to make it over, I am created to re-create my Creator, and thus render him truly complete in his creativity. For certainly he is not complete as Creator till he brings forth a being as creative as he is in essence; it is the complete Man that makes the complete God.

Such is, then, the psychological (or pampsychical) Norm, whose formulation means a new World-Discipline through which all science is to be organized afresh. The philosophic Norm, though it has the same general content, namely God (or the Absolute), World, and Man, is different, since it leaves out the Ego recreating the entire process of the Universe, and projects this process into abstractions, such as Cause, Law, Essence. But now we are to reach back and take up the Ego which has made Philosophy, and has thrown out of itself these abstractions; every Ego is henceforth to have as its own the making of its own Philosophy, which is no longer to dominate it autocratically from the outside, even in form. Not the Philosophy as doctrine is alone to be received, but the creativity of the philosophy-maker is what is to be ultimately imparted, so that the recipient Ego becomes also creative, being taken up into the process of the Universe, and formulated with it as an integral part of it, as returning and re-creating that which created the Ego creative. Evolution is the regnant word in the Philosophy and in the Science of the Nineteenth Century. The Ego is indeed evolved; but not till this evolved Ego evolves the All which evolves it, making itself both sides, and completing the cycle of the Universe (which is our psychological Norm), is Evolution completed, being seen and expressed as a part or stage of the total process of Being. For if Evolution be universal, must it not be itself evolved? The psychological Norm shows the Universe evolving through Nature the Ego, but also it shows this Ego evolving the Universe, and thus rounding out the Great Totality.

We have alluded to the religious Norm which

posits a supreme personal Will as the creative source of the Universe. On the other hand the philosophic Norm takes an abstract principle, as Cause, Law, Atom, to be the essence of Being. (For a further discussion of the three Norms, religious, philosophical and psychological, the reader is referred to the introduction in the author's History of *Ancient European Philosophy*, particularly pp. 25–32.)

We may next ask, What is the meaning of this psychological Norm in the progress of nations, in the development of institutions, in the movement of humanity? Very distinctly does it put chief stress upon the worth of the individual who is now to take his pivotal place in the Universe, and even to be formulated as a necessary element of all science. Hitherto he has done the work, but has been largely left out. He is now to determine that which determines him, make the law which governs him, in fine re-create afresh what has created him. This does not mean that Law, Institutions, God are to be abolished or to be lessened in any way; on the contrary their influence will be heightened, when they no longer stand over against the individual, dominating him from the outside, but are perpetually re-created by him as an element of his deepest nature. He too belongs in the process of the All in spite of his separate, seemingly isolated individuality.

That institutional world which has developed the worth of the individual to its highest place and potency, is undoubtedly found in the Occident. Psychology in this new sense could not be the offspring of European Society, still less of Oriental. Every great period and indeed every great territorial division of civilized man has its own social and institutional character, which ultimately finds its highest expression in a World-Discipline. Creatively Religion belongs to the Orient, the prolific home of many Religions, among others of our own. But Philosophy in its truly genetic soul, belongs to Europe. Must not the Occident too have its expression in a World-Discipline sprung of its deepest spirit, which has already manifested itself in Institutions and especially in the State? Such is at least our view. Accordingly in the historic evolution of these World-Disciplines, Psychology will be creatively developed in the Occident.

XVI.

It is time to glance back at the preceding exposition, and to re-state the three leading psychical forms or Psychoses which have been unfolded. This statement will be given in psychological nomenclature, to which the reader will have to get used, since it is what definitely formulates and inter-connects the science. Technical terms cannot be avoided in any strict presentation of a scientific subject. We have already spoken of the word *Pampsychosis*, through which we seek to suggest that the Universe is psychical and also a process, as distinct from the divine Ego in itself, which is conceived as a stage of this process. Thus we hope to escape in Psychology the everlasting seesaw between Transcendence and Immanence (see following pp. 326–8), which has given and still gives so much trouble both to Theology and Philosophy, especially to the Kantian Philosophy and to all its students.

Here then, are the three main Psychoses, which may be deemed the fundamental sweep as well as the grand inter-connecting links of our science in its completeness.

1st. The Ego as the primal or elemental Psychosis, with its three stages metaphysically expressed. This we may regard as the germinal transition from Philosophy into Psychology, since the latter has to conceive and employ the abstract terms of the former in order to declare and to define itself. Having gotten the Psychosis we possess the organizing and uniting activity of Psychology and all its sciences.

This elemental Psychosis, or the process of the Ego as it is in itself, proceeds to grapple with the non-Ego, or the World, and passes over into the following.

2nd. The Ego as psychological Pychosis with its Feeling, Will, and Intellect, which arise through the Ego's attempt to take up and appropriate its *other*, the external world. We need a common word for Feeling, Will, and Intellect dealing with the object or the world, and taking it up emotionally, volitionally and intellectually, and thereby being determined to many activities which it is the function of Psychology as science to evolve, describe, and put in order. For this purpose we have often used the word *appropriation*, with some similar terms, which the reader has to make his own in the given sense. Feeling, Will, and Intellect, then, manifest various grades of appropriating the object.

But the Ego as this psychological Psychosis moves through the given, created world up to the All-Ego which has created it (the Ego) and the world. Here then is a new turn downward into creation.

3rd. The Ego as pampsychical Psychosis, or the All-Ego composed of God, World, and Man which constitute the psychical process of the Universe or Pampsychosis.

Often we have said that Man or Ego is the child of the Universe and bears the impress of the same in Consciousness, which is also, in itself considered, the elemental Psychosis above mentioned, or the primordial process of the Ego. The Universe is fundamentally self-creative, for what is there to create it but itself? Still its self-creativity must be a process, which involves the created Ego returning and recreating its Creator. It requires the whole Universe to produce man (Ego), but this product must in its turn be productive of what produces it, else this producing principle is not the Universe, which, to be itself, has to produce itself as productive, has to create itself as Creator. That is, the All-parent must impart to his child (the Ego) that which makes him All-parent, namely the power of begetting anew the All. Thus through the Ego begotten of the source, yet returning and re-begetting the same, the cycle of the All or of the Universe is completed, the Ego being that oft-mentioned pivot which finishes the round of the Great Totality, whose expression is now the psychological (or pampsychical) Norm.

This Norm we may briefly indicate in its three stages as follows, (*a*): The Absolute Ego as creative, the First Self, (*Urselbst* of Schelling, the All-Ego in itself; (*b*) the World as created, the not-Self as the utterance, or externalization, or appearance of the First Self; (*c*) Man, the Second Self, created but also creating and self-creating as conscious, whose supreme function is to go back to his creative source, recreating and formulating the same through its entire course.

Such is the grand Totality of Being in its process psychologically conceived. It is not the philosophical Norm of that same Totality, nor does it assert the primacy of any special mental activity. On the contrary the Ego is taken as the complete process of Feeling, Will, and Intellect rising to its genetic source, in the All-Ego through its own psychical act, the Psychosis.

If I say that the essence of Being (the *ousia* of the *on* in philosophical speech) is the Psychosis, this is no longer a mere abstract principle like Cause or Law, but is the Ego itself declaring its process to be the essence of Being. The philosophic Ego of all time, seeking the essence of Being in some abstraction projected out of itself as universal, has now discovered that it (the Ego) in its own process is what it has been searching for down the ages. So it necessarily makes the transition from Philosophy to Psychology, the latter supplementing and completing the former.

Thus Psychology gives primarily as the science of the Ego, the inner movement of all Being. Considered in this light it is a kind of logic, formulating in its categories the essence of whatever exists. As already stated it is etymologically the *Logos* of the *Psyche*, which penetrates and interconnects both the inner and outer worlds. The old logic of Being is thus supplemented if not supplanted by what originally made it, namely the process of the Ego.

But our Psychology remains not engrossed in

its own pure movement; on the contrary it has its side of application, yea it applies itself to the other sciences, giving their inner fundamental movement and connection. We have seen Psychology proper evolving itself by appropriating the object through Feeling, Willing, and Knowing, till it attains the creative All-Ego creating and putting the impress of itself upon all creation. When the Ego, rising through its psychological ascent, reaches its pampsychical process as God, World, and Man, it finds the creative principle not simply of itself, but of the Universe, which it proceeds to re-create in thought, that is, to psychologize. Here lies the realm of its application to Science, whose material the Universe must furnish. The Ego goes forth from its inner subjective realm with the certainty of finding its own creative process in everything. Thus the Ego having psychologized itself, must proceed to psychologize the Universe, not merely as a Whole but in all its special divisions, which give of course the special sciences.

In another and possibly more technical way we can state this matter. The Psychosis, having evolved the Pampsychosis as the creative process of the Universe, itself included, will proceed to identify this process (the Pampsychosis) particularizing itself in every special department of science — in Nature, Art, Institutions, etc. That is, the elemental Ego (Psychosis), being itself the created process of the creating Universe (Pampsychosis) will seek, recognize and formulate this process as the fundamental creative fact of every science. Psychology thus has to re-create the subject-matter of every department of which it treats, giving the origin thereof from the All, as well as formulating the details in their psychical order.

The next topic naturally will be a survey of the sciences psychologized. As Psychology starts its movement in Feeling, Will, and Intellect, these are to be taken as the ordering principle of the sciences. First comes a Psychology of Religion, since the Feeling of the All-Ego or God is the primordial act of the Ego, is indeed our very consciousness. Out of Will, with its native sense of Freedom, spring the sciences of Ethics and Institutions. From Intellect mainly we have to derive Art, Poetry, and what we may call the alethic sciences of Nature, History, and Philosophy. This brief summary we cannot here expand; we can only say that Psychology is their one normative science. (A somewhat fuller account of this subject is given in the following pages under the head of Absolute Feeling, since all these sciences, though unfolded from and organized under different psychical activities, call forth Feelings of their own. See the introductory statements at pp. 309, 336. 363, etc.)

The main thought is, however, that Psychology, when it attains its supreme purpose, is to show and formulate each activity of the mind interconnecting with all things and with the very All, through their common process, the Psychosis.

XVII.

We have now reached the point at which we can take up the divisions of Psychology proper, and give some idea concerning them in advance of their detailed exposition. These divisions are our well-known Feeling, Will, and Intellect, each of them a vast subject in itself. As already stated they all are seeking to appropriate the Object, are stimulated by it in some way to their own respective inner activities. The Ego, in thus endeavoring to make the world its own, is really trying to find its own origin (always the deepest instinct in man, as the poetry of all peoples shows). Upon this origin or creative source of itself it will come when it fully attains the All-Ego or the Pampsychosis, which will also reveal the genetic element not only in it but also in the world, its counterpart. At present, however, we are simply outlining the total process of Psychology, in its three main stages or divisions.

1. *Feeling.* This is the process of the Ego within itself turned inward, immediately, by some

outer determinant. The object or the world stirs the Ego to its primal psychical act which varies according to the different stimulating objects outside. (Feeling is specially set forth in the succeeding portion of the present volume.)

2. *The Will*. The Ego with its elemental process is stirred by the object to go forth out of itself, and to meet and to transform the same (the object) after its own pattern. Hence the Will is psychologically the stage of primal separation, and develops various inner forms of its own which gives the basis for Ethics and Institutions. (This subject is specially treated in a volume of the present series called *The Will and its World*.)

3. *The Intellect*. The Ego with its elemental process is stimulated by the Object to reproduce this object in some form within itself. I reproduce within myself the thing sensed, represented, thought, though in different degrees of reproductive energy. Thus I know it, Intellect giving knowledge as distinct from feeling and volition. (This subject has likewise its special treatment in a volume of the present series entitled: *Psychology and the Psychosis—Intellect*.)

Some general observations upon these three divisions may be discursively added. Feeling is the native, elemental, almost automatic Psychosis; the object is not known by it, but influences merely. Nor does the Psychosis strictly know itself in Feeling, though it has what we call self-reference (see p. 58). Consciousness is primarily a Feeling, and even Self-consciousness has its roots in Feeling, and cannot be divorced from it in treatment. (See following p. 147.)

Moreover these three — Feeling, Will, and Intellect — form a Psychosis together, and each forms a Psychosis in itself—which fact has been set forth in the section on Method.

It may be here remarked that Psychology has unfolded more and more toward a complete development of each of these three stages. Feeling, for instance, though the first in order has been the last to develop, in fact it is not yet developed in science to the same degree that we find in Will and Intellect. The reason for this backwardness is that it cannot get hold of itself, it has to be organized through another power, namely, Intellect. On the other hand Intellect, though the last in order, has been the first to develop, since it knows and formulates itself in thought, and thus is the organizer and formulator of the other mental activities and indeed of everything.

XVIII.

The educator who has entered into the meaning and scope of this preliminary essay cannot have failed to note that it has certain far-reaching pedagogical implications. If the method of the

Psychosis is the true method of all mentation and indeed of all science, then the science of Education is assuredly to be psychologized after this norm. Education deals primarily with the human Ego, particularly with that of the child. If the Psychosis is the fundamental process of this Ego, which on the one hand is to be unfolded in itself into its complete activity, and on the other is to be seen and formulated as the essential principle of God, World, and Man, then the Psychosis must have the supreme stress in pedagogical science. Moreover it is to enter the class-room practically, and become the organizing principle of the recitation, since it is the deepest inner bond between teacher and pupil. Particularly if our American pedagogy is ever to move out of its present chaotic distress, it must be through a world-discipline which is sprung of and images our social and institutional life.

And here we feel compelled to insert an observation which is derived from personal experience. In teaching this Psychology a class can be easily wrecked by following the old rectilineal way of going straight through the book, instead of proceeding cyclically with the whole subject and then with its parts. For instance, if the class is studying Intellect, the Psychosis of the entire subject must be first given; at the start we must grasp the totality of the theme and its process as Sense-perception, Representation, and Thought. Then each of these stages is to be formulated as a Psychosis, before descending to further details. That is, Sense-Perception, the first stage of Intellect, has itself three stages of the Ego, which is present as a Whole in it, these three stages being Sensation, Perception, and Apperception. Then each of these three, being the mind in one of its special activities, has likewise its Psychosis, which connects it as a part not only with Sense-perception, but also with Intellect, yea with all Psychology, and indeed with the Universe itself, which is a Psychosis. Such is the method here employed, which internally interlinks every special activity of mind with all other special activities and with the whole mind, and finally with the All. Now unless this process is brought out by the instructor in its lesser round as well as its largest sweep, the main fruit of studying Psychology is lost, and the science drops dead, which otherwise is and can be made the ultimate communication to the very Self of the pupil. The true teacher is always dealing with that soul before him, and the Psychosis is the common bond between the two, which in Psychology is to be brought out from its lurking place and is to be manifested through the activity of both minds in a kind of mutual integration. But when this integration does not take place, the two souls remain outside of each other, and the Psychosis falls down to a shriveled and ghastly formalism, which causes the Ego to shiver, as if in the presence of its own corpse. The formalist, particularly the formalist trained by metaphysical science, is apt to wreck concrete Psychology, till he gets the discipline of the Psychosis, his procedure being so different from it.

The mental particularism and narrowness which comes of the infinite division and specialization in the science of to-day, is to find its corrective in Psychology, of course in the right Psychology. For this moves in the other direction: it brings to unity all the scattered particulars, which are the result of special investigation; it gathers the products of many minds and indeed of many centuries, and stamps them with the impress of one mind, which can organize them after their fundamental principle. Such was once the function of Philosophy, and this discipline is by no means yet to be dispensed with in a complete education. There must come a new University, the *universitas extra universitatem*, which will show itself truly universal by universalizing the mind, by making it go through and appropriate the very process of the Universe Such is one of the tasks, now getting urgent, of Psychology.

In conclusion we re-affirm the new position and worth of man in the Supreme Order, as set forth in Psychology, He is to determine what deter mines him, is to make the law which governs him, is to re-create what created him. Philosophy posits dogmatically its principle which the Ego is to accept and follow, but Psychology trains the Ego finally to make its own doctrinal system, to be creative in the highest sense, and so to formulate its own Absolute. I am to acquire from Psychology not merely a body of principles, but also the creativity behind them; every one is ultimately to be his own psychologist making his own Psychology, to be not simply the learner but to become the master. Moreover the true teacher is to have his calling transformed by Psychology, for he is endowed by it with a new function. He is not simply to propagate his doctrines and his formulas to a band of devoted disciples whose life-work is chiefly to repeat him, though this may have to be done at first and even continued for years. He is to impart not alone his organized thought but the power to organize it, which is the great ultimate end of education, even if it be yet an unattained ideal. The pupil is indeed to learn and to learn thoroughly the formulated system of Psychology, but this is only the means for bringing him to make his own formulation. We have to think that every Ego as the child of the Universe must be endowed with the latter's creativity in some degree, if this be but brought out in the right way; and to bring it out is just the function of the teacher, who shows his highest capacity by rearing pupils who surpass him. When the philosophic master has his school with its members bearing his name — Platonist, Aristotelian, Herbartian, Hegelian — and thinking only in his categories after him perchance with a certain chivalrous sense of loyalty beautiful and admirable in its place, that we call European, feeling in it a certain autocratic or aristocratic supremacy of the master which Psychology is to transcend when it becomes fully matured. But not this alone: Education has now the outlook of making every Ego not only his own psychologist, but even of making him his own Genius (see following pp. 377-8).

With a little gasp at such a prospect, far-off as yet, we may wind up these Prolegomena (fore-words), and start to grapple with our main task, by no means inconsiderable, of defining, organizing, and interconnecting the science of Psychology, in its three grand divisions of Feeling, Will, and Intellect. When this task is fairly done, another and much greater looms up, that of applying our central creative science to the total cycle of special sciences, re-creating them psychically, and uniting them together in a universal order, from every part of which, even the smallest details, gleams the creative soul of the Universe.

Introduction to Feeling.

Of the three divisions of Psychology — Feeling, Will, and Intellect — there is no doubt that Feeling is in the least developed, most chaotic condition. In fact, it has been called just the chaotic part or stage of mind, which the other stages (especially Intellect) are to organize and to bring into some sort of order. Will such an order be Feeling still? Certainly; otherwise there can be no science of Feeling, which is a chaos till it be ordered. A chief difficulty is that Feeling has in itself small power of self-ordering; this has to be done from the outside, has to be largely imposed upon it through the self-conscious Intellect.

We often say and truly say, "my feelings in

this matter cannot be described." Some psychologists accordingly have affirmed that language is inadequate to tell what Feeling is, since " the essence of Feeling consists in being felt." Nevertheless these same psychologists continue to talk and to give us good long Treatises upon Feeling. After having decapitated themselves, they still walk around without difficulty, holding their heads in their hands (like St. Denys) with no diminution of the power of speech. Now it must be granted that the description or definition of Feeling is not the Feeling itself. But the same objection would hold against any other department of mind, and could be directed against all science. Feeling, however, can be described fairly well, and ordered too; at least the beginning already made can be continued. The object of the Psychologist is not to feel, but to know Feeling. Another favorite statement found in the works of most Psychologists of to-day is that Feeling is " the subjective side of mind," its internal phase, and hence its interesting aspect to itself (*Sully* and many after him.) But certainly Will and Intellect are just as subjective as Feeling — all three being stages of the subjective Self. And it is difficult to see why Feeling is more interesting to the Ego than its Will and Intellect. These categories or descriptive terms pertaining to Feeling tell us nothing distinctive, and hence are inadequate.

I. In the treatment of Feeling we have to start with the concrete Ego as assumed, though this assumption must be unfolded into a proof of itself in the course of the exposition. The Self is to reproduce itself in its development, and thereby show its origin. Thus it reflects the Universe, which must be its own eternal self-reproduction. Moreover we may also take for granted at present that the Ego is a process in its Feeling, is what we call a Psychosis, which is the underlying unitary movement in all forms of mentation.

At this point, then, we shall give a preliminary definition of Feeling as *the process of the Ego within itself turned inward.* Such a preliminary definition must be in the first place as general and as all-embracing as is the entire field of Feeling; but, in the second place, it must be capable of being specialized into the definition of every particular Feeling within this field. Now the starting-point of specializing Feeling in general lies in the question: *Turned inward* by what? By some object or class of objects which stimulate it to activity or determine it. With such a determinant variety of Feeling enters and classification begins.

Going back to the other part of the definition, we find the statement: *the process of the Ego within itself.* This indicates the subjective character of Feeling; it is the process of the

Ego within itself. But both Will and Intellect are also such a process; hence this part of the definition expresses what is common to all three primal divisions of the Ego, to Feeling, Will, and Intellect. Each is a process, and a psychical process or Psychosis, not a dead or quiet result; moreover, the Ego has this process within itself, which fact makes it subjective, as distinct from an objective process, which takes place outside the Ego. For this reason (we may repeat) it is a mistake to say that Feeling is the subjective side or aspect of mind, as if differing in this regard from Will and Intellect.

But there is in the above definition a point at which Feeling is seen differentiating itself from Will. If Feeling is *turned inward*, Will is *turned outward*. We may consider the Will to be *the process of the Ego within itself turned outward* toward the object, which it endeavors to possess or transform. This is, of course, subjective Will, the original of all forms of Will. Intellect, the third stage of the Ego is in its way a union of Will and Feeling, the two other stages of the Ego. It is primarily turned outward toward the object which it appropriates and then turns inward, assimilating the same to itself in knowledge.

In this way we define Feeling and contrast it with its two correlative elements in the process of the Ego (Will and Intellect). If the fore-

INTRODUCTION. 9

going exposition be correct, we have a general formula which covers the entire domain of Feeling, and from which all its particular forms can be derived through its varied determinants.

II. We may state the general fact of Feeling to be the reception of the world immediately into the Ego, which is stirred thereby to its primal, native, automatic activity, to what we may call its elemental Psychosis, or the Feeling of Self in its primordial manifestation. The world, or we may say the Universe, is, therefore, the first determinant of the Ego to Feeling.

Now this Feeling cannot know, and cannot express itself. Hence the Psychology of Feeling as a science must employ Intellect, which goes back and knows Feeling. Through Intellect Mind is self-knowing and thus becomes conscious of itself even as unconscious, conscious of itself as Feeling. It is Intellect which can determine by definition the undetermined, universalize the particular, express what cannot express itself. A twofoldness we note here in the science as distinct from Feeling itself; the first stage of the Ego (Feeling) must be taken up and organized by the third stage (Intellect), in order that it become known, which is indeed its higher destiny. In Feeling we simply feel; in the science of Feeling we no longer feel (or perchance we feel a little) but we know Feeling. The Ego as Feeling has to move forward to Intellect in order to complete itself; the Ego as Intellect has to move backward to Feeling in order to complete itself. Feeling has in it a negative, grinding, self-triturating element, from which it obtains a certain relief, if not total release through the Intellect, which separates the Ego from its Feeling and brings it to look back at the same as a stage transcended.

It is evident that Feeling properly comes before Intellect in the psychical order, not after it, as many psychologists affirm. Feeling is more individual, capricious, and even irrational, while Intellect is more universal, self-reflecting and hence deliberative, having as its culmination Reason, which Feeling in itself has not or has confusedly in the form of instinct. The so-called training of the heart is not the work of Feeling alone; rather is it the work of the Intellect putting a rational content into Feeling and making it permanent in our emotional nature. In fact Feeling as such cannot discipline itself, though it certainly can take discipline the profoundest, and be completely transformed and even transfigured.

III. It is, accordingly, my Intellect and not my Feeling which can create and utter the foregoing formula of Feeling as *the processs of the Ego within itself turned inward.* Feeling does not know itself, though we may well say that it feels itself, having an inner resonance or echo of itself. Feeling has this element of self-separation and self-return, which act, however, never rises to a full self-consciousness, such as we see in Intellect. Still the total process of the Ego is present in Feeling, though implicit. (More about this dual character of Feeling later, particularly under the head of Pain and Pleasure.)

Now Intellect, being the explicit self-conscious process of the Ego, can unfold and make explicit this implicit unconscious process of the Ego which is Feeling, giving to the same a language and an organization.

It is evident that Feeling is much more difficult to formulate than Intellect, which is in a manner self-formulating, self-conscious, knowing and expressing itself. The word is universal, Feeling is particular; hence the two are opposite till their contradiction is harmonized by thought. The words *fear* and *love* express Feelings but are not Feelings, being the thought thereof, which properly has no Feeling. Thought can think Feeling and define it, but Feeling cannot feel Thought except remotely and implicitly, and cannot define it at all, having strictly no articulate speech of its own, though we speak metaphorically of a language of the emotions. Properly the Psychology of Feeling is its right language, though quite devoid of Feeling.

There is, accordingly, an immediate element in Feeling which escapes our science, because the one is immediate and the other mediate or knowing. Feeling thus has its own right and its own place in the process. Here again we must insist upon the order of these two activities: Feeling is to come before Intellect, whose chief function in the present relation is to turn back upon Feeling as given, to know it and to formulate it in a system of definitions, which constitute its science. Intellect must be grasped or rather grasp itself as the third or self-returning stage of the Ego whose first stage is Feeling as immediate.

IV. The world and all that is in it are made to be felt, as well as to be known. Feeling may be said to have this end: it is to take up and appropriate all that is external to it including its own echo or reverberation. It is primarily to make inside what is outside, putting the All into the form of the unconscious Ego which is a stage in the grand journey toward self-consciousness. The Universe must be felt as well as thought, indeed before it is thought. Thought itself may be deemed a clarification of Feeling, a working-over of the unconscious into the self-conscious.

From the standpoint of Feeling the Ego must be regarded as capable of feeling all things and the All (*panaisthetikon.*) Out of this primal stage, which is merely a capacity or potentiality, the feeling Ego will advance till it feels the All organized in Religion, Art and Institutions, which organization or order (the work of an organizing Ego) it will take up into Feeling and thereby mount to its supreme point in the present sphere. In other words the Psychosis will feel the Pampsychosis as ordered, and attain what we call Absolute Feeling.

Thus the feeling Ego runs through a vast gamut of tones from lowest to highest, being struck like an instrument of music by an ever-varying outside world to whose lightest touch or hardest blow it thrills in response. Or we may compare Feeling to the chameleon which is said to take the color of the object upon which it rests, having its own inner process as alive, yet also changing with its determinant. In like manner Feeling remains the one subject ever shifting and turning in accord with its environment. But for such adjustment it has to have its own movement within; a stone cannot thus change, and so cannot feel.

If now we revert to our formula of Feeling as *the process of the Ego within itself turned inward*, we find that it is turned inward by the world, which thus is felt. An omnisentient Ego on one side and an omnisensible world on the other may be regarded as the two given extremes of Feeling, between which lie all its varied forms.

V. That feeling is one of the three stages or

elements in the tripartite division of the Ego or Soul has long been seen. Indeed the conflict between Reason and Feeling is as old as rational man, who, as soon as he began to reflect upon himself, must have discriminated between the two sides. With the rise of Philosophy and especially of Ethics, the nature of Feeling must have been recognized and described.

It is, therefore, a serious mistake to say that the threefold division of Mind originated with Kant. Such is generally the statement of German writers, who are largely followed herein by English and American psychologists. A far better case could be made out for ancient Plato with his triple division of the soul, though there are uncertainties in such an interpretation. But we need only consider his *Philebus*, which is essentially a treatise upon Pleasure, in order to find Feeling examined and emphasized with great distinctness. It is curious to observe Sir William Hamilton denying in the most dogmatic manner Plato's claim in favor of Kant's (*Lect. Met.*, p. 560), and then to see him citing the *Philebus* in regard to the nature of Pleasure and Pain, which Hamilton regards (erroneously, we believe) as quite the sum total of Feeling.

We shall have, then, to think that Feeling had been observed separately and designated clearly as a leading division of the mind, together with

Intellect and Will, long before Kant. Still it must be confessed that Feeling has been the slowest of the three to get organized; in fact it is not yet satisfactorily organized. The divisions of both Will and Intellect are pretty generally accepted by psychologists, at least such is the case with their primary divisions. But how to divide Feeling is still an unsettled question. This comes from its indefinite nature, in which all limits seem to run together into one indistinguishable mass. Still these limits exist though they have to be dug out and brought to light by Intellect, which is the self-defining and hence the all-defining.

Such is the task which lies at hand. We shall attempt, before preceding to details, to give some notion of the three leading divisions of the total realm of Feeling, which must, however, find their justification later, when their complete sweep is seen with all the subdivisions.

VI. At this point, then, we must again pick up our formula and show it differentiating itself into the three fundamental stages of Feeling. If this be *the process of the Ego within itself turned inward* by various determinants, we must first seek to find the leading classes of the latter in the present sphere. Already we have noted the extremes — Ego on one side, and on the other the Object, the World, the Universe. These two sides begin interacting in Feeling; the function of the one is to feel the other in all its gradations. Let us call the determinant of the Ego to Feeling the All in the present very general outline of the total movement of our theme.

(I.) *Turned inward* by the All in itself, which stimulates the Ego immediately, as member of itself (the All). The Ego here is not separated from its determinant, the Universe, but is an organic part of it, and as such feels its influence, as the limb feels what affects the whole body. So the total organism of the Universe determines the Ego as member to a Feeling of that Totality. I feel the All in every glance upward at the starry sky in the night.

The movement in this sphere is from the Ego given, to the Ego reproduceed, individualized, separated from the All. The All in its turn has its process likewise, moving from an implicit unity with the Ego to an explicit condition, which divides from it the Ego. This stage of Feeling we call the *elemental*, being an element of the All, as well as the earliest form of Feeling.

(II.) *Turned inward* by the All separated and particularized, which is the outer world of manifold determinants moving the Ego to Feeling. The All must now be conceived as divided into the Ego and itself, each being taken as outside of the other. This, however, is really not the case, the separation between Ego and Universe is an appearance, which is to be overcome.

The movement is now from this dismemberment to a re-organization, from a separative individual Feeling to an associative Feeling (sympathy), in which the Ego begins to re-unite itself with the All. This second stage of Feeling shows the Ego asserting its individual freedom (as Feeling) against the determination of the external world limiting it and making it finite. So we call this stage of Feeling *finite*.

(III.) *Turned inward* by the All organized and formulated as the process of the Universe (the Pampsychosis) which is creative of the Ego now determined by it. That is, the Ego as recipient is stimulated to take up into Feeling and to unite with itself the Universe as self-mediated, or as absolute.

But this formulated process of the All or Universe is the work of an Ego endowed with the creative power of thought (genius), which work determines many recipient Egos to a common Feeling with it, and so unites them in Religion and Social Institutions, in Ethics and Aesthetic. This is the third leading stage of Feeling which will be named *absolute* in the present exposition.

Thus we find that the third stage of Feeling as just set forth returns to the first stage and takes up the unorganized All which the Ego there felt, and organizes the same into a process which every Ego is to feel — it is to feel the ordered Universe (third stage) not merely the unordered (first stage) or the disordered or dismembered (second stage). Such is the purpose and end of the entire movement of Feeling: to bring the Ego to feel the order of the Universe in the latter's psychical process (the Pampsychosis). This we may well deem the highest development and cultivation of Feeling.

The whole subject of Feeling will, accordingly, be considered under the three following heads: —

(I.) *Elemental Feeling:* the Ego united with the All as organic member, is determined to Feeling by the same.

(II.) *Finite Feeling:* the Ego disunited from the All which is itself disunited and dismembered, is determined to Feeling by the same.

(III.) *Absolute Feeling:* the Ego re-united to the All re-organized, is determined to Feeling by the same.

The nomenclature of Feeling offers peculiar difficulties. The English word (Feeling) has the same form as adjective, participle, and noun. This linguistic defect is fundamental, and makes the formulation of the present subject more difficult in English than in any other European tongue of equal development. And no different word can be found to take its place. We shall help ourselves out in part by writing the word with a capital letter when a noun (Feeling), and by using a small letter to begin it when an adjective or participle (feeling). So we can distinguish between *the Ego as Feeling* and *the Ego as feeling*.

Part First.

ELEMENTAL FEELING.

This is the first general division of the entire realm of Feeling. The process of the Ego within itself is now turned inward immediately by the All of which it is a part. Conceive your Ego to be an organic member of the total Universe, and as such member to be determined by this Universe. Your arm is an organic member of your entire body and responds in many ways to the determinations of the latter; it feels the corporeal Whole immediately, acting spontaneously in defense of the same or dropping helplessly when its source, the body, is incapacitated. Carry this relation up into the All and behold yourself as a member of it receiving its influences and making them an element of your own inner life. Such influences springing from the Great Totality and wrought over directly into the process of your own Ego, become Feelings, since they are the process of the Ego within itself turned inward, its primal activity (or Psychosis) roused and thrown back upon itself. And more specially, they become Elemental Feelings of the Ego, since the latter is not separated from the determining Totality, but is an element of it, organically connected with it as member. Later the Ego, having attained its free individuality, will hold itself separate from the Totality — in which state it will have a wholly different kind of Feelings called Finite, which are to be considered hereafter.

In the present sphere of Elemental Feeling we must not forget that the Ego is inside the universal organism, of which it is a directly connected limb or member, in immediate unity with the same. The human Ego as individual soul with its body is determined by the All-soul with an All-body (cosmos).

And now having fairly settled the limits of Elemental Feeling as a whole, we are next to grasp its inner movement. In it we first find the idea of Feeling, as this is taken by itself, abstractly, quite apart from the concrete Ego, though the latter is implicitly present. Next comes the fact that this abstract or ideal Feeling is determined by the Totality as **ext**ernal or as Nature (or the world), which thus becomes the content of this otherwise empty form of Feeling and produces what is often called natural Feeling. Finally rises the all-feeling Ego which has lain back of the two preceding stages, but is now become explicit, distinct, yet still elemental, being kept in organic relation to the determining Totality, though reacting against it, and struggling to get free of it.

In accordance with these statements, we shall definitely bring together under the following heads the process of Elemental Feeling:—

I. SELF-FEELING; this shows the feeling Ego taken by itself, abstracted from its outer content, as formal, ideal. Yet this abstract Self-Feeling has to be determined to its activity by the All, of which it is a part. The subjective process in itself or the pure Psychosis.

II. WORLD-FEELING; the feeling Ego is now filled with a content from the external world which is outside of it, yet which with it belongs to the same great Totality or the All. The subjective process is here really determined by the object, both being within the All.

III. ALL-FEELING; the content or the determinant of the Ego is now the All in its Self-reproductive process, which stimulates the Self-feeling Ego to participate in the process of the Universe, that is, to become All-Feeling (Feeling

ELEMENTAL FEELING. 23

of the All). The process of Self-Feeling (pure Psychosis) is determined by the process of World-Feeling (reproductive) to the process of All-Feeling.

Such is the round of Feeling in its present stage (the elemental) showing respectively as its determinants Self, World, and All. Other terms we might apply, as the adjectives formal, real, concrete. But the main thing at present is to observe the cyclical movement, which is that of the Ego primordially (Psychosis), verily the elemental one of Feeling, in which there is the participation of the inner Self, of the outer World, and then of both together in the Great Totality.

This process remains elemental, since it is an element of the one organic Totality, being conneced with the same organically, that is as an organ or member. Such is, then, in our nomenclature the Elemental Psychosis of Feeling, composed of Self, World, and All as determinants, whose subordinate stages we shall next unfold.

SECTION FIRST. — SELF-FEELING.

In the study of this subject we first seek to describe and define the basic process of the Ego in Feeling — that process which underlies and organizes into unity all the diversified states of the feeling Self, from the simplest to the most complex. We are to find and to formulate the one fundamental fact of Feeling, its common principle, or Feeling as it is in itself. This we shall call by the name above given. It is the primal Psychosis of the Ego in its immediate stage as Feeling, being the original psychical process which is to take up into itself all externality as its stimulus and thereby produce the vast multiplicity of Feelings. Yet it must be ultimately conceived as a part of the All, else it could not feel, having no determinant and hence no activity.

Self-Feeling, regarded as Feeling in itself, implies abstraction, as if it were taken from a concrete or real Feeling. Still it is the first, being the underlying Form or Idea of all Feelings which have a content derived from the outside world. Now it is the inside world of Feeling taken by itself which we are at present trying to conceive and organize. For it is a world having its own process with many states and kinds of Feeling.

In this way we reach back to what may be named Simple Feeling, or First Feeling, which, however, is always a process even if implicit, a Psychosis, and not a fixed substrate or supersensible substance. If we regard it as originative and primordial, it is still Feeling which in its passivity receives all outside determinations, and then in its activity transforms them into its own special forms.

The question will come up: How did this primordial Feeling of the individual Ego get to be? Not now can such a question be fully answered; still we may note here that the Ego as Feeling is the child of the Universe as Ego, of the Pampsychosis, which has also the process of Feeling, as well as of Will and Intellect. Hence arises the fact, which is destined to have a very important bearing upon the coming Psychology, that through the Psychosis of Feeling the individual may be brought into a more direct connection with the Psychosis of the All than through any other form of mental activity, and becomes more amenable to its influence.

We have already noted that Feeling is subjective, very individual; man in Feeling is exclusively himself and nobody else. Indeed it has been maintained that Feeling is so completely itself that it can never be truly known, even by that Ego of which it is a stage. In other words Intellect cannot understand Feeling in the same person. But if such were the case, there could be no Psychology of Feeling, since science would be unable to reach it through knowing.

Nevertheless we may well say that all men are most alike in this primary Feeling, but most unlike in Intellect. In fact man and the animals resemble each other closely in Feeling, but very remotely in Intellect. The law then runs: the more individual the stage of mind (such as Feeling), the more similar it is in all individuals; the more universal the stage of mind (such as Intellect), the more dissimilar it is in individuals.

We have called this sphere of Self-Feeling a world; it is indeed the innermost circle of the feeling world. All Feeling is internal, still it has various grades of internality, according to the degree in which it is influenced by the outer world. But Feeling in its present stage of Self-

Feeling is wholly divorced from externality and grasped as it is in itself, purely, abstractly, ideally. It is, however, not merely one abstract Feeling but a world of such Feelings which is now to be organized, constituting the system of Self-Feeling.

I. *Simple Feeling*, or the act of Self-Feeling in its primal simplicity and pure abstractness; the original movement of it taken by itself. It is the primal Psychosis of Feeling as abstract, formal, having the form of the feeling Ego, but not its content. (The original typical *aisthesis* underlying all the stages of Feeling.)

II. *Double Feeling*, or the twofoldness of Self-Feeling manifested in Pleasure or Pain, which is the accompaniment of every act of Feeling. All Feeling is in some degree pleasurable or painful, necessarily having such a concomitant. Thus Feeling shows its first real separation, being itself as pure Feeling and as its own echo (or otherness) in Pain and Pleasure, which are likewise Feelings and have their own process (co-sentient Feeling, *sunaisthesis*).

III. *Total Feeling*, or Self-Feeling as the total process of the Self in Feeling, which is now individualized. This completes the movement of Self-Feeling, whose inner world has herein reached the point of the Self feeling its total threefold inner process of Feeling, Willing, and Knowing. Recollect, the Self *feels* this process now, does not will it or know it; feels it as abstract, as taken by itself, without other content than itself.

Such are the primal lines of our pure inner world of Self-Feeling, or, Feeling as it is in itself. Still we are to see that it belongs under the head of Elemental Feeling, being the ideal element thereof, and hence a necessary constituent or stage, in contrast with, yet also in union with, the real or natural stage.

As to Pain and Pleasure, we shall always find in them a separation from the pure act of Feeling and a reference to the Self. This Self now appears, being called forth in the present case by Pain-and-Pleasure, in which the Feeling (so to speak) feels itself, returns upon itself, and so posits Self or Ego, whose special characteristic through all its stages is its self-returning power. Intellect has the corresponding manifestation in its self-conscious act. That is, Intellect knows itself and Feeling feels itself; in like manner Will wills itself in order to be self-active. All three (Feeling, Will, and Intellect) are forms of the Ego and show the Ego's self-reference or self-return in every act, each in its own way.

The foregoing Elemental Feeling of the Self in its full process reaches back to the primordial act of simple Feeling, takes up the double Feeling of Pain and Pleasure, and thereby becomes not merely the bare Psychosis of Feeling but the Psychosis of the Self as Feeling — which distinction the student will do well to note, since it shows the movement from implicit Self-Feeling to explicit.

I. Simple Feeling.

There is a first Psychosis of Feeling which does not properly feel, since it has not yet that inner separation and return which bring to it Pain-and-Pleasure. It is abstract, being quite without any concrete content of Feeling; it is formal, being the form which all Feeling takes; it is universal, being applied to each and every Feeling. In such way we attempt to grasp this primal act of Elemental Feeling, the fundamental type which all kinds of Feeling have to assume. Or, since it is not a fixed mould but a psychical process, we can conceive it to be the basic movement which constitutes Feeling.

Taking a Greek conception, we may call this stage the *Panaisthesis*, a kind of archetype of all Feeling, which is of course nothing more than that first wholly simple Psychosis already mentioned. We begin with it as something given, as the starting-point taken for granted, of which, however, we must see at last the origin. This goes forward to the Universe as Psychosis (the Pampsychosis) between which and this first Psychosis of Feeling lies the whole gamut of Feelings.

We have already stated that this act of Feeling, though simple and primordial, is a process

SELF-FEELING — SIMPLE. 31

and hence must be seen in its stages or component elements. These are the following: —

I. *The Sensorium* (or *Panaisthetikon*). The mind is here conceived as the absolutely passive totality of Feeling, wholly potential and so not yet real in any special Feeling. This is not yet the first act of Feeling, but its antecedent possibility. We may deem it the all-containing womb of every Feeling yet to be born, the mother-principle of the future world of Feeling. The Sensorium in its present meaning is supremely receptive of what determines it to activity; in itself it is just active enough to receive its determinant and to become real Feeling.

We have called it a totality, which contains potentially the Universe in the form of Feeling, and is the Ego's primordial impress of the All. The Universe asleep in the Self is the Sensorium which, however, is to be stimulated, awakened, determined by some determinant outside of itself.

Of the two words mentioned in the caption, our preference is for *Panaisthetikon*, though never before employed, as far as our knowledge goes. It means that which is capable of all Feeling, capable of the Universe of Feelings from the lowest to the highest. It expresses the Ego's potentiality of the All. The word *Sensorium* may have the same meaning, but it is entangled with the notion of Sensation, which is something quite different from Feeling, as we shall see later. Still it will answer the purpose.

II. *The Determinant.* This is the second principle which we must conceive as stimulating and even impregnating the Sensorium to an activity which brings forth the Feeling. It is external to the Sensorium as such, separated from it and producing separation within it as the condition of its new life. Thus it is the second stage of that primal act of Feeling which we are seeking to grasp.

What is to be the Determinant in the present case? All externality may impinge upon the Ego as Sensorium and set it to work. Every form of the outer world may be thus transformed into Feeling. In fact it is the destiny of everything unfelt to be felt, to become transmuted into a Feeling through the Sensorium. We may truly say that the end of the Universe is to be felt as well as to be known, to be a Feeling as well as to be a Thought. And both the Feeling and the Thought of the All are to be organized into a system which shows each of them as an ordered totality.

In general the All, both in its wholeness and in its separation, is to be the Determinant of the Ego as capable of feeling all and the All (*Panaisthetikon*). In this sense the Ego may be regarded as absolute potentiality, which calls for an absolute reality as its supreme determinant in Feeling. This we shall see later under the head of absolute Feeling.

III. *The Coalescence (Panaisthesis)*. The Determinant, having stimulated the Sensorium, coalesces with it and produces the determined Feeling, which is thus the potential All of Feeling realized, particularized, metamorphosed into an actual Feeling. Now the primal act of elemental Feeling is complete; this Coalescence is the unity of the universal Sensorium with the particular Determinant whereby both sides become one in the process of Feeling.

Still this process we must see to be a formal one, properly the Norm of every special Feeling which is to rise hereafter. It is the universal as Sensorium becoming particular: which statement is just that of the normal or typical Feeling in its process. Infinitely elastic and variable we shall find this Norm to be, yielding to the untold diversity of Determinants yet remaining itself in all this diversity. The ever-shifting emotional coloring of our inner life springs from its Norm yielding to every influence coming to it from the outside. This is likewise the weakness of the purely emotional nature.

Such is, then, the process of what we here term Simple Feeling, the form of Feeling which contains all Feeling. It may be regarded as the vast deep sea of the Soul, at first quiet but capable of all sorts of billows and surges (Panaisthetikon) when stirred up by some Determinant. It has its regular rhythmic rises and falls, like the daily flow and ebb of the tide. The winds blow upon it in certain places and in certain directions, causing special upheavals; the external cause may stir in us a similar tempest. The winds of passon, we say, blowing on the soul produce the interruption of its diurnal rhythm. Then from the bottom of the sea there rise volcanic outbursts, unseen earthquakes which disturb this same regular order; nobody sees the cause, but there is a vast overwhelming tidal wave, circling the earth possibly, or crossing the ocean, and engulfing the land. Finally, from some peculiar obstruction the regular tide mounts higher at certain points every day, as at the Bay of Fundy.

The sea is indeed a kind of material earth-soul, an outer visible manifestation and counterpart in nature to the unseen soul within. Water with its absolute movability and formability, taking all shapes yet losing them at once, is Feeling externalized. Yet water has its invisible phase (vapor in the air), and the soul its visible phase (the bodily reflex). Water too has its winged form in the cloud, rising from the earth against gravitation, mounting visibly and invisibly toward Heaven. Poets have used the sea as a metaphor of the soul with its Feelings both peaceful and tempestuous. The Odyssey is largely a sea-poem reflecting in its transparent depths the inner nature of man, and especially of its hero or world-man, Ulysses. The storm in *King Lear* is directly connected by the poet with the soul's tossings of the old king.

But Feeling cannot remain simple and be itself; it has to be something more than the mere Norm of itself. Now comes the fact which has always created surprise and investigation: Feeling divides within itself and duplicates itself, passing from its simple to its double stage.

II. Double Feeling.

When I bite into an apple of a certain kind, I find it has a sweet taste; this taste is a sensation, in which the Feeling is as as yet quiescent or potential, a mere Norm. But when I declare this sweet taste to be agreeable, the Feeling is not only aroused, but has a determinate character; I not only feel, but feel pleasure. I may also feel the opposite which is pain. A Sensation is conceived as single, but a Feeling has to be double; it must not only be, but be agreeable or the opposite. Here then we enter the realm of Pain and Pleasure.

In order to avoid misconception at this point we are always to recollect that the doubleness lies not in the two Feelings of Pain and Pleasure (which we shall later find to be threefold), but in the first Feeling and its echo, the latter being painful or pleasurable.

Pain and Pleasure are conceived together as counterparts, opposites yet belonging to one and the same process. This fact we shall seek to suggest by the hyphens in the expression, *Pain-and-Pleasure (Algedonism).*

Moreover Pain-and-Pleasure in some form is the concomitant of every act of Feeling, though not the act itself. All Feeling, we say, is pleas-

PAIN AND PLEASURE.

urable or painful; Pain-and-Pleasure is therefore, the predicate of Feeling, not the subject, not the Feeling itself. Still Pain-and-Pleasure accompanies Feeling, inseparable from it yet distinct; thus it is the second stage of a Psychosis of Feeling taken as it is in itself (Self-Feeling).

Thus Feeling has, through Pain-and-Pleasure, a kind of an echo of itself, which, going forth, comes back to itself, a process self-separating yet self-returning. This is the doubleness which now appears in the movement of Elemental Feeling, a resonance issuing from it, encompassing it, and accompanying it always. Pain-and-Pleasure is a sort of atmosphere springing from and enveloping the sphere of Feeling in all its movements and variations.

Having thus indicated that Pain-and-Pleasure, taken together, is the second or separative stage of the total process of Self-Feeling or Feeling in itself, we pass to the fact that this stage (Pain-and-Pleasure) is a process within itself, a full Psychosis with its own three stages. The member of the Whole, in order to be truly such a member, must have as its own process that of the Whole.

Accordingly we look for the three stages of Pain-and-Pleasure. On the surface there appear but two. But now comes the fact which has always provoked much discussion: the mind seems to discern two quite different kinds of

Pleasure, which, however, with their common name produce confusion. But here, without untangling the many opinions upon this subject which we find in books on Psychology, let us state at once our conclusion: there is a first Pleasure before Pain, there is a second Pleasure after Pain. Thus Pain is the middle or divisive stage of the total Psychosis of what we have named Pain-and-Pleasure. Consequently in the ordering of this subject we shall have the following movement: first is that immediate Pleasure which spontaneously rises with the free primal act of Feeling; second is Pain which springs from that act interrupted; third is the second or mediated Pleasure resulting from Pain overcome wherein the primal energy of Feeling is restored. These three stages which form the Psychosis of Pain-and-Pleasure in its complete process will be next more fully described.

I. THE FIRST PLEASURE. — All free energizing of the Ego has in it Pleasure, as a kind of harmonious response to itself. The primal act of Feeling is declared to be agreeable, it agrees with — what? Certainly with itself — which agreement is our First Pleasure. The Psychosis of Feeling at its start separates indeed within itself, but only to be the more completely one with itself and to enjoy itself. As Ego it must divide in itself, but just through this self-division it can feel with itself or indeed feel itself in

Pleasure. Thus Pleasure is a kind of sympathy, the fundamental one, in which Feeling becomes sympathetic with itself. The first instance of fellow-feeling is Pleasure, which is thereby the fountain of all other sorts of fellow-feeling. Co-sentient with the first Feeling is the First Pleasure which is always the companion, and of course the pleasant companion, of its mate.

The First Pleasure is the innocent, the unfallen, never having passed through its opposite, which is Pain. It may be deemed the Pleasure of the angels, of the cherubs, of the celestial hosts who never followed Satan into Sin and Pain. The little child seems often to be a sharer in this pure Pleasure, which is the joyful accompaniment of that primal Psychosis of Feeling which may well be deemed the most immediate impress of the Pampsychosis upon the human soul. Perchance also for the adult man there is a sphere in which the First Pleasure still remains in its pristine purity. The Pleasure of living is a First Pleasure, and usually continues to the end.

Still the negative element will not fail to creep in and mingle with life. The finite being has not escaped and cannot escape his own limitation which interrupts and even corrupts this First Pleasure, introducing a new and opposite stage of its process. So it comes that in this First Pleasure the process begins, the very process of the aspiring Ego, and drives the same in various ways upon its limit, making it tragic. As it is finite, it shows itself transitory, self-canceling, dialectical. This fact we may note in three different aspects:—

(*a*) *Quantity*. It is well known that the simplest Pleasure of the child, going beyond a certain amount, begins to pall, to turn to its opposite. Sweetness gets to be loathed through its excess.

(*b*) *Quality*. Pleasures generally, and particularly the First Pleasure, may be of different kinds in different individuals, being determined perchance by heredity. The earliest play of children indicates a special quality in their First Pleasure. Still even this will undo itself and demand a change, and of change also we get tired.

(*c*) *Intensity*. The degree of First Pleasure is likewise manifest and tends to rise to the point of self-undoing and passing into complete lethargy and fatigue. Intensity of delight turns even to Pain.

These three aspects of the First Pleasure we may compare with the three aspects of musical sound, which has loudness (quantity), timbre (quality), and pitch (height, intensity). Sound is indeed a kind of soul of the material object expressing itself at some assault or stimulation. It gives an outer response or resonance which may be loud or low merely, or fine or coarse, or high strung or unstrung. But the First Pleasure has an inner resonance, and is primarily self-stimulated to its states. It feels itself, hears its own echo, enjoys its own song. Still it can be and is stimulated from the outside to this activity of itself, particularly by the Fine Arts.

Music, through its sound, which has also a Quantity, Quality, and Intensity of its own, stimulates primarily this First Pleasure and sets it to moving in its own sphere of activity. But music, increasing in its complexity, appeals to the more complex Feelings. The correlate to the inner world of Feeling with its organization, is the outer world of music with its organization, which reaches its culminating point in the orchestra. The ordered social life of civilization finds its musical instrument in that body of players which also represents a social life of sound. But the First Pleasure has its First Music in the simplest self-returning vibration of sound.

Into this little inner Paradise of First Pleasure, being very limited and as innocent as Eden, creeps the real original Fiend, bringing with him all our woes.

II. PAIN. — Such is the demon who breaks into our pure First Pleasure, which knows not itself, but simply feels itself. There comes sooner or later an external power, a Determinant which stops it, diverts it, transforms it to its opposite.

Hence Pain on this side has been called negative, in contrast to the positive First Pleasure just mentioned. It is an interruption, an assault, and may be a destruction. It is that stage of Feeling in which the outer Determinant weaves itself into the soul-life, which, previously quite homogeneous, now becomes heterogeneous.

It is evident, therefore, that the Determinant of Pain is the main ground of its variety, and hence the principle of its classification. If this Determinant is external, coming from the outer world through the senses, we may call the result Sensational or Organic Pain, but if it is internal, springing out of the inner life of the mind, we may call the resulting Pain Ideational; finally if it is universal, coming from the All-life (or the Pampsychosis) we may call it the Universal Pain.

These Determinants of Pain (the sensational, ideational and universal) are the main, though not the only ones; they are crossed by other influences which have to be taken into account. There are the quantity, quality, and intensity of the stimulating Determinant, which distinctions have been already noticed in connection with the First Pleasure. Stimulated beyond a certain point it turns to Pain. That point of transition has been sought for, and the line of the rise to the supreme Pleasure and of the descent to Pain at the crossing of the boundary has been marked in diagrams.

Here, however, we shall note only the main divisions and their facts.

(*a*) What we call *Sensational Pain* springs from sensation, or from the outer world intruding into that inner round of the happy Self already designated as the First Pleasure. This intrusion comes through the Senses. As this Pain is measured largely by the external Determinant it can be to a certain extent measured and tabulated. That is, in this sphere the quantitative principle is dominant in the Determinant, even if the quality and intensity be not wanting. The outer force with which one person strikes another is mechanical and calculable in its production of the effect which is connected with Pain.

(*b*) What we call *Ideational Pain* springs from the inner world with its idea, image, or conception. To be sure there may be the outer sensuous stimulus which stirs this inner movement of the soul. But an intermediate Determinant between Sense and Feeling has arisen from the depths of the Ego and asserts itself as the dominating power. Or we may consider the present as *emotional Pain*, since its character is determined by an emotion as stimulus.

There is no doubt that the qualitative principle, that of kind, enters this stage of Pain and gives to it not so much quantitative mass as qualitative character, which belongs to the endless diversity of subjective spirit. The pangs of remorse and of the tooth-ache are qualitatively different, and it is not so easy to compare them quantitatively (to say which is the greater in magnitude of Pain). The variety of subjectivities is far greater than that of organisms. Still here too quantity has its place, and the Determinant is quanti-qualitative.

(c) What we call the *Universal Pain* springs from the Universe which is a thought and is not directly presentable through the Senses. Still it, like the object of Sensation, is external to the Ego, which, however, is inside of it and hence a part of it. Thus the Ego feels itself within the object, not the object within itself. But the Determinant to Pain is now the totality, the Universe, which not only includes the Ego but produces it; the First Pleasure is interrupted by what creates it, and the Feeling of separation is absolute. The First Pleasure is not only cut off from its source, but is transformed into the Pain of hostility against the All.

Such is that peculiar Pain of existence called Pessimism, which is not only a doctrine of Intellect, but a state of Feeling, a permanent disposition which sometimes defends itself by a Philosophy, by a view of the Universe in correspondence with the mentioned Feeling. A lighter form, usually transitory, of universal Pain is known to Germans as *Weltschmerz* (world-pain). The French have also their word (*blasé*) for a person with a similar affliction, which is rather that of disgust or satiety, the cosmical egg having been sucked absolutely dry. The horror of the Englishman is the Pain of being *bored*, which utterly destroys his First Pleasure, while the Determinant lasts; but when the Universe gets to be a bore, he has reached his stage of universal Pain. Closely allied is the Pain of Civilization, which is rampant in older civilized lands, and makes its victims look back with longing eyes to their pre-historic barbarism and even to their ancestral animality.

Thus to some minds an omnipresent Pain is the great fact of the Universe which becomes, when formulated, the principle of a Philosophy. Germans have not been slow in evolving a scheme of thought of this sort, which indeed lies implicit in their modern philosophic beginning, in Kant himself of whom in this aspect Schopenhauer is the spiritual child. Such a doctrine hardly belongs in a new country, like America, with the possible exception of Boston.

If Pain be negative, then universal Pain must be self-negative; Pain, made universal comes back to itself and undoes itself, becoming the Pain of Pain. The Universe as Determinant has turned out the destroyer of the First Pleasure which it created. But the Universe is to overcome Pain as its enemy, or its disturber. So really the Determinant overcomes the Pain and we have a return to Pleasure. The All cannot be painful, cannot be negative without self-contradiction.

If all activity be in itself pleasurable, then Pain as active, must have underneath itself the possibility of Pleasure, by the very fact of its activity. Nature heals, it is said, is self-correcting; disease, sin, Pain is unnatural. The denial of truth implies at least the truth of denial. Still the Negative with its Pain is a part of the process, we cannot refuse to it an existence, even if it be inherently self-destroying.

Pain is, therefore, an important thing in this world of ours, particularly has it had an important place in Religion. What shall we do with Suffering, especially undeserved Suffering? The Christian Religion has been called a Religion of Pain; rather is it of Pain overcome or even self-overcome. Whereupon follows a new Pleasure, which certainly cannot be the first.

III. THE SECOND PLEASURE. — There are, then, two kinds of Pleasure, as regards origin and also quality; both have the common element of being agreeable, but each stands in a different relation to Pain. The next fact is that both belong together in one process with Pain, which process is that of the Ego itself — a Psychosis.

Such are the two basic facts upon this subject, which, if clearly seized, will be a guiding thread through the mazes of the numerous theories, ancient and modern, concerning Pleasure-and-Pain. Of some of these theories a brief survey may here be taken.

Plato (in the *Philebus*) holds that Pain is the first in order, the source, the condition of Pleasure, which is simply a restoration from a disturbance; that is, Pleasure is only the negative of Pain, by which it is determined and upon which it is dependent. Pleasure is the vanishing, the becoming, the appearance, not the essence, which is Pain. Out of this doctrine has been inferred the pessimism of Plato.

Aristotle (in his *Nicomachean Ethics* X 3) traverses the foregoing view of Plato about Pleasure, maintaining that there are many forms of Pleasure which are not preceded by Pain. Intellectual delights, such as those which Mathematics furnish, and also certain sensuous delights, such as those of taste and hearing and vision, have no antecedent Pain which must be overcome before there is enjoyment. In other words they do not result from a negation of the negative (Pain) but are primordial, and are the accompaniment of the native energy of the mind. Such is Aristotle's view — Pleasure is the concomitant of mental energy unimpeded by any outer obstruction.

Now it may be said that each of these views has its truth but not the whole truth. We can well say with Plato that Pleasure follows and with Aristotle that Pleasure precedes, Pain. The real solution of these ancient difficulties as well as many modern ones about the theory of Pleasure-and-Pain is to grasp them in a process together. This process, as already set forth, is threefold, and has the native Pleasure of the act of Feeling as its first stage, which is followed by its negative (Pain) as the second stage; but this Pain is negated in turn and succeeded by a new kind of Pleasure which is thus mediated by Pain, and which we call the Second Pleasure. Such is the Psychosis of Pain-and-Pleasure, whose final stage we are here considering as the Second Pleasure.

Now comes another curious fact in regard to these two greatest Greek philosophers. Plato, whose main drift has been above given, also declares (particularly in the *Republic*) that there are pleasures, both intellectual and sensuous, which have no preceding pain. Thus he acknowledges the existence of a First Pleasure as the immediate concomitant of energy in mind and also in body. On the other hand Aristotle affirms that Pleasure results from the fulfilling of a want which is otherwise painful. Here the Stagirite, the great supporter of the First Pleasure, acknowledges even in his refutation of Plato, the

Second Pleasure. Thus the two doctrines stand opposed again, though each has shifted to the other's side, seeking somehow to come together, yet not finding distinctly the way.

Next let us introduce the modern philosopher. Hamilton who affirms strongly the opposition between Plato and Aristotle as above given (*Lect. Met.* XLIII), seeks to reconcile them by a theory or rather a distinction of his own. "The counter theories of Plato and Aristotle are right in what they affirm and wrong in what they deny," says he. But this is not an adequate view of the old philosophers. So he affirms that Pain and Pleasure are, each of them, both absolute and relative — a view which hardly meets the problem.

The foregoing may be taken as a sample of the voluminous discussion of this subject down to the present time. The two Pleasures are duly recognized, analyzed and speculated upon, but a distinct comprehension of them as stages of a process with Pain and the corresponding formulation of all three in such a process, are wanting.

Under this head of Second Pleasure we place states of Feeling which show the long, multifarious and often desperate struggle between Pain and Pleasure. This struggle ends in the return out of Pain, and the triumph of Pleasure in its new form. The divisions of the subject must show the main ways of enfranchising

Pleasure, which in its first form has been (so to speak) captured and imprisoned by Pain. These we may regard as follows: first is the interaction, or the commingling of Pain and Pleasure, a compromise, often ending in a neutral result; second is the liberation from Pain, the separation from it and suppression of it through the Will; third is the theoretical liberation, in which the contemplation of some form of the All is the Pain-releaser.

1. *The Interaction.* This brings about some adjustment or compromise. All Pain may be deemed a separation between form and content — the form being activity and the content being some impediment to that activity. In the present case form and content interact, and thereby come to a kind of equilibrium. A little lyric says: " I'm pleased and yet I'm sad." There is, moreover, a kind of inebriation of sorrow, a revelry of pain, a luxury of suffering — in which statements the two opposites are united.

We can often experience in ourselves and others that Pain and Pleasure conjoin in producing a feeling which partakes of both, a shading off of one into the other. They are by no means mutually exclusive or always antagonistic to each other. Indeed if all energizing has in it a Pleasure, Pain must have the possibility of its opposite. A violently repressed or an overstrained activity produces Pain, according to the degree of excess. Hence Pain creeps into Pleasure when excessively repressed or stimulated. Perhaps here lies the ground of the paroxysms, the rises and falls of grief, for example; they show the struggle of activity against interruption, of form against content.

(*a*) We may observe a rhythm between Pain and Pleasure, a sort of mutual yielding and opposing, quietly billowy or boisterously paroxysmal, both in body and mind. It has a sympathy with the vibration of sound, and hence is roused or soothed by music. Finally these opposing forces may neutralize each other and settle down into an equilibrium.

(*b*) The inner opposition may reach defiance, refusal to surrender, Stoicism. Men have courted bodily pain as the enemy of Pleasure, particularly of the sensuous sort. The crucifixion of the flesh seems to mean that the Second Pleasure (as bliss) can be attained by destroying the First Pleasure through self-inflicted Pain.

(*c*) Not only physical Pain, but an ideal Pain as in Tragedy is employed as a means for reaching the Second Pleasure, which is also ideal in this case. Aristotle called Fear and Pity a catharsis (purification).

2. *Liberation (practical)*. Now comes the second main act in this movement of the Second Pleasure — the Liberation from Pain by its complete mastery and suppression. For Pain is

allied to enslavement, and Pleasure both First and Second, to freedom. First Pleasure accompanies the primal free activity of the Self, and the Second Pleasure is the enfranchisement from Pain and a return to the primal Pleasure. The present sphere involves particularly the Will, which is stimulated to interfere against Pain. — Three kinds of Liberation.

(*a*) There is first the outer Liberation from Sensational Pain, and the restoration of the body to its free organic activity — the corporeal overcoming of the interference. Thus the body has a limit-transcending power.

(*b*) The inner Liberation from Ideational Pain, from the mind as determinant to Pain (see under Pain). The Ego within triumphs over its own negative states, and returns to Pleasure through its Pain, thus showing itself transcending its limit and asserting its supremacy.

(*c*) The universal Liberation from the Pain of the All, or of the Universe, whose thought produces this sort of Pain (World-pain). Goethe says that he obtained release from suicidal thoughts by writing his *Werther*, in which novel the hero instead of the writer kills himself. All activity has a liberating power in this direction.

The struggle for liberation from Pain has in it an analogy to the struggle for political freedom. Coming so emphatically from the Will, we may call this liberation the practical one, in contrast with the theoretical one which springs from the Intellect, and to which we pass next.

3. *Liberation* (*theoretical*). This is, in general, reached by seeing the Universe and its process as creative of the Ego. The latter feels the response within itself as Pleasure, to which the Ego returns from finitude and Pain. Such is the result of contemplating the divinely creative Soul in Art, Poetry, and Science. This is the supreme Liberation, through the Intellect, which beholds the Pampsychosis. The accompaniment of such an act is the Feeling of Pleasure again attained after interruption — not by action as in the preceding case, but by contemplation.

Here we speak only of the Pleasure which accompanies the highest contemplation. Its content, or that which is productive of it, cannot be now given, but belongs to the last stage of what we call Absolute Feeling. At present we shall note merely the following points, whose full meaning will be understood later: —

(*a*) There comes a liberation from Pain (World-pain, pessimism) through the contemplation of Art which is positive (negative Art, on the contrary, fosters it).

(*b*) There comes a similar liberation through Poetry, which reveals the Negative undone, indeed self-undone.

(*c*) There comes a similar liberation through

formulated Thought as Science, Philosophy, and specially Psychology in its wide sense.

Such is a slight outline of the scheme of the Liberation from Pain, which in its complete sense is the enfranchisement of the individual from whatever interrupts his free activity, and brings him back to Pleasure, which is thus not the First but the Second, and has in it the full process embracing the return. The great thinkers of the 17th century saw the completeness of this Second Pleasure, and from it derived their notion of Pleasure as some sort of perfection. Descartes rather vaguely says that "Pleasure is the consciousness of some perfection of ours," which could hardly mean the First Pleasure. Spinoza regards as Pleasure the state "in which the mind moves to a greater perfection," overcoming its obstruction. Leibniz also holds that Pleasure is the Feeling of perfection. In all these examples we find the conception of a movement out of limitation and Pain to a transcendent condition, the process of the Ego therein being taken as implicit.

Pleasure with its counterpart, Pain, has played an important part in Philosophy, Ethics, and Psychology. As philosophical it has been taken as the fundamental principle of being. As ethical it has been regarded as the ground or end of all conduct, and has given rise to many forms of moral science as Hedonism, Epicurianism, Utilitarianism. As psychological we have discussed it in the preceding account, showing it to be a stage of the process of the Ego in the sphere of Feeling.

Such is, then, the threefold process (or **Psychosis**) of the dual Feeling of Pain-and-Pleasure. Recollect that the duality consists not in the two forms, one being Pain and the other Pleasure, for these forms or stages we have found to be really three. Properly the duality lies in the Feeling itself, that it divides within itself and is pleasurable or painful, by an inner necessity of its nature. All Feeling is thus self-separative, self-echoing, double; it agrees with or disagrees with the total process of the Ego, hence we call it agreeable or disagreeable. If I sense an object I always have a feeling in connection with the sensation; but the feeling separates itself and lets itself be felt as a pain or a pleasure, or, more exactly as First Pleasure, or as Pain, or as Second Pleasure, in each of which stages the Feeling is dual. Hence we call the present the threefold process of the dual Feeling of Pain-and-Pleasure.

We have already implied repeatedly that the total Ego lies behind this Double Feeling, which agrees or disagrees with it, and so becomes agreeable or disagreeable to the entire Self. " I do not like it," I say; why? Something *felt* within me stirs a *feeling* which obstructs or assails my total Self in its inner process. This total Self here begins to rise into the horizon of Feeling; or rather it has been present all the time, though unrecognized. But now it must be brought out to light and unfolded by Intellect, of course as Feeling.

The outcome is that a new stage has appeared — the feeling Ego in its complete process, or Total Self-Feeling. When we say, "the Ego feels Pain-and-Pleasure," we have introduced the background (Ego), which is next to become foreground. In this expression lurks the entire process of Self-Feeling, namely Simple, Double, and also Total Feeling. This last stage is now before us for special consideration.

III. Total Feeling.

The caption is intended to suggest that the Self-feeling Ego at present feels its total process of Self, which it has not hitherto done. This process is what is to be unfolded in the following account. We are to see the Ego advancing to the point of feeling its own process as Ego. Total Feeling may also be grasped as a return to Simple Feeling, or to the Norm whose empty abstract form it fills with the movement of the Self. Thus the Norm becomes truly concrete, a very real object in the possession of every man, namely his Ego which feels.

So we have attained the third stage of Self-Feeling, of the inside world of Feeling taken by itself, removed from the outer world and grasped in its bare abstractness. In this sphere Feeling reaches the point of finding or feeling its own pure process, and has thus become total and threefold as distinct from its preceding dual condition. It feels both itself and the echo or reflex of itself (in Pain-and-Pleasure) to be one and a process.

Total Self-Feeling is, therefore, the Feeling of the process of the Self, not the Knowing of it or the Willing of it, though Intellect and Will are certainly implicit in this process of the Feeling of the Self. The whole Ego with its Psychosis is here, but in the form of Feeling, which is everywhere (according to the formula) the process of the Ego within itself turned inward — in the present case turned inward through itself, and not by any outward Determinant.

Elemental Feeling has, accordingly, completed the round of its first general stage by attaining Self-Feeling as this Feeling of the process of the Self, or the Psychosis as it is in itself, such Feeling being stimulated by itself directly, though ultimately by the All. Thus Feeling has manifested its primal simplicity or its Norm as Simple Feeling; then its self-separation as Double Feeling, which finally unites itself in the threefold process of the Self as Feeling.

The preceding stage, Pain-and-Pleasure, implies self-reference, or the Feeling of Feeling. Feeling feels itself and hence calls for the Self as such. When you feel a smooth piece of wood, there is a sensation which pertains to a knowledge of the object (Intellect); but there is likewise a Feeling stimulated which is primarily a movement of the Ego, a bare Psychosis, yet is also a pleasure or a pain. The smooth piece of wood is not only felt (rouses an act of Feeling), but is felt to be agreeable (rouses the act of self-reference). Feeling feels itself as process; that is, it separates within itself and refers its determination back to itself; it feels smooth (agreeable) to itself. Feeling cannot think the term *agreeable*, because it does not think at all, it simply feels. The Intellect is the power which gives to it language. Feeling is not Self-knowing, but is Self-feeling.

In comprehending this Total Self-Feeling, the difficulty common to the science of all Feeling, rises up with a special force. Intellect has to know Feeling and its process, not simply feel it; the mind as Self-knowing has to separate itself from Self-Feeling, then turn back and grasp the same as a Feeling which does not then feel. And that is not all. Self-Feeling must contain implicitly Self-knowing as a part or stage of itself, otherwise it does not feel the total process of the Ego as feeling, willing and knowing. Thus Intellect must explicitly know itself as implicit in Self-Feeling and formulate such knowledge for the science of Feeling. This will give the Ego knowing itself to be the Psychosis of Self in the present form of Feeling.

We have already noted the Psychosis in the Norm or Act of Feeling (first stage), since every possible thought and formula must be a Psychosis. This also appears in the movement of Pain-and-Pleasure (second stage). But now the abstract Norm of Feeling and its concomitant or resonance in Pain-and-Pleasure have developed into their fundamental substance or genetic source which is the feeling Self. For it is really the Ego or Self which primordially feels, then feels Pain or Pleasure as the accompaniment of its first Act of Feeling. But Ego is essentially activity, process, hence the feeling Ego we may deem the third grand Act of Self-Feeling, the concrete Act, not the abstract one (as is the first), which is now filled with a content making it concrete.

I. Accordingly, when Feeling gets to Total Self-Feeling, we have the Feeling of Self or of Ego. We see that Feeling separates within itself (as we have already observed in Pain-and-Pleasure) and then reaches back and overcomes the separation, uniting with itself in this act of self-reference. Now, the foregoing process is just that of the Ego, which divides within itself, and out of this self-division returns to itself, performing the primal psychical act called the Psychosis. But it is the Ego as Feeling thus dividing within itself and returning to itself, not as Intellect, nor as Will. For the Feeling which feels itself, does not yet know itself, is not self-conscious. It is that first self-reference of the Ego which is the basis and beginning of all mentation. Nor is Feeling self-active, as the Will is, going forth out of itself and grappling with its opposite, the world. On the contrary Feeling is more the passive principle of mind; its very activity is to show its passivity; it seeks not to transform its externality (as does the Will) but it turns the same back into itself, employing it as a means or determinant to make itself feel.

Here again we may recall the basic distinctions in Psychology as the Science of Feeling, Will, and Intellect, each of which is a form of self-reference of the Ego. Now self-reference of the Ego as self-knowing or self-conscious belongs to the Intellect; but self-reference of the Ego as dominantly self-active belongs to the Will; while pure self-reference of the Ego, without its self-consciousness or self-activity, belongs to Feeling. To be sure the most passive Feeling has an element of self-activity (or Will) and also a strain of self-consciousness (or Intellect), though neither of the latter has the stress or dominates the Ego. When I feel, I have to act and I have even to know, perhaps in a faint subordinate way. In fact, we are to see that unless every Feeling of the Ego had in itself the complete process of the Ego, that is, had Will and Intellect-as well as Feeling, it could not be a stage or phase of the Ego. Unless the part has in it the reflection of the totality, it cannot be a part of that totality.

In the complete cycle of mentation, therefore, Feeling has the fundamental essence of the Ego, namely self-reference, or the psychical act of self-separation and self-return, but in the main as unconscious and passive.

We may now see that the Ego as Feeling throws out its fringe of Pain-and-Pleasure in every activity of itself, which also follows the Norm or the primal Type of itself. Thus, we repeat, the abstract Norm becomes real, concrete, an existent entity in the world, namely the Ego. This has been implicit from the beginning, but now it is explicit, an actual fact, describable, yea self-describable in its supreme manifestation as Intellect. But as regards Feeling we have in the foregoing view the elemental principle; this is specially Total Self-Feeling, which embraces and unifies into its process the three given elements: the primal Act or Norm, the second stage of Pain-and-Pleasure, which then drives forward to the third factor, the Ego which feels Pain and Pleasure.

II. Necessarily the question rises here and elsewhere: Whence comes this Ego, Self, Soul? It has been taken for granted, inspected, or rather self-inspected; but has it no prototype, no Creator? Hardly can it stand in the Universe in mere isolation.

At this point, then, we have to take note of the counterpart of the individual Ego, namely the All, the Absolute, the great Totality, which must have likewise the process of the Ego. Thus the extremes of the Universe come up before us, both of them Egos, the individual and the universal. Between these two extreme Egos lies our Psychology, which is the record of the one Ego, the individual finite, created Ego, seeking to find, to know and to appropriate the other Ego, its creator and his works. For understanding this fact aright, we need a new nomenclature; at least we need two words to express afresh these two extreme Egos and to suggest their process. Hence we shall employ the terms *Psychosis* and *Pampsychósis*. The latter is the psychical process of the All which creates the individual Ego in its own image, that is, as a psychical process. Thus the creating is implanted in the created, whose destiny must be to return and to re-create its creator.

At present, however, we seek to catch a glimpse of what the feeling Ego has to do with the Pampsychosis. This has its own process composed of the Absotute (as Ego), Nature, and Man, who is a commingling of both. But the destiny of Man is to be also an Ego with its process; though a product he must also reproduce what produces him. Now the first impress of the Pampsychosis having its process stamped upon man is the process of Feeling or of the Ego as Feeling, or more fully stated, of the Ego feeling in itself the process of the All.

We must often repeat to ourselves and make real within ourselves that every man is the child of the Universe. His original ancestor is just the All, and this is what he feels primarily. His Ego is his inheritance from his father the Universe, and the first form or stage of this Ego is Feeling. And having it he has all or rather the All with its process which is likewise Ego (the Pampsychosis). To be sure he has to take possession of his heritage just through his Ego; the Psychosis must be perpetually re-creating its source, the Pampsychosis, in order to dwell in harmony with itself and its world, in order to receive and enjoy its own.

III. With this outlook upon what is to be soon more fully set forth, we turn back to our view of Total Self-Feeling with its process. Primarily we have noted that it is the third stage of the process of Self-Feeling in general. All three of these stages are contained in the statement: *I feel Pain-and-Pleasure.* First is the Feeling (simple), second is the Feeling of Pain-and-Pleasure (dual), third is my Self or " I " feeling Pain-and-Pleasure. Such is a kind of theorem or formula of all Feeling taken as it is in itself, abstractly, ideally. We have attained the feeling Self, which, however, must be seen to have its own inner process.

This process we have already set forth quite fully in the foregoing account of Self-Feeling. Here we need merely summarize the result as follows: —

1. The feeling Ego feels itself to be Self-Feeling as such, as immediate, as potential — feels its own possibilities and inheritances human and pre-human. The original chaos of Feeling which is to become cosmos; in it the process of Feeling is implicit, unborn, yet is existent.

2. The feeling Ego in Self-Feeling *feels* itself to be Self-willing also, but it *is* not Self-willing, it simply *feels* itself to be such. That is, Self-willing means here not the going-forth to the outer world, but the purely internal act of self-separation of the feeling Ego, in order that it attain its complete process.

3. The feeling Ego in Self-Feeling *feels* itself to be Self-knowing, but it *is* not Self-knowing, it simply *feels* itself to be such. That is, Self-knowing means here (in the process of Self-Feeling) not the self-conscious act of Intellect but simply the self-returning act of Feeling, its mere self-relation, which does not rise to self-knowledge, though certainly on the way thereto.

We may now see the end and purpose of this movement of Self-Feeling: the unfolding of the threefold process of all mentation in the form of Feeling. The development of the feeling Ego this is, not its reproduction, which belongs to the coming chapter. The present stage shows the Ego with its process of Feeling, Will, and Intellect, but as Feeling; moreover it is this Ego turned inward *through itself*, hence we call such Feeling Self-Feeling. But next this feeling Ego, having been won, is to be turned inward, not through itself, but through something external to itself, which is nevertheless one with it in the All. A new movement of Feeling therein commences with a new end and purpose.

Looking back at the three stages of Self-Feeling, we find that we have attained the following results: the simple Norm of all Feeling whatsoever, then the Feeling itself in its doubleness, finally the Ego which lies back of all Feeling. These results we are to keep and unfold in what follows. The feeling Ego has deepened till it has reached down to its own process and made the same explicit. Still even thus it is a part which seeks to be the whole, and hence through itself it is driven forth to complete itself by appropriating its counterpart — the World. This will give to it a new content and a new character.

SECTION SECOND. — WORLD-FEELING.

The Self-feeling Ego is to take up the World into itself and thereby become the World-feeling Ego. The felt process of the Self we have just had; the felt process of the World we are next to have. The latter is what really stirs to activity and develops the former. The World is the primordial teacher of the Self, calling forth the inner through the outer. As such educator the World must be grasped in its movements, which will always be found to be self-returning, or in cycles, which thus correspond externally to the internal movements of the Ego.

In the previous section the feeling Ego taken by itself or the Self-feeling Ego was considered, being its own inner Determinant. But now we come to the World-feeling Ego, having the outer World (Macrocosm) for its Determinant. Thus a separation manifests itself between the two Determinants, the inner and outer, and two corresponding Worlds rise into view — the inner and outer, or the Microcosm and the Macrocosm.

Still our World-Feeling is elemental, the World-feeling Ego is a member of the great cosmical Body which determines it and which is distinct from it, yet is in immediate organic connection with it. That is, the World-feeling Ego is embodied, and is often called the soul. Thus in the present field two Bodies appear, the microcosmic and the macrocosmic, each with its own soul. At the same time we must not forget that these two Bodies with their souls are parts of the one great pampsychical organism within which they mutually interact and determine each other.

The Soul is Life, but it is something more. Life is the central principle (or ideal unity) of the Body merely; it unifies all the corporeal organs, but is confined to the bodily organism and passes away with its exit. But the Soul indicates a central principle outside of and higher than the Body, and uses the Body as a means for that principle. I give my Life for a higher end than Life, for my soul's existence or eternal Life. Soul is that Life of which the total Body is but an organ or member, hence Soul is the manifestation of the macrocosmic whole which determines Life and Body, and to which they belong.

So we see the outer Universe with its process is the ultimate and ever-present Determinant of the individual Ego as Soul with *its* process. The Macrocosm is what stimulates the Microcosm, which is to take up the movement of the former, and thus live in the great Whole, enacting verily the integral life. It is true that the All would not be itself unless the Ego performed its part in the universal process, and creatively reproduced its source. The Psychosis is necessary to the Pampsychosis, even if the latter be the Determinant primarily.

And now we are to bring before ourselves the All determining the individual Ego to its process of Feeling. This All is at first outside of the Ego, is in the form of non-Ego, or Nature. Such is properly the second stage in the total movement of the All; we begin with it as the immediate external world (Macrocosm) determining the individual Ego (Microcosm) which is also here the immediate, the given, the assumed for a starting-point, though this Ego has been unfolded in Self-Feeling. But the course of the exposition is to show both these extremes, as mediated; what is now picked up and taken for granted must be reproduced and so proven in the end.

The above mentioned function of Nature

grasped as a whole, and employed as the Determinant of the given Ego to Feeling we may call the Natural Totality, which will show itself working in the following three ways.

I. *The World-Feeling as cosmical.* The Natural Totality (Macrocosm, Nature, World) determines the Ego to Feeling (here World-Feeling) directly through the individual Body as given, untransformed. This Feeling is essentially the cyclical, as seen in the Heavenly Bodies, as felt in the round of the seasons, of day and night, etc. The Feeling of the external or mechanical cycle.

II. *The World-Feeling as somatic.* The Natural Totality (Macrocosm, Nature, World) determines the Ego to Feeling (World-Feeling) through the individual Body transformed in Race, Age, Sex. This second (separative) stage leads to the great bifurcation of all animate Nature into the two sexes, whereby the individual Body reproduces itself as sexual, and thus completes its somatic cycle.

II. *The World-Feeling as reproductive.* The Natural Totality determines the Ego to Feeling (which is a World-Feeling) of self-reproduction through the individual Body, whereby Nature as Totality reproduces itself. That is, Nature taken as a living Whole, as All-Life, has to reproduce itself through the self-reproduction of individuals in their bi-sexual process. Thus the Totality of Nature makes its reproductive cycle.

Such are the three stages of World-Feeling or the Ego within itself turned inward by three leading forms of the World's process, and receiving their impress. This process of the World or Macrocosm taken by itself we may grasp as follows for our present purpose: first its simple spatial oneness, with movements in it external and mechanical; then its self-division within itself culminating in a bi-sexual Totality of Nature, in order that, finally, the living World may be renewed and be eternally self-renewing.

A favorite conception of certain philosophers has been to endow this Natural Totality with a Soul (World-Soul) in correspondence with the individual Body and its Soul. Plato has the thought, though he was not the first Greek thinker to broach it; Bruno started it afresh, Schelling elaborated it, Hegel mentions it but passingly. The World certainly has its process, which is a Psychosis, and which stirs the Ego to a correspondence in Feeling.

I. Cosmical Feeling.

The World-Feeling Ego (Soul) is determined directly by the Totality of Nature (World) through the Body as intermediate, without transforming the latter (which transformation takes place in the next stage — somatic). The resultant Feeling is called Cosmical, the Feeling of the Cosmos, which may be said to have its soul also (often called World-soul). Thus the two souls, individual and cosmical, communicate through their physical bodies, producing primarily what is here named Cosmical Feeling. Each is a soul incorporate, separated as bodies yet coming together as souls.

The fundamental fact which Cosmical Feeling stirs in the soul is that the Universe is cyclical, eternally self-returning and therein like the soul itself. The Cosmos is forever rounding itself out in nature, and its separate elements, as sun, stars and earth, have the same characteristic. Now all the cosmical shapes rouse the primordial movement of the Ego (or soul), which is also a cycle (Psychosis), but unconscious, a Feeling. Thus Cosmical Feeling is the correspondence of the feeling Ego with the Cosmos, or of the Microcosm with the Macrocosm; we may deem it the harmony of the individual soul with the World-soul, both being incorporate and working through their bodies.

Elemental is such Cosmical Feeling inasmuch as both bodies with their souls are organic parts of one Whole, and ultimately belong together. In fact, it is just this Cosmical Feeling which unites the individual with the Cosmos, makes him cosmical, a member of the grand Totality of Nature. Through it he feels himself to be this Totality within, and a link of it without; it revolves with him inside, and he revolves with it outside. I take up the motion of the cosmical All within me, and it takes me up into its motion outside of me. Our respective spheres, each with its own process, form one process together, which is elemental and is given in the present form of Elemental Feeling.

And now we are to see this Cosmical World-Feeling in its own psychical movement, being determined by the external World to its activity. Such activity will be varied according to the diversity of cosmical Determinants, to which belong Space and Time for instance, as well as Sun and Earth. Taking these together and getting their process, we shall find the following stages in order: —

I. *Cosmical Feeling uncentered*, yet struggling to get a center; the feeling of pure outsideness with which the external World starts.

II. *Cosmical Feeling centered*, in which the

Ego feels itself to be the center of the cosmical cycles, beholding these with its outer vision.

III. *Cosmical Feeling self-centered*, in which the Ego comes to feel that each cosmical body has its own center and cycle, beholding with its inner (intellectual) vision.

The individual looking out upon the Macrocosm feels it as a Whole. It is what stirs the Feeling of the Infinite, of that which has no bounds. The Cosmos thus starts in man the primal Feeling of his limit-transcending Self, which is the potential source of all his future activity. He seeks to encompass the All by passing from limit to limit, from Beyond to Beyond — in one sense a vain search, but in another sense very fruitful. For he is driven to look not outward but inward for his Infinite.

I. THE WORLD-FEELING UNCENTERED. — Here we have a World-feeling Ego, but it has no center as yet without or within. That is, the Soul feels itself to be immediately one with the cosmical elements which determine it. The Ego hence feels no true inwardness, and still it feels, yea feels itself. In fact, it feels itself to be outside of itself; even when turning inside it is carried ever beyond and beyond itself. Here is the Feeling of the World without a center, and our feeling Self is a part of such a World. Very vague is this Feeling and even contradictory when stated; still it exists and must be grasped.

Nay, it has its process with the cosmical forms of Space, Time, and Motion as Determinants.

1. *Space*. The Cosmos or the Totality of Nature is outside the Ego and determines it to feel this outside as self, to be self-outside in Feeling. The World-feeling Ego first feels the world as pure externality or outsideness, which is the primal Feeling of Space. The World in the beginning is not only outside, but self-outside, chaotic, unordered, potential. And this is the first and naturally the easiest condition of the feeling Ego, for it has no self-separation, no self-effort. On the other hand such a condition is the hardest for the thinking Ego, being so remote from the same. Still I must be in Space, and also it must be in me; my Ego must be spatial and feel itself spatial.

Space is the pure continuum of the World without anything in it, containing only its empty self. It has no division, though the possibility of all division, which is now to become actual.

2. *Time*. The Totality of Nature has in it division, active division, which is Time as distinct from the static continuity of Space. The Cosmos is this endless self-division within itself, as Space is an endless continuity or extension outside itself. This Time-form of the Cosmos also determines the Ego to its Cosmical Feeling of Time, that of pure division eternally active. Time impresses upon the Ego that the Universe

is and must be self-separative as against the simple, immovable fixity and self-sameness of Space, which is the primordial oneness of the All taken by itself. Space is divisible only from without, Time is self-divisible, eternally dividing itself within itself.

The main point to be here noticed is that Space and Time stimulate correspondences to themselves in the Ego, which we call Cosmical Feeling (spatial and temporal) since the Ego within itself is turned inwardly by them, and is made to feel harmonious with these forms of the Cosmos, re-enacting an inner Time and Space as stages of the soul. Moreover we are to see that external Time and Space are stages of the Cosmos which is also a Psychosis, having a soul or World-soul with its process. So we catch the thought: the soul-process of the Cosmos with its two stages of Space and Time rouse the corresponding two stages of the soul-process of the individual.

But there is a third stage to which we must pass.

3. *Motion*. The Feeling of Pure Motion divested of every substrate may be grasped thus: Time, the self-dividing Cosmos, returns and divides Space, the undivided Cosmos, which is only divisible from the outside; through which process rises the moving Cosmos, or the Cosmos as Motion. Time thus measures Space, giving to the same a unity which now has division in it,

and is no longer the first undivided processless unity of Space. Motion begins to have, therefore, the cycle in itself, even if not fully developed. A limited body as Space-occupying when it moves, is always returning to occupy spatial limits co-terminous with those which it leaves. What it separates from, it goes to. Ancient Zeno's dialectic of Motion glimpsed this contradiction.

On the whole Space, Time, and Motion are without the center, though calling for it and going towards it. The center of Space is said to be everywhere; the center of Time is everywhen; the center of Motion (as pure) is everywhere through everywhen back to everywhere. Thus Motion is not a real cycle but the potentiality of all cycles.

The individual must feel himself, not only in Space, Time, and Motion (external) but as Space, Time, and Motion (internal). Possessing them as Feeling, he will begin to separate them from their unconscious condition through Intellect, and thereby start to know them. Unless they were in him as Feeling, he could not know them, in fact he would never be stimulated to know them.

Philosophy finds its first difficulty in grasping and formulating Space, Time, and Motion. Very simple and natural for Feeling, they are very abstract and alien for Intellect. They are the easiest to feel, but the hardest to think. The outer and inner worlds seems to flow together and coalesce in Space, Time, and Motion; the individual soul and the World-soul in them seem twinned in Siamese fashion and very difficult to separate. Hence it comes that Kant, the famous German philosopher, makes Space and Time subjective forms of Sense-perception, belonging to the Ego and not objective.

We may well deem Cosmical Feeling, especially in its spatial form, as the first Feeling of the beginning Ego, as the primal turning inward through a Determinant (Space) which has no center except anywhere. And this first Feeling is equally indeterminate and unfixed, hardly more than the possibility of getting fixed. The movement out of Space through Time into Motion, though still indefinite, begins to define the cycle externally, and hence to start it or to wake it up. Indeed Motion may be said in a sense to wake up the Ego, not so much to itself as to the outer world, which now appears circling about it, and therein manifesting to it the primal order of the All.

II. THE WORLD-FEELING CENTERED. — When we behold or seem to behold the Heavens turning around above us in the night, or the Sun revolving over our heads in the day-time, we acquire the notion of a cycle of celestial bodies, of which we are the center. Definitely, materially, visibly does the circular movement of the Great

Totality now appear, and it appears circling about us. Space, Time, and Motion had no such center apparent, being disembodied, immaterial, and only relatively visible, though fully felt. But they have become incorporate, materialized, individualized in the multitudinous spheres of the physical Universe, which have a self-returning movement in their orbits, elliptical for the most part.

Of this cyclical education imparted gratuitously from above to every son of man, we may note the following colossal instructors: —

1. *The Solar Cycle*. The Sun impresses itself upon my sense of sight as revolving around me every twenty-four hours, rising in the East and setting in the West, bringing to me light by his presence and leaving to me darkness by his absence. The illuminating principle of our visible Universe moves for me in a cycle, and my Ego responds in Feeling. Moreover he has an apparent variation in his motion; he shifts his place in the course of the year and returns to it, producing another cycle, the annual, which I feel specially in the change of the seasons. The Sun, therefore, seems to have two cycles, the daily and the yearly; if it varies from the regular cycle, the variation is seen to be cyclical, dispensing thus its gifts of the seasons as well as of daylight and darkness. But its chief gift to the Ego is the educative one, the cycle ever self-re-

turning, without which the Universe would rush to chaos in a day.

2. *The Celestial Cycle.* When the sun has disappeared under the sea, another cycle makes its appearance by way of counterpart. The whole Heavens break out into stars, which also seem to revolve about the Ego, rising and setting, each of which must make a cycle. It is as if the sun had been cut into millions of shining pieces and flung by the almighty hand through the skies to the remotest limits of the Universe. But each piece insists upon being a sun and moving through its cycle with the rest. The stellar world seems to individualize the cycle, filling the celestial spaces with an infinitude of these self-returning lines.

Thus the Ego through outer vision comes to feel itself the center of an infinite number of cycles. Impressed upon it not only day and night, but *by* day and night literally is the cyclical as the universal fact of Great Nature. Such as the primary education which the visible Universe gives to the Ego under its training. At the same time the Ego is such a cycle internally but undeveloped. The World-soul in its outer manifestation is unfolding the individual soul into the possession of the All (the Pampsychosis). The centering of the World-feeling Ego is a great step which the child as well as the primitive man must take in its spiritual development.

Thus by day and by night the Ego beholds itself a center for a complete revolution of the external All. It feels likewise that it has passed through two corresponding conditions, waking and sleeping, which form a diurnal cycle always turning around. It is the center of the revolving Whole, and it revolves in its way with the same. The great fact is that through this experience the Ego gets centered, passing out of its drifting, uncentered state in Space, Time, and Motion to its primal cyclical condition in which it finds its place in the All. Thus the Self takes its position in the Universe, making itself the center thereof.

3. *The Planetary Cycle.* Yet some of these seeming stars do not move with the rest, but have a motion of their own which cuts across the regular paths. Hence they are called wanderers (planets), which assert their own particular orbits, though these are also cyclical in the end. Thus the eye observing these celestial bodies, marks a difference, an individuality in the motions of some of them which seem to break loose from the universal frame of the circling universe, and to go their own way. Still they always get back to their starting-point, they return into themselves. The satellite, the moon, is another variation of the cycle perpetually

drawn round the skies. Even the comet bursting into our Solar System is cyclical and will return after hundreds, and in some cases possibly after thousands of years. This vast cycle, however, lies beyond individual vision and also beyond individual life.

Such is the training of our cosmical vision by day and by night, which are themselves recurring or in a cycle. Our Ego gets centered fundamentally in and through Feeling, beholding the whole heavenly sphere and all its individual spheres sweeping around ourselves as a center. But not only vision, life itself moves through this circular course in the seasons with their heat and cold, and in the diurnal circle of light and darkness bringing into our day waking and sleeping. We live the cycles of Nature as well as see them. Thus man finds everywhere the cyclical Macrocosm impressing itself upon him, and calling for the correspondence in his Ego, the Microcosm.

But now soon this external orbital motion of the celestial body round the center is to pass into the rotary motion of the body itself around its own center.

III. THE WORLD-FEELING SELF-CENTERED. — It was a mighty step in man's training through the Macrocosm when he found that it has its own center outside of himself and the earth, and that every moving body of it is also self-centered, or at least has such a tendency. Thus we pass to a new kind of cyclical motion in the Cosmos, the axial or rotary as distinct from the orbital. The heavenly body turns upon its own inner center, while revolving around its external center.

In the history of science this is known as the transition from the geocentric to the heliocentric theory. The sun is center of the solar system; the Earth revolves around it in an elliptical orbit producing the seasons, and also revolves upon its own axis producing day and night. Such a statement contradicts our outer vision, we have now to behold the motion of the Macrocosm and its bodies not with the sensuous eye merely, but with the mental. We pass from what *seems* to what *is*, we have to see the Universe now as God sees it.

The Ego now makes itself universal as center; having centered itself in the All, it must see that every Ego is thus self-centered; and then that every celestial body is likewise self-centered. That is, the self-centered Ego begins to behold itself as the principle of all things; it begins to feel that what the Universe is, it is, and what it is the Universe is.

1. *Single Rotation (Terrestrial)*. In the present sphere we note the self-contradiction of the sensuous world. We see no longer a rising and a setting sun, but the earth rotating on its

axis like a wheel and thereby causing the cycle of day and night. Herein certainly lies a great training for the race out of the immediate sense-life. The sensuous manifestation of the physical Universe remains, but we must view each part through viewing the Whole. The Earth taken by itself stands still, while the Sun moves about it, but taken as a part of the cosmical Totality, just the opposite is true. Hence we must consider the heavenly bodies together, centering each part as we center the Whole.

2. *Associative Rotation (Planetary).* Each individual planet of the solar system rotates on its own axis in its own way, at a certain distance from the sun, also at a certain inclination of its axis to its equator which helps produce climate. Thus it has its own individual character.

But all the planets have their common character in revolving about the center outside their bodies yet inside their orbit — which center is the sun. Thus they are associated, and form a society; each indivividual as self-centered has its own life, but as centered outside in a different body it has a communal life. The solar system is thus a social system, and the planets form a little village of the skies.

But this total solar system, composed of sun and planets, is said to be revolving around some far-off center, and moving in an orbit of yet uncalculated dimensions. But what does it meet

WORLD FEELING — COSMICAL. 85

in its journey? Other stellar communities, which must have also their cycles.

3. *Universal Rotation (cosmical).* It is generally agreed that each star is a sun, often much larger than our sun, with its planetary retinue, and the corresponding cycles, orbital and axial. Thus the starry Heavens, filled with constellations, is really a kind of social order made up of millions of communities also moving in their orbits. Each of these communities we may suppose to have its own law expressed cyclically. Thus we conceive of a Federation of Solar Systems, to which all belong, and which also revolves in some unknown way. Such, when we can grasp it, will be the Astral Republic.

The Ego within itself is turned inward by the Cosmos, and produces the foregoing cosmical Feeling, wherein the Ego feels not only its own centering, but the universal self-centering, in which the Totality as well as each of its parts is self-centered. The heliocentric view of our solar system is known as the theory of Copernicus, and has a most important place in the Renascence, or the New Birth of the Spirit. In Philosophy the Ego comes to the front as the chief object of speculation. For the Ego begins to see its own process in the great Totality of Nature, and very naturally it turns back upon itself to find itself out. The formula of Descartes, " I (Ego) think, therefore I (Ego) am," expresses at least the search after the essence of the Ego.

The relation between man and his cosmical environment has always been felt, and has led to many exaggerations and superstitions, of which astrology furnishes a striking instance. So much delusion has had its source in this sphere that many are inclined to regard it as containing nothing but delusion and fraud. But the Cosmos has been and still is a great educator of man, particularly in bringing him first to feel and then to understand his cyclical Self.

II. Somatic Feeling.

The second stage of World-Feeling is called somatic since the Body is transformed by the Totality of Nature or the physical environment of the individual. In the previous stage (cosmical) the Body was indeed the means, but it was not organically changed: it was taken as it existed then and there without being wrought over by the Totality of Nature. For instance Race lies in the body, even in the external color of it as well as in shape, size and structure of organs, being a product of physical conditions.

Accordingly our World-Feeling becomes distinctively somatic in manifestation, showing itself now in and through the corporeal organism adapted to its environment, which is of course still macrocosmic. The result is that every individual, each one of us, has a Body with characteristics which have been produced by the physical Universe, and which bring with them Feeling. I have a Feeling which comes from my facial angle, and which is roused at the view of a human being who is more prognathic.

Thus the Totality of Nature keeps transforming the Body, while this transformation has its echo in the Soul and Feeling. The Soul is more distinctly incorporate than in the previous (cosmical) stage, in which the Body was relatively implicit. But now it is intermediate between Cosmos and Ego and has the explicit stress.

The attempt to locate certain activities of mind in certain parts of the body is very old and is always renewing itself in one form or other. Physiognomy sought to read the soul in the face; Phrenology in the conformation of the skull; Palmistry in the lines of the hand. Undoubtedly the greatest scientific success in this field must be accorded to Physiological Psychology, which deals particularly with somatic stimulation in order to bring about psychical reaction.

Somatic Feeling shows itself in three leading forms, all of which spring from a transformation of the Body by the Totality of Nature, though in various ways.

I. *Racial Feeling*, arising from Race in which the Body as a whole is transformed by the Totality of Nature, but is varied according to its locality on the earth. This variation produces difference of Races, out of which a separation of Feeling is born, Racial Feeling.

II. *Periodic Feeling*, arising from the Periods of Life (Youth, Manhood, Old-Age), in which the Body is transformed by the Totality of Nature, but is varied according to the years passed through by the Individual, with which variation always come changes of Feeling, here called Periodic.

III. *Sexual Feeling*, arising from the difference of sex in which the Body is transformed by the Totality of Nature, but is varied by a special set of organs out of which variation springs Sexual Feeling.

Here it should be noted that Sexual Feeling is different from Reproductive Feeling. The one asserts the difference of the sexes, the other is the overcoming of that difference. There is a prejudice of Sex as well as a prejudice of Race. When the man will not take the woman as preacher, lawyer, or doctor, he manifests his Sexual Feeling, affirming his masculinity. The woman in literature has also roused protests which have their basis in sex.

Somatic Feeling is, accordingly, the process of the Ego within itself turned inward through the human body transformed by the Totality of Nature, of which it (the body) is an integral part. Thus somatic Feellng is an elemental World-Feeling rising from some special transformation of the corporeal organism, and dividing itself into three stages above given. When I say, "I belong to this race" as against other races, or "I am in this period of life" in contrast with other periods, or "I am of this sex" and not of the other (thank the Lord), I give expression to a somatic Feeling, with its worth and possibly with its narrowness.

The movement of somatic Feeling is from the body determined and transformed by the Totality of Nature to the body reproduced through itself as sexual. This likewise we are to grasp as a round or cycle in which the individual body returns into itself in its offspring, which is also racial, periodic and sexual.

I. RACIAL FEELING.—Every man is a member of one of the races which are usually given as five. Primarily Nature has made him racial in Body, and with this special form of the Body is the corresponding Feeling as somatic. Moreover his Body is the product of a long development in a certain environment.

The Totality of Nature produces a diversity on the surface of the earth in various ways, and this diversity is most strikingly manifest in the grand divisions of the globe. Races are geographical, each has its locality. The Mongolian is found in Eastern Asia, the Negro in Africa except in the northern part; the Caucasian has had his home in the lands around the Mediterranean in Northern Africa, and also in Western Asia and in all of Europe. Thus the Races have seemingly developed in different grand divisions of the Earth's surface, being determined and differentiated by physical conditions, or the Totality of Nature. These geographical boundaries of Race still prevail, though they are being broken into on all sides by the Caucasians of Europe.

The marks of Race are, therefore, indelibly stamped upon every human organism and are read at a glance. Every man recognizes at once and primarily the man of a different race, and draws the racial line. He manifests his racial Feeling, and probably his racial prejudice. As if a printed page he peruses the conformation of the head, the more or less protruding jaw, the shape of the nose, the slit of the eye, the kind of hair: all of which and much more are printed on the skin of man in a printer's ink of many colors.

The simplest classification of the Races — simplest, because most manifest — is that according to color, which is best seen in the following scheme: —

1. *The White Race* — Caucasian, the dominant Race at present, with a tendency to rule other Races.

2. *The Black Race* — the least developed physically and institutionally, with the least racial Feeling probably.

3. *The Yellow Race* — The civilized counterpart of the White Race. More nearly allied to the Yellow Race than to the White or Black are the Malay with a brownish-yellow tinge, and the

American (Indian) with a reddish-yellow tinge (copper-colored).

That there is a great process going on between these Races at present, is apparent to all who can read a newspaper. It looks as if the future World's History is going to be racial more than national, having been chiefly the latter hitherto. The historic process of Nations is to be widened into that of Races and is to pass out of Europe and her colonies into all the grand divisions of the globe.

In particular the American Republic has to grapple with the problem of the Races, whose chief difficulty lies in racial Feeling. We have in the midst of our population the extremes, the White and the Black, not to speak of the vanishing Red man. In the outlying territory is the Brown Philippino, along with various other racial layers. Nor should we leave out of the account various backward elements of our own Race. Europe never had such a problem, not even Rome; its political units have been nations of the same Race. But now the political units are getting to be the different Races which are working toward some kind of an institutional union.

II. PERIODIC FEELING. — In every individual, whatever may be his Race, there are Periods of Life through which he passes, and which manifest themselves in a change of his Body. These corporeal changes determine Feeling; every person feels different at different times of Life, he is not the same in old age as in boyhood. Thus somatic Feeling is not only racialized, but individualized, and moreover diversified in every individual according to successive Periods of Life. Such periodic Feelings spring from periodic transformations of his Body which have their course or cycle. They are differentiated in Time, while the Races are differentiated in Space. These somatic Periods are the work of Nature in the organism and outside of it, the work of Nature's Totality.

As the human organism receiving the sun's rays is transformed into a kind of spectrum which shows its varied colors in the skin of the several Races, so that same sun manifests in that same organism its daily rise, culmination and decline, as well as its yearly circle of the seasons, in which Nature is born again, matures and declines. Wider still than the daily and yearly cycles, is the Period. The Body has thus a Feeling of the World and its movement (World-Feeling) which reflects itself in the above mentioned cycles, and permanently in the so-called Ages of Man, which may be ordered in many ways. Shakespeare has the well-known seven, but they are presented on their negative side by the melancholy (pessimistic) Jaques. Simple and more organic is the following.

1. *Youth* moves physically from being born (infancy) to being sexed (adolescence). This is the period of acquisition, of education, of mastering both in body and in mind the racial heritage. The individuality of nature is made complete by sex.

2. *Manhood* is physically sex realized, the individual does not remain a mere individual, but becomes the generic process which reproduces the individual. With this natural element is connected a corresponding spiritual trait of creating through Will and Intellect. Or we may say in abstract terms, the individual universalizes himself. The character of the sexual and the reproductive Feelings which form the basis of this division into Periods, is set forth under the next head (of sex).

3. *Old-Age* has the tendency to break with the living Present, and to turn toward Past and Future. The vital vigor declines, the elasticity of the Body becomes hardened into routine, custom, regularity. The Spirit may follow the Body or it may rebound from it and become more active and original than ever. The Nineteenth Century has been famous for its great old-men.

The Feeling of Old-Age gets to know itself by the contrast with the Feeling of Youth, which hardly knows itself but feels itself with all the greater intensity. Hence Old-Age is more self-conscious, more reflective. In fact we see that these three Periods are in the main dominated by Feeling (Youth), by Will (Manhood), and by Intellect (Old-Age). Undoubtedly there are many fluctuations and exceptions in this Psychosis of the Periods of Life, still it holds good in general, and has long been recognized.

It is evident that each of these Periods is capable of sub-division. Particularly Youth as the time of education must be separated into special epochs from the suckling (and even from the pre-natal condition) through various school-ages. Moreover Youth passes through a far greater number of changes in a brief time than either of the other two Periods, since it has to re-enact in small the evolution of its race.

III. SEXUAL FEELING. — In the Body sex is manifested organically, having its own organs, with their corresponding Feeling which hence belongs to the somatic class. In the preceding Periods of Life Nature changes the Body symmetrically, all parts being transformed equally, though some member may become disproportionately old through some defect or injury. But sex is individualized in a special part, and sexual Feeling is correspondingly special, not general like the Feeling of Age (periodic). You feel young or old all over and all the time, though in this sphere too there are variations.

The fact before us here is the sexing of the

living Universe. There is this line of separation through all life from the highest to the lowest vegetable as well as animal. Nature dualizes itself into the two sexes, male and female. It makes each individual a half, so to speak; the two halves of humanity are said to be almost equally divided, as if there was some kind of control in this matter. The Totality of Nature splits itself into two sexual halves, making every individual even pre-natally on one side or the other. As to race each person is the whole of it; but as to self he is only the half of it — Man and all living creation being bi-sexual.

Many duties of life divide on the sexual line. Man has sexual Feeling in all that he does; the same is true of woman. He goes forth into the world, does its business, fights its battles, rules its political Institution. He does not like being governed in the State by woman, who sways particularly in the domestic sphere. The dual sexual Feeling thus tinges human existence through and through, dividing it into symmetrical moieties which form or ought to form an harmonious Whole. This division of sex pays no attention to other divisions such as Race or Age, but cleaves across them both through their whole length, and reaches down to the first forms of life.

So we bring before us this great fact of sexual separation throughout the Totality of Nature.

It has always excited wonder and speculation, particularly about its origin. Plato has fabled of a unisexual being, who was primordial, and who became bisexual. But a more famous passage is the following: "And the Lord God caused a deep sleep to fall upon the man, and he slept. And he took one of his ribs" and made the woman. Man is thus conceived as unisexual at first, and out of the first sex the second is created. Then the Race becomes bisexual.

Along with the problem of origin rises a more searching question: What is the ground of this separation into sexes? To the end that the individual reproduce himself and thereby preserve the species, the Race. But herewith a new kind of Feeling comes into view, springing from, yet quite opposite to the sexual Feeling in the proper sense. For sexual Feeling affirms the separation into the two sexes, while reproductive Feeling unites them.

In the Totality of Nature the component parts of the sexual process are male and female; to these the offspring must be added as the end and purpose of this process. But the offspring is also sexual, in this respect following one or the other of its parents. Hence with it the process begins over again, and we see what may be called the somatic cycle or round complete, ever returning into itself. Such is the pivot of the great

Natural Whole of Life turning on the self-reproduction of the individual body.

But this vast process with its varied reflex in Feeling cannot be here given; we can only make brief mention of the human sphere: woman, man, child.

1. We place the *Woman* first in the psychological order, since she undoubtedly represents the stage of Feeling more than the man whose distinctive trait in the present relation is rather the Will. Her Ego is inclined within itself to turn inward at the outer Determinant; the world stimulates her to Feeling more than to Action, though she is not without the latter. Nature has made her part a recipient one in the reproductive process; she overcomes her one-sidedness of the sexual separation by the acceptance of what comes instead of taking the offensive.

2. The *Man*, as already indicated, is Will when considered as a part of the psychical process, of which both Man and Woman are stages. And yet each must have the total psychical process of which each is a part, in order to be a part or member thereof. Nature has made him the aggressive, assailing, outward-going element of the total human Psychosis; he goes forth into the world to transform it, to re-create it. And of this kind is the share that he has in the present process of sex.

3. The *Child* is the result and end of the

somatic process as sexual, the third stage of it, and its fulfillment. If the mother is Feeling and the father Will, the infant ought apparently to be Intellect, which sounds contradictory. Developed Intellect the Child is certainly not; rather is it Feeling, as all Youth is dominantly. Still the main function of child-life is to know the World; and this knowing is the process of Intellect. In play, in school, even in mischief the Child is grappling with objects that it may know them for its future activity and culture. In this sense the Child is mainly an intellectual process, and its Feeling is for knowledge, not always, however, by way of the school. Thus the vocation of childhood is to rise from an emotional toward a rational state of mind.

If we accept the idea of progress, of evolution, of a continued betterment of the human race on the whole, we have to say that in the average the Child is an improvement on the parent, is greater mentally and morally. Relatively therefore he has more Intellect. Everybody knows the many individual exceptions to this statement. We are, however, speaking of the total movement of mankind. Every parent feels some such possibility in his infant and prays that it may become reality. Hector on the walls of Troy takes his boy Astyanax in his arms and holds him up toward Heaven with the fervent petition to the Gods; "May he be a better man than his father!" Such a possibility even the hero feels to be in his child, imaging harmoniously in his soul's supplication the movement of humanity.

Hence comes the interest in the Child as the bearer of all future progress and civilization. With every people who have faith in their own worth, and who-wish, therefore, to perpetuate their social and political life, the education of the Child is becoming a chief national end, and is calling forth a new Institution just for this purpose. Not simply one is to be educated to be ruler and the rest to be ruled, but all must be educated to be rulers and ruled.

The Child is the product of two reproductive processes united; he inherits traits from each parent separately, but he also inherits from both taken together, what neither has separately as individuals, namely himself, his own individuality. For he is the product of both, not of one or the other. Something is added to every born Ego from the stream of descent. Each parent is the product of the process of his or her parents, and so has something which neither had, and which may be transmitted. Heredity means not simply the transmission of what is like to the ancestors but also of what is different. This difference lies in the very nature of the reproductive process. This fact comes out strongly in the improvement of the breed of animals and also of vegetables. If their creative or reproductive process is protected by domestication, there takes place an evolution which imparts something more than the transmitted qualities of individual ancestors. But in man the great inheritance always is his limit-transcending nature.

Here we have reached the conclusion of the somatic process as determining World-Feeling and have found its purpose to be the reproduction of the individual body. But this body reproduced is still sexual, and must reproduce the same process which produced it, and thus the creative round begins anew with every reproduced individual of Nature, who is endowed by inheritance with the same originative Feeling which gave to it its own origin. Such we name the somatic cycle, the cycle of our own bodies, in contrast with, yet also in deep harmony with the outer cycle of the heavenly bodies which we observed in cosmical Feeling.

Though the self-reproductive individual drops back into sex and its division, he has brought to light a new and greater process, namely that of the self-renewal of all Nature through the self-renewal of the individual. This gives rise to a new kind of World-Feeling, in which the Ego feels the universally reproductive energy of the Totality of Nature.

III. Reproductive Feeling.

In order to understand the present Feeling, we grasp the Totality of Nature in itself, or the World in its complete self-reproducing process. We recollect that in the movement of Self-Feeling we reached in its third stage (as Total Feeling) the complete process of the Ego in itself, or as the subjective Psychosis. In like manner we have at present reached the third stage of World-Feeling, in which the Ego feels the total World-process as self-reproductive.

In thinking out the problem before us, we may first ponder the following proposition: the Ego feels the World-process, or the World reproducing itself through the self-reproduction of the individual. The renewal of the World is the renewal of all its individuals. Thus the individual as self-renewing or self-reproducing determines the living All as self-renewing or self-reproducing, which in its turn determines the individual to be self-renewing or self-reproducing. Let the reader observe this new total cycle of self-reproduction in the individual, in the world, back to the individual. Such is what the World-feeling Ego finally feels as its complete manifestation.

Another fact we may note at this point: the

individual Body with its process (somatic) does not now determine the feeling Ego, but is determined by this Ego and reduced to being a part of its present process of Reproductive Feeling. Thus we distinctly pass from Life which is corporeal to Soul which is supra-corporeal, using the body for its purpose, and making the same a member of a greater Whole. Hence we are no longer in Somatic Feeling which reached its conclusion in the self-reproduction of the sexual body. But now this process is subordinated to the self-reproduction of the living Universe.

So the new individual comes to light — the purpose and end of the sexual separation of the Totality of Nature. We have seen how the All as Life, the All-Life, divides within itself and becomes sexual in order to re-create itself. The object of the All (as vital) is to produce the new individual who keeps the process going by reproducing himself. The child is not only the renewal of both parents, but of the whole Universe, by which it is reared as well as by father and mother. The sun and moon and planets take part in the training of every child, giving a cosmical education, as we have already seen. His body is transformed and made racial; then he is also sexed, that he may participate in the reproductive process of the Universe and keep it moving. Thus he is a link of the All as it returns into itself and remakes itself in a perpetual round of creation. On the other hand he individually must make this round also, participating in the reproductive process of the Universe in order to get and to beget himself in harmony with the movement of the All.

Here likewise we are to see the fundamental movement of the Psyche, the Psychosis, which manifests itself both as soul of the Universe and soul of the individual. There is the first undifferentiated unity, then the separation into the sexes, out of which state both Man and the Universe are to return through the reproductive process, which makes creation creative. Such is the Psychosis underlying and determining what we have above called World-Feeling, of which Reproductive Feeling is the third and self-returning stage.

But in Reproductive Feeling taken by itself there is also the Psychosis as has been already indicated. Man, Woman and Child form a Psychosis, are parts of a process including them all. Yet each member of this process is also a Psychosis, being a Psyche, an individual soul or Ego, which is now the produced, though at the start (in cosmical Feeling) it was taken for granted.

These discursive statements we may bring together in the following order which indicates the underlying thought in its general sweep.

1. The Universe grasped immediately can only

be self-reproductive, for there is nothing outside of itself to produce it or to cause its reproduction. The All or the All-Life must be conceived as dividing within itself and generating itself; it is the self-reproductive process within itself. The Universe is its own Self-Life, the rounded Totality of animate existence, ever turning back upon itself and reproducing itself.

But what is the pivot upon which it thus turns? For it is making its vital cycle now, not its mechanical, as in Cosmical Feeling.

2. This pivot is the individual with its self-reproducing process through the sexual separation. We have already in somatic Feeling noted this process which manifests itself especially in Woman, Man, and Child, returning to itself in the new sexed individual (offspring). We call it the pivot (or the axis) since all animate Nature renews itself through the self-reproducing individual, vegetable and animal. The living Whole of the World divides itself on this line of sex from top to bottom, and out of this division it returns to itself and forms its process of All-Life through the process of the individual, who is driven thereto by what we above designate as Reproductive Feeling.

The individual sexed or halved by the Totality of Nature, *feels* his halfness, feels his lack of being a Totality in himself, and so he seeks the other half or the other sex in order to complete himself as a self-creating Whole. For he feels this Whole, though he is not it corporeally; this Feeling is what drives him to make himself entire through the process of reproducing himself as individual. He is not wholly himself till he recreates himself.

The Body is not transformed in the present sphere, hence it is not somatic in the sense above given. Nor is this the Body of the cosmical sphere, in which it was taken as a whole receiving the impress of the Macrocosm and its cycles. Thus we have here a new stage of the World-Feeling, which is now determined by the Totality of Nature to the reproduction of the individual hitherto given or taken for granted. The reproductive process presupposes also the dualism of sex whose separation and isolation, and we may say selfishness it must overcome by the Feeling of completeness through another of the opposite sex (Love), which Feeling is realized in the family.

3. Each living thing is a self-reproducing individual with its own round of life, moving through its orbit of birth, bloom, decay. The entire organism of Nature is, therefore, composed of an infinitude of living cycles, crossing each other, intertwining, struggling for existence, and forming the colossal panorama of the All-Life. We may compare these vital orbits of animate objects in all their varied interaction to

the vast complex of the cosmical orbits drawn through the skies by the numberless heavenly bodies of every description. From both cases we see that the Natural Universe, as a whole and in its parts, moves in self-returning cycles, whether these be external and cosmical or internal and reproductive.

Thus all living things with their individual process form a Social Whole, or animate Universe, which is determined by them reproductively, yet which in turn determines them reproductively.

The World-Feeling has now become reproductive, determining the individual Body to reproduce itself, and thereby to reproduce, for its part, the living All. This is the final purpose of World-Feeling, which always works in and through the human organism, and brings it at last to complete its cycle, by turning it back upon itself and causing it to reproduce itself and the World. This is the cycle of Nature in the individual, who reproduces himself in another individual, his offspring, going back to his pre-natal starting-point, and passing through birth and youth again. Such, too, is the movement of World-Feeling herein set forth: as cosmical it assumes the Body as something given, as somatic it transforms the Body in its parts and organs, as reproductive it re-makes what it assumed at the beginning in Cosmical Feeling.

Thus reproductive is a return to the first or given Feeling, which it accounts for in the true way, namely by creating it anew, wherein the sexed individual becomes generic, creative of itself, by returning to itself out of the sexual dualism through another individual of the opposite sex.

Here we have the natural basis for the Family, which has also its institutional element, by which the union of two sexes is elevated out of its purely physical side and made permanent.

With the idea of the Individual reproducing itself (axial) and in this act also reproducing the animate Universe (orbital) in connection, of course, with all other living individuals, we have reached the conclusion of Reproductive Feeling, and also the greater movement including it, namely, World-Feeling. The individual with which we started as assumed has now been generated, having been through Feeling turned back upon itself and made to reproduce itself, and therewith also the World-Life. The Ego from being a recipient of the Totality of Nature, has wheeled about on its own axis (so to speak) and reproduced itself, and with itself the Totality of Nature. Such is the cycle of the present sphere of the World-feeling Ego, embracing both the Ego and the World as self-reproductive.

Casting a glance over this entire field, we observe a common movement in all three stages of World-Feeling. Cosmical Feeling brought out the axial and orbital cycles and also that of the Totality of Nature as determinants. Somatic Feeling ended in a similar movement of the sexual individual with its reproduction and return to itself as a new individual. Reproductive Feeling manifests likewise in its way an axial, orbital, and universal cycle — the individual self-renewal in itself, the individual self-renewal as means for renewing the living All, finally the universal self-renewal of the living All, or the animate Universe.

Still the self-reproductive process of the animate Universe or of the World is an outside process in the sense of producing individuals which are born in separation, and remain in separation to the end — this being the second or separative stage of the present sphere. But the true Universe as the complete All is an inside process, self-reproducing through itself, since there is no outside to the Universe; even the self-reproducing individual is now inside the total process, and a part or stage of the same.

But now comes the thought that every part or member of any Whole must have the process of that Whole within it as its own ideal principle or soul in order to be such part or member of the given Whole. The individual as part or member of the Universe must have the latter's process within itself as its very Self or Soul in order to be such individual. This is now the Ego itself produced by the All, the child of the Universe with the latter's process.

Herewith we have come to the end of World-Feeling which has the World as its determinant more or less external, and we have reached the feeling Ego which has within itself the self-creative process of the Universe as its very essence. We must now conceive the self-generating All as producing the individual and imparting to the same its own universal process, thus calling into existence the conscious Self or Ego, which as Feeling is the Feeling of the All or All-Feeling.

With this thought we have moved into a new stage of Feeling, which we call All-Feeling, and in which we are to witness the unfolding of the new individual as Ego, with its All-process. The Universe is now felt in its self-creating movement: first as the one primal Whole, secondly as self-separating, thirdly as returning out of this self-separation to its concrete unity. Such becomes the movement of the Ego within itself, stamped as it were by this self-creative process of the Universe, whereby we designate it as conscious. This is a great new dawning in the history of man who now begins to possess consciousness. Mind as conscious is eternally self-begetting, self-creative, like its first parent, the Universe, who endowed this conscious Mind with his own self-creative power, which enables thought not only to create itself, but to re-create its parent, the Universe.

We may use somewhat more familiar terms, but more vague, to express the order which we have passed through. (1) *Life* — the self-reproducing individual in himself, or as physical Body, reproduces another individual as Body — the corporeal round. (2) *Soul* — the self-reproducing individual as pivot reproduces the Totality of Nature, not merely single Life but the All-Life — the mundane round. (3) *Consciousness* — the self-reproducing individual reproduces, not another individual, nor the Totality of Nature, but the absolute Totality or the Universe within itself, which thus has created after its own image (or process) the individual as conscious Ego.

Consciousness has probably given more trouble to the psychologist than any other mental activity, with the possible exception of Free-Will. It is often said to be indefinable, being that through which everything else is defined, but not itself. Some regard it as feeling, others as knowledge, still others as volition. We shall find that it is all three and yet neither. Then its origin has given much trouble. Is it a state of the nerves or does it come from some other source? A distinguished psychologist has proposed to drop the term from the science, as if the difficulty lay in the word and not in the thing. Other psychologists will keep any view of its origin out of psychology proper as such a view belongs to metaphysics. Only the phenomena of Consciousness belong to the psychological domain, and can be truly known.

These limitations we shall have to disregard. Undoubtedly the word has several meanings, according as it is applied to larger or smaller fields of the self-recognizing or self-relating mind. But such an obstacle is found everywhere in the formulation of thought. Consciousness, which for us is the Ego as All-Feeling, must be seen in an order from which flow all its divisions and their definitions.

SECTION THIRD. — ALL-FEELING.

We have now come to a new stage of Feeling, the Feeling of the All, or the All-feeling Ego, which feels the Universe as self-reproductive. It is the process of the Ego within itself turned inward by the process of the All and determined by the same to its own inner self-reproduction or self-activity. Such Feeling is still elemental; the All-feeling Ego is still in an organic unity with the All determining it. But it differs from the two previous stages of Elemental Feeling, Self-Feeling and World-Feeling; in the former the Ego reaches the point of feeling its own inner process (as Total Feeling), in the latter the Ego reaches the point of feeling the process of the external world or of the Totality of Nature, whereby this is self-reproductive. All-Feeling, however, is determined by the All; it is the All-feeling Ego which is stirred by the All to feel the All and its process, not simply the process of the Self or of the World. The Totality now determines the Ego as Feeling to feel the Totality.

All-Feeling is, therefore, the third stage of Elemental Feeling, and forms a Psychosis with the two previous stages, Self-Feeling and World-Feeling, embracing them both in one process. The interaction of the two psychical movements of the Self and the World is that which is to be reflected as Feeling in the Self. Or the Self as All-Feeling is to take up both itself and the World into its own process of Feeling.

In World-Feeling the feeling Ego came to feel the self-reproductive process of the Totality of Nature, which pivoted upon the individual self-reproducing. Thus the Totality of Nature took up the individual into its process. But now it is taken up in its turn by the individual which in consequence feels itself within itself to be the self-reproductive process of the All, which means that the conscious Self has arrived, that the Ego has attained consciousness, self-dividing yet self-returning wholly within itself.

Our leading proposition under the head of All-Feeling is, therefore, that the conscious Ego here reached has in it the Feeling of the All as self-reproductive process, is properly All-Feeling. Every act of consciousness is the individual feeling the Universe as self-creating. The conscious Ego has the self-separation and self-returning power of the All whose process it re-enacts in its movement. The consciousness of the individual is, therefore, the impress of the Great Totality upon Man, who has to be internally the All in order to be conscious.

Let us take an example. The conscious Self not only sees yonder object outwardly, but sees itself at the same time inwardly performing this act. It turns back upon itself and beholds itself separating from itself and then returning to itself with the external percept. Now this inner process of the self-separating and self-returning Ego is the truly universal one, that of the Universe eternally self-creating, which process the Ego has to pass through in order to see consciously. Nothing in the Universe has the Ego's process except the Universe. The individual thing outside of it can stimulate it, must stimulate it to behold the All in beholding the part. Lying back of my sensations, my volitions and my thoughts is my conscious Ego, which as conscious has in it immediately the process of the All, or is the Feeling of the All. Now this process in the Ego and in each of its activities has been designated by a special name, the Psychosis.

We have already found that the process of the

Ego in itself, or as purely psychical, has the three forms — Feeling, Willing, Knowing. But now we find that each of these forms has behind it consciousness, or the Ego as conscious, as Psychosis, re-enacting in the individual the self-separation, and self-returning All, which is properly its source. We shall set down these points in order: (1) I feel, will, and know; (2) I am conscious that I feel, will, and know; (3) this consciousness of mine is the All-process in me, which I feel as present and active (All-Feeling).

Such may be deemed the basic act of Mind. Not till the self-reproducing process of the Universe is internalized in me, this individual, am I universal, or a mental member of the Universe, having its self-creative movement in me as an ever-active Feeling. Consciousness is the mark of humanity. Every animal, yea, every vegetable is a physical member of the self-reproducing Universe, participating in its self-reproduction. But when the Ego feels itself to be All-Feeling, feels within itself the self-reproducing process of the All, it has become Mind, Spirit, Consciousness. To sense even the particular external thing, it has to reproduce internally the Universe which creates that thing of sense.

Self-Feeling (first stage of Elemental Feeling) is now to *reproduce* itself, not merely to *find* itself as already existent. The Self-feeling Ego we came upon in Total Feeling, as it lay back of the process of Feeling, Willing, and Knowing. But how does it get to be? We are to penetrate behind it and see its origin. This origin, as already stated, lies in the self-reproducing Universe, which gives to the Ego All-Feeling and makes it conscious.

The Ego as Consciousness is self-creative wholly within itself, making itself over in a perpetual round of self-activity, which is its primordial gift from the Universe also eternally self-creative. But in this getting of Consciousness by the Ego there are stages, we behold a movement which must be set forth. The Self internalizes gradually the self-reproducing Universe, which in some special form of itself stimulates the individual to the act of inner self-reproduction, to All-Feeling.

It is the object of an exposition of All-Feeling to show the various stages of the same as it unfolds in the All-feeling Ego as determined by the All in its self-reproducing process. For this All has as its end to determine the Ego to determine itself, to assert its own freedom as self-reproductive or self-conscious, and thus to liberate itself from the stage of Elementalism, that is, of being determined immediately by the All as an organic part of itself. The All-feeling Self must attain finally the point of determining its Determinant, of determining the All which determines it.

The stages in this movement of All-Feeling or of the All-feeling Ego, from being wholly determined by the All, to its determining the All are as follows:—

I. *Feeling of the Endowed (Pre-conscious) Self;* the sphere of what is often called natural endowment, the gift of nature to the Self, which is wholly determined by the same. Yet the Self must have the capacity to receive.

II. *Feeling of the Conscious Self;* the individual Self begins to determine itself and hence to separate from the All which determines it; the sphere of interaction and struggle between the two sides. Rise of Subject and Object.

III. *Feeling of the Free Self;* the Self now not only determines itself against its Determinant (the All), but determines the same.

It should be observed that in the course of the exposition we shall employ three terms expressing essentially the same fact, but from different points of view: these terms are All-Feeling, Consciousness, and the self-reproducing All as individual Ego. We may put them together in the statement that the Ego feels the All in becoming conscious.

Such is the round of All-Feeling as here conceived, in which the feeling Self is a member of the Universe felt, being inside (so to speak) the determining All. Moreover each is self-reproducing within itself; this power has been imparted by the All to the individual Ego, which is thus the latter's child. Now this child, at first determined wholly by the parent, we shall see develop till it determines its parent.

I. Feeling of the Endowed Self.

There is a pre-conscious state of the Ego when it is ready to receive its endowment from the All-Giver. This state is the potential one for the coming Consciousness, which is the primordial gift of the Universe giving itself to man in order to make him man. That is, the All imparts its self-reproductive process to the Ego which thus becomes internally self-creating, or the primal Psychosis as the All-feeling Self.

But man had already the capacity to receive and to appropriate this gift. Whence such a capacity? This we are to see in the Ego as Re-productive Feeling, in which the individual exercises its own self-reproductive power and thus makes itself the pivot of the process of the All. Having assisted in producing the animate Universe, the individual has the latter in itself implicitly and is a part of the great Whole and its process. Such is its capacity for being endowed, its potentiality which is now to become real.

What then is the endowment which the All imparts to the Ego, of course with the latter's capacity and co-operation? It is in itself a process with stages of its own, though it be also a stage of a larger process. The endowed Ego we shall classify thus: —

I. *The general Gift*, given to every Ego that it be Ego.

II. *The special Gifts*, indicating how the endowment varies in individuals.

III. *The absolute Gift*, which is the All endowing the Ego with its own self-creative power.

Popular speech furnishes a hint of the present sphere when it designates a man as gifted by Nature, which thus endows his Soul or Self with a certain mental or spiritual attribute. The mind therein is recipient, receiving from the outside a present, really the present of itself as having this particular bent or talent. Its donor is declared to be in general terms, Nature — Nature imparting not a physical but a spiritual Gift.

I. THE GENERAL GIFT. — The common Gift to all mankind is Consciousness, which comes from the self-reproducing Universe internalized in the Ego, whereby the latter reproduces itself wholly within itself, self-separating and self-uniting in one process. This inner power of perpetual self-reproduction is the universal Gift from the All to man, being his primordial attribute of humanity. Such is Consciousness as given, as passive or potential, not yet as active and realized.

We have seen the Totality of Nature at its highest as self-reproductive, keeping up its perpetual round of life through the sexed individual reproducing himself. This process of self-production, having become internal, and completing itself in one individual, makes the same a conscious Self, elevating it out of the dualism of sex. We may, therefore, say that Nature in its Totality as process determines the individual to be in itself the total process as self-producing. In this way we behold Nature as the Whole endowing man with the supreme gift of itself, namely Ego, which divides within itself like sex, and then returns to itself out of such division, in an eternal round of self-production.

The Endowed Self, of which we are treating in the present sphere, is, accordingly, gifted by Nature, or better, by the All which imparts its self-creative process as the endowment of the Self. Such is, in general, the endowment. The Endowed Self does not simply feel the All as cosmical or as somatic, or as even reproductive, but it does have the All-Feeling of creativity; it feels the tendency or the ability to recreate in one form or other its Determinant, the Universe. It is not only the given, but the specially gifted.

The Ego, therefore, being primordially endowed with the process of the Universe, and thereby becoming universal, begins to get its first Psychosis and to employ the same in order to re-create for itself the world. It feels the process of the All and thus has All-Feeling, which is a present from the All-parent to every Ego on its becoming conscious.

II. SPECIAL GIFTS. — But not only all men receive a common endowment, but each man has his own special endowment. From the side of the Ego and its inherited past many a modification of the General Gift plays in. The process of the Universe being passed into and through the limited Ego, becomes laden with and confined in the latter's limitations. Thus the Ego reproduces itself in a certain way, the self-reproducing All being made to go through the individual alembic of heredity. Every stage of the Ego as Feeling, Willing and Knowing manifests some form of the self-reproducing All limited and specialized. We call these Gifts special, and designate them by special names, as Disposition, Character, Talent. Upon each of these a few words.

1. *Disposition.* Every Self is endowed with what is called a Disposition, a natural bent, or temperament. It is hardly yet an activity, but rather the possibility of what he will do. It is not simply a Feeling, but a Feeling as Feeling, not as as Will, or Intellect. The Disposition of the man is the original protoplasmic Feeling which has not yet become definite even as Feeling.

Still we may and do define certain general tendencies of Disposition. We say that a man is of an optimistic Disposition, or he may be pessimistic. Formerly a good deal was made of the classification of the temperaments, of which four were usually designated, sanguineous, choleric, melancholic, and phlegmatic, each of which was supposed to have its counterpart in the fluids of the body, and to be somatically determined. Rightly has such a scheme been abandoned as chimerical. The Disposition (or Temperament) simply reflects in its special way, which is indeed very aqueous, the self-reproductive All as its determinant; it is an All-Feeling, a primordial endowment of the Self from the All.

But this Disposition, or Feeling of the Endowed Self merely as Feeling, quite passive and potential, has to become active and real, in order to be of the Ego.

2. *Character.* The Endowed Self has also specially a Feeling of Character, which implies Will. Character means a distinct mark stamped upon the Self, which others may read. A man of Character leads, rules; he is the gathering point, the concentrating energy for united effort, great and small. Disposition is only the *may-be* which in Character solidifies into the *must-be.* The result is that Character may beget a failing, obstinacy, by holding fast to the small and unimportant matter as firmly as to the greatest. Hence Character must be supplemented by

another Gift, that of Talent or Intelligence in order to save itself from its own grip.

Thus Character must have a content adequate to its power. A great Will should have a great Intellect to give to it something worthy of its doing. A man of Character we consider not only as having great energy, but also as having an universal end in his energy — especially a moral or institutional end. This brings us to our next endowment of the Self which we name Talent.

Goethe in a famous distich has contrasted the two endowments as follows: —

> *Es bildet ein Talent sich in der Stille,*
> *Sich ein Character in dem Strom der Welt.*

These lines speak of their development rather than their origin, the one unfolding in the world of contemplation, the other in the world of action.

3. *Talent.* The essential element of Talent is the Intellect, in contrast with Character which is Will, and with Disposition which is Feeling. Yet all three are in Feeling, and in Elemental Feeling. We may set down these three stages of the specially Endowed Self as follows: —

The Feeling of the Endowed Self as *Feeling* — Disposition.

The Feeling of the Endowed Self as *Will* — Character.

The Feeling of the Endowed Self as *Intellect* — Talent.

In the present division, the Feeling, Will, and Intellect of the Ego, endowed severally by the All with its self-reproductive process, form together a movement which is the Psychosis of the All-Feeling of the specially Endowed Self. Each is more or less distinctly the Feeling of the All self-creating. Talent has this Feeling along with the content of Intellect, and hence is more definite than the other two, than Disposition and Character. When a person has Talent, he feels himself able to grasp and to appropriate intellectually what is universal. For the typical act of the Intellect is the Ego consciously taking up, appropriating, and identifying with itself the objective world and its process. Talent is primarily a Feeling in which the Ego feels (but does not fully know or formulate) the process of the All in its own, being stimulated thereto by that process, and being receptive of it as a definite process. On the contrary, Character being Will throws this primal Feeling out of itself into action and conduct. But Disposition simply receives, and feels this process of the All, and remains still therein an indefinite Feeling.

Talent thus shows more or less distinctly the cycle underlying itself and all mind: the Ego feels the All determining it (the Ego) to reproduce itself (the All) in its process, the Psychosis. Talent as intellectual has, therefore, various grades, according to the ability of the Ego to reproduce this process of the Universe, or to make itself universal. The following stages may be noted:

(*a*) *Appreciation:* This is Talent as receptive, capable of receiving the impress of the universal process, and hence of recreating the same as given. A person should be appreciative, it is the first stage, that of assimilating the divinely creative movement of the All. Education has to begin with appreciating, in order to rescue the Ego from mere feeling and sensation. It must receive the stamp of the Universe, which is already within it potentially, and then proceed to recast or to make over the same. This, however, comes next in order.

(*b*) *Imitation:* This means that we must not only receive passively but reproduce actively the given thing or process. Here, then, Will enters decidedly into Talent. Much has been recently made of Imitation in educational books. Undoubtedly it holds an important place in the child's training; and the man, the most highly developed and original, never wholly gets rid of it, particularly as a means of learning, of the acquisition of knowledge. Talent usually signifies the gift for acquiring what has been already elaborated by time; it is deemed acquisitive more than creative. Undoubtedly by this kind of Talent the process of the All is reproduced in the Ego, but as something already formed, given, transmitted. Hence the question must arise concerning what forms it, concerning that original power which has the unique endowment of being able to put into an enduring form the divinely creative process of the Universe, so that the rest of mankind can appreciate and perchance imitate the same.

(c) *Adaptation:* We would still place under the head of Talent the gift of adapting the old invention or the known general principle to new contingencies. This is not strictly Imitation which makes the copy, but the power of Adaptation which can change the copy to make it suit changed conditions. Undoubtedly a creative strain begins to show itself in Adaptation; the idea as given though it creates for itself a new body.

But is there any endowment which can bring forth the new idea, the creative principle itself? This has its process, which is ultimately that of the All, the self-reproducing process of the Universe, of which we have had a good deal to say hitherto. But the question now is, Does it descend into the individual Ego with anything like its native genetic energy? Certainly men have thought so and have given the appearance a name — Genius.

III. THE ABSOLUTE GIFT. — This is not the common Gift of all mankind, like Consciousness, but the most uncommon one. In a sense it is the universal Gift, being the Gift of the Universe, which now imparts itself as the very process of the All to the human Ego, who may feel it, act it, think it, formulating it also in words. Thus Genius is the most special yet the most universal of Endowments. In a general way we may deem it the creative power of the Universe humanized, individualized, Egoized.

We can still regard it as a kind of Talent, but the all-embracing, all-creating kind. It is at its best intellectual, though not without strong Will and strong Feeling, if it ever accomplishes anything. It has the Feeling of the endowed Self as Intellect (to use our formula), but the Talent has risen to Genius, whose root *gen,* means to create and is found in old-Aryan speech and in many Greek and Latin derivatives (among them are *generation, regeneration,* and also *degeneration*).

In Literature the distinction between Talent and Genius is most striking. Tasso is a great Talent, imitating and reproducing a previous poetic form (the epic) with transcendent ability; Dante, on the other hand, is a great Genius, really creating his form as he goes along, in spite of his predilection for Virgil. A similar distinction holds between Milton and Shakespeare, the latter re-creating the transmitted dramatic form. Something of the sort can be said in regard to Schiller and Goethe. The same difference can be traced throughout all human activities.

Genius has also its negative side and through this can go to pieces. It is divine yet can become diabolic, in fact it always has a demonic power in its endowment. What is more often seen wrecking itself than Genius? A man of Talent often does more for himself and for the world than the man of Genius. Can the Genius train his demon to work in the harness or must he rush headlong into chaos? Goethe came to have the best-trained Demon of any modern poet, though in early life he passed through great danger. Hence the recent talk about genius as a form of degeneration, putting stress upon the negative side.

The man whom the All has endowed with Genius has always to be recognized as unique, and as having a unique work to do in the world. It is the Genius who feels most intimately the creative process of the All, and re-creates it in a new form for mankind. In Art there must be the Genius to reproduce the Absolute Self with His process, and to make Him appear (in marble, color, sound, etc.) to the senses that even the common man may participate in the Divine. The Genius is the originative man, the founder of Religions, Sciences, Institutions, and usually evolves at the turning-point of the new epoch in the World's Order. We call his the absolute Gift of the Absolute, which imparts to him its own very essence.

In the present book we shall have to consider Genius again in its relation to Absolute Feeling, which is the third and highest form of Feeling. Then the function of Genius as man's creative power of the Universe, which he has to re-create and organize anew for human participation, will be dwelt upon more fully.

We have thus gone through the round of what we call the Feeling of the Endowed Self, or the Ego feeling its natural endowments, which culminate in Genius. But now this passively endowed Ego must begin to show itself active; having received the gift of the process of the All, it must manifest that process within itself as distinct from All, yet in connection with it. The Ego having received its gift of inner determination has to make it valid against the determinant — in which fact lies the twofoldness of Consciousness. Thus we pass from the feeling Ego as pre-conscious to the feeling Ego as conscious.

II. Feeling of the Conscious Self.

The process of endowing the Pre-conscious Self with Consciousness has just been given. The self-reproductive All has imparted itself to the Ego, whereby the latter has this All-process within itself, as its own. Such is the power which the Ego now receives, whereby it becomes truly Ego, passing from its potential condition as pre-conscious into its conscious reality. The All self-reproducing is made over into the individual who as conscious separates within himself and returns to himself in the one subjective act of consciousness, which is an eternal self-begetting of the Self. We have already spoken of the conscious Ego as the dualism of sex internalized, for Consciousness still shows the separative, dualistic character of Nature, but as overcome and transformed into the inner process of Mind.

But now a new separation takes place. We have before us the created, produced Ego endowed by the All with its own creative process. What is the result? Just this: the Ego becomes creative, self-reproductive on its part, like the All. Thus we have the Universe apparently split in twain, revealing two self-reproducing centers, namely itself and the Ego. Or rather, as there are many Egos, we have many individual centers, and one All-center. Each Ego, through the very endowment of the All, has become an All within itself, having its own inner world with its process which is the Psychosis. The gift of the Universe to the Ego is the gift of separation from the Universe, of aloofness and independence, perchance of Adam's and even Satan's fall. Such is the Feeling of the All (All-Feeling) as conscious, with its two elements.

We are, therefore, to see the Universe in its supreme self-movement nourishing, providing for, evolving the new-born individual as Ego, stimulating in the latter its own self-creating Process, so that the Ego will also possess in its way the genetic power which is that of the Universe. Thus the Ego gets to be universal, and performs the Process of the Universe, first in Feeling and then in Thought and Will. It is the grand Totality which causes the Ego itself to be total also, and to have in itself the genesis of the All. This is the meaning which is really lodged in that much-misunderstood term *universal*, which should be seen as the essential characteristic of the Universe. The Ego can be endowed with universality only by the Universe.

The Ego is now to be stimulated by the All with its self-reproductive process to the Feeling of itself as likewise self-reproductive. Such is the twofold interaction and even opposition: the

Ego on its side is to assert its own creative Self, while the Universe must do so, too, in order to remain Universe. So it comes that the conscious Ego, having been endowed by the self-reproducing All with its own inner power of self-reproduction, starts to reproducing itself against its Determinant, its creative source. It turns back upon itself from the All, and becomes conscious of the All within itself.

In spite of this separation, yea through it finally, the conscious Ego is still a member of the Universe, from which indeed it derives its innermost nature, its consciousness. It is a part, which, however, is endowed with the process of the Whole, whereby it truly becomes a part, and in the present case a conscious part perpetually recreating the Whole in itself. Here we behold the theoretic origin of the process of the Ego, of the Psychosis, which is the impress of the All-process (Pampsychosis).

In the present (conscious) sphere of All-Feeling we are to grasp the Ego as actively determined by the self-reproducing All, not merely endowed passively by it, as in the preceding sphere. The Ego must itself be self-reproductive now, though stimulated thereto by the All. But there are various stages of this response of the conscious (internally self-reproductive) Ego to the stimulation of the process of the All. The feeling Ego can be stirred to conscious activity without being aware of its Determinant, without being self-conscious. The stimulating thing though present, is not yet known though its influence works. But the outcome must be that it becomes known, whereby the Ego passes from what we call its sub-conscious state to its self-conscious one. But this self-conscious Ego is again to be submerged into the process of the All and lose for a time its self-consciousness (for instance in sleep).

These stages of the All-feeling Ego as conscious we shall summarize in the following way.

A. *The sub-conscious Ego*, the movement into self-consciousness, in which the new individual is still mainly passive, recipient, asleep, receiving its native endowment from its ancestry and from its original parent, the Totality, till it obtains the complete Process of the latter, which is self-consciousness. The Ego gets its division within itself into subject and object.

B. *The self-conscious Ego*, in which the new individual wakes up to a knowledge of itself and of its environing world, being determined thereto by the Process of the Totality. Here is the great separation of the present sphere, the Ego now consciously separating itself from the Totality and putting the same outside of itself. The Ego as subject-object gets the non-Ego.

C. *The supra-conscious Ego*, the movement out of self-conscious separation back to the sub-conscious condition (in sleep). The Ego returns to its first unity with the All, yet takes its inner division into subject-object along. That is, the outer separation into Ego and non-Ego is cancelled, but the inner separation into subject and object is preserved.

More briefly we may characterize the three stages: the Ego gets to be subject and object (within); the Ego gets to be Ego and non-Ego (within and without); the non-Ego (without) gets the Ego as subject and object (within). In single words: the Under-Self, the self-conscious Self, and the Over-Self.

Such is the general sweep of the present sphere, in whose movement we observe the universal psychical process (the Psychosis). Looking at it from the standpoint of the Ego, we note the first Sleep of unconscious growing Self, then the great awakening into Self-consciousness, then the second Sleep which comes after this awakening and recurs periodically or cyclically during life, repeating its process till the third and final Sleep.

We may also glance at the present sphere from the standpoint of the Totality which is likewise a Self, just the universal Self, whose function is to create an individual Self which, rising through its sub-conscious life, becomes self-conscious and separates from the Totality which brought it forth. But this separation it renounces in sleep and goes back to its parent and becomes one with the same again, receiving in that unity many impressions and intimations from the universal Self not obtainable in its waking self-conscious state.

In this movement, then, we must grasp two Selves, the individual and the universal; or, better stated for our present purpose, the subconscious and the supra-conscious Selves (the Under-Self and the Over-Self) between which is interjected the self-conscious Self, or the realm of self-consciousness which is in opposition to and in a struggle with both the other Selves. Hence it is the realm of division outer and inner, whereof more will be said in the special treatment. At present we shall set forth some details pertaining to the first stage.

A. THE SUB-CONSCIOUS EGO. — All the forms of World-Feeling, cosmical, somatic, reproductive are gathered up from the past of the individual and preserved in the sub-conscious Ego. Not as active (unless stimulated by some special cause) but as potential, implicit, quiescent do they lie slumbering in the little universe of the Under-Self.

And not only experiences of the past quite from Nature's beginning, but also the endowments of Nature given to the pre-conscious Ego are not lost but are secretly laid away in the sub-conscious Ego till called for by the emergency. Chiefly that Gift of Consciousness lying back of and really constituting the Ego is not only conserved but developed in this nocturnal world of the Under-Self, till it breaks forth into the self-conscious dawn.

We make a distinction between the *pre-conscious* and the *sub-conscious,* the one belonging to the endowed Self, the other to the conscious Self. The Endowment as such is a given thing, given by the All to the Ego when pre-conscious, which Ego, when it possesses and stores up this Endowment as its own, becomes sub-conscious, having in itself primarily the Gift of Consciousness though not yet of Self-consciousness. That is, Consciousness becomes now twofold, being the Ego as recipient (subject) and as the thing received or endowment (object); within itself the Ego becomes subject and object, and both together in one process. The object is the given, yet this given object is the Self, which also must be subject or recipient. Hence the Ego as the total process of itself is often designated as subject-object.

Every person is aware of having within himself a vast reservoir of Feeling which on some provocation rises to the surface from unknown depths, we may say, depths of the past. For in the house of the Ego, in its cellar as it were, are stored the results of an untold past evolution, potential, quiescent, till duly stimulated, and roused from their dark resting-place. We may deem them the successive layers of the submerged Ego, building itself and being built upward to its self-conscious condition.

Beneath the threshold of consciousness, as the expression now runs, lies this wide domain belonging to the Ego, which is being explored more and more by a certain class of recent psychologists. Even the adjective is coming into usage which designates it as under the threshold (*subliminal*). It is often called the sphere of the Unconscious, though a stage of Consciousness in the wide sense of the word. It is the world of Feeling extending immeasurably beyond the sun of Self-consciousness, like the Space of the Cosmos. We may call it the Under-Self, in which the Self exists, and is secretly working and developing its own germ of Selfhood, but is not yet fully aware of itself and of its process, though going that way. It is a dark Netherworld of potential shapes of mind, some of which (but not all) are destined to rise out of the abyss of the Ego to Self-consciousness.

Whence do these shapes come into the Under-Self? From the unknown predecessors with all their transmissions; from all the ancestral forms reaching back to that primal hoary progenitor in whom Darwin and Haeckel behold the origin of human kind, glimpsing the first faint spark of life in animate creation. Still within our sub-conscious Ego lie the worms, fishes, and mammals of the geologic ages down which we have traveled in our descent to the present. We have in us still the deinotherion, the megalosauros, and all the stages of savage man stored away in the millions of nooks of our souls. Former stages of evolution, now transcended but once actual, now asleep but once awake, now past but once present and alive, repose in the Under-Self of every man and may sometimes be made to stir in him and even to assert for awhile their former possession of his being. In general this is the original generative realm of Feeling, whose sub-conscious origin often reaches back for untold æons to some remote ancestor whose species has long since disappeared from the face of the earth.

These past stages of the sub-conscious Ego, which once existed and had reality, but now are possible only as Feeling, were determined then as now by the Totality which fosters, cherishes and unfolds the individual. And the end was also the same as now: the getting of a self-conscious individual or Ego as the outcome and bloom of this sub-conscious world. Yet it took a long labor to bring forth this flowering of the individual, this birth of the self-knowing Ego.

Dim outlines of a movement we may catch here, though the Under-world of the Ego is not sunlit by the self-conscious Intellect. A searchlight, however, may be thrown down upon, if

THE SUB-CONSCIOUS EGO. 141

not into, these abysses, and reveal some indications of what is there going on.

1. The human embryo may be deemed, for our present purpose, the starting-point of the Under-Self in its rise through the manifold strata of sub-conscious life. The sexual process we have seen reproducing the Ego as the embryonic form which is to relive the life of its race from the start onwards. Already as unborn child it receives the endowment of its kind transmitted from the past; it assumes states of antecedent animate existence and transcends them with great rapidity. Of course it is largely unknown what primeval conditions the foetus passes through; but we may consider that vast areas of early life with their corresponding Feelings rise again to the surface and become active once more, perchance only for a moment, and then again are submerged in the sub-conscious ocean of the Ego. The bearing of an individual Self is the re-bearing of the whole race, indeed of all animate existence, and possibly the line may extend still farther back.

In this embryonic state influences are taken up by the Ego with great facility from the outside. It is the *passive* condition of the sub-conscious Ego which is ever responsive to the external determinant by which it is often molded both in body and in character. Pre-natal influences coming through the mother from the Totality give the primal bent to the new Ego in the process of formation.

2. Still this new Ego is also *active*, has its own inner movement, though it be dominantly passive; to receive requires some activity. Its gifts of heredity, which it has to appropriate, extend from the immediate parents as a center outward to the periphery of the cosmos (Macrocosm) which imparts to the germ (Microcosm) all its possibilities. Thus we note already the incipient struggle between the two Selves before mentioned, the Under-Self and the Over-Self, or in general the individual and the universe. But the outcome is that the Process of the Universe is impressed upon the responsive Ego and becomes the latter's fundamental Process for all and in all.

Still with this Process and indeed by means of it the new Ego asserts itself persistently and keeps on transcending stage after stage, all of which stages it buries in the depths of the subconscious Self, where they are by no means annihilated but continue to exist as potential, and whence they may be resurrected as forms of Feeling under the right stimulus. Herein we behold the new Ego endowed with the gift of self-evolution, always striving to rise above its real condition to a higher end.

3. Thus the Under-Self or the sub-conscious Ego becomes a vast storehouse of transcended

stages which were once actual but which have dropped back into sleep whence they may be aroused by some Determinant into Feeling. No human being can ever know what treasures of Time's coinage lie buried in the dark Netherworld of his own Ego, nor can he imagine what strange spectral monsters of the aforetime are crouching off in the dim corners of his far-reaching Under-Self with its antediluvian history in Time and Space. The race-consciousness of the Past every Ego possesses, put away somewhere in the cellar of his soul, possibly barreled up by itself where it can be tapped with the proper instrument and made to spirt forth into daylight at times with surprising energy.

Such, in general outline, is the work of the sub-conscious Ego. First it is passive and in this state receives manifold outer influences till it gets the Process of the All; but it is likewise active and elaborates its own contents, always transcending the given stage through self-evolution, till it finally becomes the huge receptacle of all the forms of its antecedent development. Nor does it stop with the past; the present is its actual existence which is perpetually struggling to bring forth the future, and thus will in turn be submerged, being overwhelmed into the Netherworld of transcended forms of itself which compose the great population of the sub-conscious Ego. So the city of the Under-Self, already of enormous extent, is continually receiving additions to its denizens, and these additions by no means perish, but are transmitted to coming Egos who inherit the past of their total ancestry.

The grand endowment of the sub-conscious Ego from its parent the Universe, is the Process of the latter, the threefold movement which makes the Ego what it is in itself, and gives to it the power of penetrating all things, since these are likewise products of that same universal Process. Thus the Ego divides within itself and returns to itself, therein becoming separate, even separate from the All which is its source. That is, the Ego has now reached self-conscious individuality, and knows itself as distinct from everything else. It has become the little Universe (Microcosm), yet possesses as its own the Process of the great Universe (Macrocosm).

The sub-conscious Ego has been seen continually moving toward the threshold of self-consciousness and now we may consider it to have crossed the same, entering thereby into a new sphere. The first long sleep of the Ego is broken, and it is awake, being aware of itself. During that sleep the All and the Ego were in immediate unseparated unity; the Ego was, so to speak, an incorporate member of the All, receiving and appropriating its powers till it attains the supreme one, the very process of the Universe. The Pampsychosis has imparted the

Psychosis to the individual Ego. Still in the present sphere (that of Elemental Feeling) this Ego, though it has become self-conscious, is not wholly separated from the All; it is still a member even in its separation, as we shall see later, and feels the whole as member, otherwise it would not be conscious at all.

There is no doubt that a treatise on the Feelings differs a good deal from a treatise on the Intellect whose activities stand in the full blaze of self-consciousness. But Feeling (specially as sub-conscious) cannot know itself; the Ego has to know its own Feelings by a borrowed lamp since they are not self-illuminating. Hence all the statements about Feeling repose in a kind of moonlight, or ratner twilight; certainly these sub-conscious Feelings are in a crepuscular realm, which gives them a kind of unreality, a spectral appearance. The Intellect shines like the sun by its own light, and we may compare it to sunlight, while the Will is seen in a kind of moonlight, reflected from the central sun (Intellect), from which the world of Feeling is farthest removed and hence it reposes in a sort of twilight.

Much remains to be done in discovering, defining, and ordering these layers of Feeling in the sub-conscious Ego. They are the historic record of uncounted æons of the Past; we may call it the Natural History of the Soul, not to be chronologized according to years. Not only sub-conscious but pre-conscious is this story of man, with speech welling up not in vocables, but in Feelings whose alphabet we are just beginning to decipher.

We might also call this stage the Getting of Self-consciousness, in which the Ego attains the total process of the All, rising from its undivided and implicit state to self-division or the. dual Ego, which divides itself within itself and still remains itself in such self-division — the only object in the Universe that can do so except the Universe.

This begins the grand struggle of the Ego's existence, that between itself and its creator as the All — the Ego holding its own for two-thirds of life, but yielding the other third to the All, which, however, restores and re-vivifies it, when it gives up and goes to sleep.

In the sub-conscious Ego as All-Feeling we have reached the Ego as feeling within itself the complete process of the All. The evolution of the self-reproducing Universe is stored up in the sub-conscious Ego which has unfolded into self-consciousness, whereby the Ego gets aware of itself and also of what is not itself. This last we call the non-Ego, which now enters the field of our theme.

B. The Self-conscious Ego. — The Ego is now self-centered, revolving upon its own axis in its own orbit. It turns back upon itself, and becomes fully aware of itself as distinct from what is not itself (or non-Ego). Thus it separates the All into two parts, Ego and the rest of the world. It isolates itself, though it cannot stay isolated.

We call this still a Feeling since it is the process of the Ego within itself turned inward by the self-reproducing All whose process it receives and operates as its endowment. The sub-conscious Ego had this process also, but as past, as capable of becoming self-conscious, but not yet self-conscious in itself. Moreover Feeling now rises to a kind of knowledge, or self-knowledge, since the Ego as self-conscious identifies completely itself as object with itself as subject, thus becoming subject-object as one process.

The new Ego whose sub-conscious career we have sought to follow in the preceding stage, takes another great step when it becomes self-conscious, that is, when it (actually, not potentially) divides itself within itself, and yet unifies itself and keeps itself one in that division. Thus it is like unto the All, truly made in the image of God. Such an act we call self-knowing or self-conscious, and means self-dependence, individuality, freedom.

Yet it involves also separation from the great All that created it and reared it to its present lofty condition. For now the Ego possesses the Process of the All in its own right, and thus becomes the little All, taken by itself. It is not only individualized but individualizes itself continuously in this Process. It sets up its own Universe against the other Universe, and makes the latter outside of itself, has to do so in fact. Such is the great division which now takes place between the Ego and the All, which finally reaches decided opposition and it may be antagonism. It is that wonderful tree of knowledge (here we may call it self-knowledge) which causes the grand separation from the All, from God. The Ego ejects the Cosmos, flings it from itself and asserts independence, no longer determined by it but internally self-determined. A mighty stride, audacious, and not unattended with peril. In one sense we may deem it the Fall of Man, in another sense it is his Rise.

And yet the self-conscious Ego remains a part of that All from which it separates itself and turns back into itself. It is determined to such separation by the All which has produced it, and has imparted to it just its self-conscious power, which power we have already seen to be the self-reproductive act of the All internalized. Without the All, therefore, the self-conscious Ego would not be determined to its self-consciousness, which operates not merely once but continuously. It is the presence of the Universe which insures the presence of self-consciousness in the Ego. Accordingly we must not forget that just in this separation from the All, the self-conscious Ego is still a member of it and determined by it.

Henceforth the Ego must unfold itself through its own Process, having broken loose from the direct training of the All, which it had as sub-conscious Ego. Then it received its determinations as the babe sucks in its mother's milk, till it gets the supreme endowment, just this self-conscious power, when the infant is weaned, in fact weans itself. But as Under-Self it acquires and retains all those aptitudes which constitute its gifts, its individual capacities, which well up into self-conscious life from these primal unseen sources, whereby it returns to and shares in the creative power of the Universe. In this way we shall often see the self-conscious waking Ego go back to its sub-conscious world, re-establishing there its former connection with the genetic All, and drawing thence recuperation and indeed re-generation. Such a power taking possession of the self-conscious Ego in its unknown depths and making it surpass itself is often called the Demonic, coming as it does from the dark Underworld of the Ego's ancient shapes. Not of necessity is such an energy diabolic, even if demonic, for it may make for the good, yea for the best.

But on account of the above mentioned separation there rises the struggle between the self-conscious Ego and the Totality which it projects outside of itself, making the same into a non-Ego which it must subsume and also consume, at least in part. We see the gradual rise of this opposition to the Totality in the growth of the child. With teething it starts to elaborate its own food from the outside, turning gradually away from the mother to the All-mother. When it stands erect, it resists the center of gravitation as its determinant; walking is a still further conquest of outer determination through the Totality of Nature. But with speech it begins to express what is within, to manifest its self-conscious or self-centered nature. Thus the Ego in the present stage resists external determination through the All, and begins to assert its self-determination.

Seldom can we recall the moment when we first became self-aware, though Richter thought he could remember it. Still less has the race been able to bring back from the remote past the time and place in which man first broke through into self-consciousness. Investigation is in pursuit of that notable event, and may yet be able to find it, or at least to fence it in certain limits, between a before and after.

It will be observed that the Self-conscious Ego is a stage of inner separation and self-contradiction. It puts the All outside of itself, or seeks to do so, wherein it contradicts itself and denies its own source, claiming to be different from the All. Likewise it separates from its own presupposition, the sub-conscious Ego, thrusting it down into the dark Underworld. The result will be a struggle in both directions. There will be upbursts of the Under-Self and downbursts of the Over-Self, into this middle realm which separates from these two Selves. The sub-conscious and the supra-conscious realms will break into the self-conscious realm as into the enemy's fortress, and there assert themselves with a peculiar energy often startling to the self-knowing Ego.

Accordingly there will be manifested in this movement the following phases: —

I. *The self-conscious Ego isolated*, individualized, parted from its connections, in which act is seen its separation from below and from above, and also within itself.

II. *The self-conscious Ego assailed and reabsorbed by the Under-Self*, or *the Upburst of the Under-Self* from below.

III. *The self-conscious Ego assailed and reabsorbed by the Over-Self* or *the Downburst of the Over-Self* from above.

Here again we should note with care the three stages or realms, the sub-conscious, the self-conscious, and the supra-conscious. They all are forms of the Self, or we may call them three Selves now in a process with one another: the Under-Self, the Middle-Self, and the Over-Self. On either side of the Middle Self are two borderlands, out of which rush the enemy, the antagonists of the self-conscious Ego. Forays in the night we may call them, often surprising and unaccountable to the dweller of that middle territory.

Though the stress of the sphere of the self-conscious Ego be placed upon the separation from the All, let us note again that the Ego still remains an organic link of the All in such separation, being determined by the same to its self-conscious act. Not till the Ego can determine the All, which determines it, can there take place an organic or elemental separation. At present, however, both sides are in a struggle, the one separating, the other resisting.

I. THE SELF-CONSCIOUS EGO ISOLATED. — This means that it must separate itself from its entanglements below and above, and round itself out to individuality. The self-conscious Ego is now to be shown getting itself, turning from all outsideness to its own self-movement.

In a general way we may regard the present stage as the complete awakening of the Ego, which it has gradually reached out of its first Sleep of birth and early development. The great fact here is that the Ego refuses to be a passively organic part of the All, but asserts itself as a total Organism within itself against the All. It sets up for itself, having the universal process as its own; it will not let itself be subsumed under another and be determined, but resolves to be self-determined within its sphere. It thus reveals its end to be freedom; the separated individual is to be as free as the Universe itself. Self-consciousness may be deemed the primal Declaration of Independence of the Ego in its career for the goal of its striving, freedom.

The characteristic of this sphere will, therefore, show itself in separation — separation of the Self from the Under-Self, also from the Over-Self, and finally the separation of the Self within itself. But there is likewise the return out of separation, specially of the Ego, which thus becomes self-conscious. So we have the self-conscious Ego, which having overcome its own inner separation, will fall into a new conflict.

1. *Separation from the Under-Self.* Already we have considered the Under-Self or the realm of the sub-conscious Ego as the immense storehouse or receptacle of all native endowments and past experiences, not only of our own previous life, but of our race and of our total heredity. There they lie sublated, not dead but asleep, in a kind of spiritual aestivation, till the right Determinant comes and wakes them up, restor-

ing them to a fresh activity even if but temporary. The unconscious Underworld of the Soul we may deem it, which every Ego has to pass through and appropriate in the form of Feeling.

But the Ego, unfolding more and more, separates from and leaves behind this antecedent stage of itself with all its human and pre-human elements, rising above the threshold which separates the Under-Self from the Self as such, which is to be self-conscious. The Ego has found itself and recognizes itself, it can no longer be ignorant of itself and of its process. The sunlight which illuminates All in illuminating itself has risen above the horizon.

Whence does it come? We may say it unfolds itself, it is self-evolved. Yet this only throws the question a step further back: whence comes this gift of self-evolution? Only from the All, the Universe, which is just its own evolution, its own creation, as self-reproduced, its own definition, or however else we may choose to state the fact. But the All, having imparted to the Ego this power of evolving itself and thus determining itself, can no longer determine it passively as a part or member of itself. Hence the next stage.

2. *Separation from the Over-Self.* This new separation is indicated in the fact that the Ego, having gotten the Universe as its own, declares or begins to declare itself independent of the Universe. When I am possessed of the process of

the All, I am no longer its prisoner. I put it outside of me, I make it object while I am subject. In a manner I negate it, calling it the realm of the non-Ego.

Such is the sharp dualism which has entered the Universe. The latter is no longer in immediate unity with Ego, determining the same in many ways as member of itself, and imparting to the same its potentialities. The child which it so fondly cherishes has thrown it off. The two extremes stand not only in separation, but in opposition and even hostility. The Ego seeks now to subject the non-Ego as the latter in the sub-conscious world subjected it. Great is the struggle manifesting itself in all stages of the Ego — in Intellect, Will, and Feeling.

Still it is just this non-Ego, as the All, which has brought the Ego to its present supremacy, giving to it the universal process (the Psychosis) and rearing it to self-determination and independence. It is the All, the Universe, which has brought forth the Self, has nursed it through its long pupilage in its sub-conscious career which is the Soul's School of the Past, and has finally given to the same its own chief essence, its very selfhood, namely its Process, which is that of the absolute Ego. This Process which is self-consciousness, we may now look at.

3. *Separation of the Self within.* Often we have alluded to the separative act of the Ego

which has the power of dividing within itself and still remaining itself in that act of self-division. No external body has any such power; if it cuts itself in two, it stays so. The Ego is the only thing in the Universe that can do such an act, except the Universe itself. For this has all division inside of itself, and as a part of its process, and still it remains one, or rather is a perpetual return to unity with itself from self-division.

Such is, then, the self-conscious Ego in its inner constitution. It has the complete Process (the Psychosis) primarily within itself, as self-dividing and self-returning, or as subject-object. But as self-conscious it makes a new division, separating the All into Ego and non-Ego, the latter of which it (the Ego) begins to subordinate to itself, reducing the All to a part or member of itself, subjecting the creator to the creature.

The result will be a conflict from both directions, from the Under-Self and from the Over-Self, both of which the self-conscious Self is seeking to subsume, thus making itself the Whole or the All when it is but a part or a stage. In this way self-consciousness is pretty certain to find its limit, and to be assigned to its true place in the Process of the Universe (the **Pampsychosis**).

But the self-conscious Ego at present, insists upon isolation, exclusiveness, wishing to get itself purely, or to become fully centered within itself, or to revolve freely upon its own axis. It thus attains its own pure process, it is subject-object wholly to itself; it is not only Self but perchance selfish. Still we are to see the present attainment: the Ego gets itself as its own inner process, gets individuality.

And yet the self-conscious Ego in spite of its love of isolation cannot remain alone with itself in the Universe. If it withdraws into itself, it must withdraw from something which it leaves outside. Thus its very exclusiveness posits its other, the non-Ego. In getting aware of itself, it must at the same time get aware of its not-Self. Such is the *real* dualism of Self-consciousness, the separation and indeed mutual hostility of the two worlds, inner and outer.

The next important fact is that this outer world, the non-Ego, is not simply passive, quiescent, taking the spurns of the self-conscious Ego with an unresisting submissiveness, but it becomes actively hostile and starts an assault upon its foe whose self-occupied isolation it seeks to break up. Necessarily the Totality cannot allow a piece to be taken out of itself, for thus it is no longer Totality. Here, then, the fight opens.

The first struggle will come from the side of the sub-conscious Ego, that vast, silent Underworld of endowments and experiences which the self-conscious Ego is inclined to suppress with a heavy hand. So we behold cavernous if not sepulchral shapes of the long-past Under-Self bursting into the present moment, supplanting and even re-submerging the self-conscious Ego.

II. THE UPBURST OF THE UNDER-SELF. — This we may take as the first protest of the complete Self against the autocracy of a part. The sub-conscious Ego with its world is not going to be altogether suppressed and negatived by the self-conscious Ego which is really an evolution out of itself and which presupposes the existence of all the forms of the Under-Self in order to reach self-consciousness. The consequence is a subliminal struggle followed often by an upburst of shapes from that Netherworld of the Ego, which produces a peculiar effect of mystery upon the self-conscious man living in the bounded sunlight of his own self-awareness.

We may well believe that the entire realm of the Under-Self is in a state of striving to become Self; the sub-conscious has as final object and purpose the becoming self-conscious. The whole Netherworld of the Ego is struggling upwards in accord with its deepest evolutionary nature; it longs to be self-knowing as man, and even as God, or as the absolute Process. Beneath the threshold of our self-conscious life is a vast reservoir of Feelings, which have indeed been transcended, mastered and suppressed as dominant states, but which can still be stimulated to assert themselves anew against the present authority of self-consciousness which is placed over them. Such is the struggle before mentioned, likely to arise from almost any provocation.

The suppression of these rebellious children of Erebos is the function of the Gods of Light, the self-conscious authorities of the Over-world. Religion is primarily to subject them to the universal principle; Ethics has the same duty. The passion, the hate, the uncontrolled emotions of the sub-conscious Ego have to be put down in part, and in part transformed with a new content. Irritabilities, caprices, whimsicalities are sudden wellings-up from these unlit sources. Not a few civilized people seem still to be governed by their uncivilized Self, savage and even animal. In fact civilization and savagery are perpetually fighting their battles over in every human soul with alternating victory and defeat.

We cannot pretend to organize this immense area of conflict between the two Selves. Science has begun to look at it with new eyes and collect facts, without much order as yet. Still it is possible to inspect some leading groups of these facts.

1. *The submerged Self*. Or we may better deem it the re-submergence of the self-conscious Ego, which previously had arisen and asserted it-

self by thrusting down into the Under-Self its own past shapes. But now comes the counter-stroke.

The upburst of the Under-Self may break through the threshold, and overflow a large area of self-conscious life, possibly the whole of it for a time. We may compare such an eruption to that of a volcano, which pours out over the surface of the earth the molten contents of the earth underneath, often submerging great tracts and producing a new surface which also has its peculiar life and vegetation. An unhappy love may bring to the surface an overflow of Feeling and a tendency of the mind which changes character. A sudden fright from a conflagration can call up terrors from the Netherworld of the Ego which probably belong to an antecedent condition of animality. The sight of a cat has been known to throw people into a fit of trembling which caused them to flee as if from a wild tigress.

On the other hand the self-conscious level seems at times to sink down of itself, and to pass under the threshold, while some sub-conscious state rises to the surface and takes its place. It is a subsidence resembling that of land which disappears, sometimes gradually and sometimes suddenly, beneath the waters of the Ocean which rise and fill the vacant space. What is called hysteria shows many illustrations

THE UPBURST OF THE UNDER SELF. 161

of this fact. Bodily feeling may quite vanish. A person may cut his arm and feel no pain in such a condition. Sensation separates from the organism (anæsthesia). Where vacancies occur in the self-conscious Ego, some isolated fancy rushes in and acts by itself, refusing to be regulated by the total self-conscious Ego (the fixed idea so-called). These subsidences or holes in the Ego, being filled with activities from another world (the sub-conscious) cause distraction and may end in insanity.

Thus we see an interplay between the two worlds sub-conscious and self-conscious, an activity partial, intermittent, rising and falling on both sides, an apparent struggle between the two Selves for supremacy. The upburst from below and the subsidence from above have many manifestations, which cannot here be described. But they all drive forward to the question: What if the Under-Self or some form of it takes possession of the self-conscious Ego, changing its character, making it as it were a new Ego? This question leads to the next stage.

2. *The Dual Self.* The dualism of the Self, the cleft personality, is now generally acknowledged as a very significant fact in Psychology, though it has been recalcitrant to any order in the science. The sub-conscious element not only breaks through the threshold, but stays

above it and rules that world like a conqueror. The result is a loss of one personal identity and the getting of another; a change of Selves takes place so that one man is another man, two individuals shape one's conduct and destiny.

How can such a change take place? A state or condition from below supplants the subject in the Ego as subject-object, and my Self as this subject vanishes. That is, I am a new subject, which, however, still has the same object or the same power of self-division and self-return. I am in this new condition self-conscious, going through the process of Self (Psychosis). So there is the complete conscious activity of the Ego, but I am a new subject without any connection with my former subjective side. Often there is no memory of it, the secondary subject has usurped the place of the primary

This psychologic change is, therefore, to be grasped by considering the separative stage of the Ego. But there is no return to self-consciousness of the primary Self, on the contrary the substitute enters at that point of self-separation, becomes the active subject and makes the return to itself. Thus there are two acts of self-consciousness, controlling successively and sometimes synchronously the individual. The dual Self, therefore, springs from the duality of the Ego, which is overcome not through its own subject but through another, an intruder seemingly from the sub-conscious world.

These points we shall illustrate by a concrete example. Perhaps the most famous case of the dual Self is that of Ansel Bourne (see Proceedings of Society for Psychical Research, Vol. 7, and Myers, Human Personality, Vol. I., p. 309). At the age of 61 years he suddenly left home, and no trace of him could be found. After two weeks he arrived in a distant town, under another name, and started a little store. He did his business in a proper way, and nothing unusual was observed in his conduct. After about eight weeks he woke up one morning, he did not know where he was or what he had been doing. While the secondary condition lasted he was in complete control of himself in all his transactions, but when he returned to his primary condition his memory was a blank in regard to what had transpired during the eight weeks of his secondary state, and joined on to the last event of his former primary condition.

Here the same man shows two Selves, each of them perfectly self-conscious, yet entirely disconnected. At what point does the separation enter, making him two? Not in self-consciousness proper for he is equally self-conscious in both conditions. But in the separative stage of the Ego, where he is subject and object, the second subject slips in and gets control of the total

Ego, leaving the first subject to drop back into the Under-Self, till called for. What caused such a substitution? That is, of course, unknown; all that we can say say is, some struggle between the sub-conscious and the self-conscious results in the triumph of the former and the temporary displacement of the latter. Possibly some weakness of the present subject causes it to sink down into the Under-Self, when its place is taken by some past state, wish, or endowment.

It is evident that Ansel Bourne recovered his primary subject through himself, the secondary subject seems to have run its course when it in turn was dethroned by the former occupant, his primary subject. But there are cases in which the new Self maintains its position against the old Self, though after many fluctuations and relapses, or we may say, after many battles in which the old Self temporarily wins the victory.

Significant is the loss of memory, so that when the new Self is supplanted by the old, the latter has no recollection of what has transpired while the former held sway. On the whole each state has its own retention and hence its own recall of events. We can see how this comes about. Memory is based upon the identification of the object recalled with the subject recalling; I remember that I once had a certain experience. Suppose, however, that the "I" which had that experience is supplanted by another "I;" it is evident that the latter cannot recall the experience of the former unless the second "I" has absorbed the first. This absorption seems to take place sometimes, so that the secondary state remembers all the events of the primary, while the primary has no power of recalling anything which belongs to secondary state. This fact was observed in the oft-cited case Felida X. whose life was one continuous struggle and alternation between two Selves, till at last the secondary Self triumphed, with a few brief relapses at considerable intervals.

3. *The Multiple Self.* It is now generally acknowledged by experts that the cleavage of the Ego may be not merely into two Selves, but into several, each of which has its own activity and character, is indeed a kind of independent person. The classic instance is that of Louis Vivé in whose psychical career no less than six different Selves participated, according to the French physicians who watched and studied his case. The upburst from the sub-conscious world is not a single dominant state, but a number of states from below rise up and determine the self-conscious Ego. The arena of such a person's soul is indeed a strange spectacle, being a kind of dramatic presentation of the various characters which his race has passed through in their development. Thus it seems likely that every former

condition of man from his first animate condition upwards may become personalized and brought to appear on the stage of the real living man and made to play its long-forgotten part.

Another peculiar fact about this Multiple Self is that two or perhaps more of its sub-conscious States may rise up together and perform their actions contemporaneously, like personages in a drama. Previously the states followed one after the other, but now they co-exist, acting and talking in relation to one another, since each is an Ego in his given character.

A very curious case is reported by Dr. Prince, an American physician (Proceedings of Society for Psychical Research, Vol. 15). The one Miss Beauchamp developed into several Misses Beauchamp, no less than four altogether. Miss Beauchamp No. I " is a very serious-minded person, fond of books and study, of a religious turn of mind and possesses a very morbid conscientiousness." But Miss Beauchamp No. III, who named herself Sally one day in a fit of jollity, " is full of fun, does not worry about anything, hates books, hates church." The one is well-educated, the other is not; the one knows French, the other does not. Now comes the curious fact that Sally took a strong dislike to Miss Beauchamp No. I, and said to the Doctor: " Why, I hate her, Doctor Prince." Many tricks and practical jokes Sally played upon her other Self.

Finally Miss Beauchamp No. IV appeared, when there was a new adjustment of the personal relations of that curious group called the Misses Beauchamp. Suffice it to say that all had different characters and acted different parts in this strange drama of multiple personality. So at least it is set down in the amusing account of Doctor Prince.

On the whole we may consider William Shakespeare as the greatest example of the multiple Self that ever lived. What a variety of characters do we not find in a single play of his! Yet he must have been all of them in the course of his life, and very often several of them at once. Sometimes we find a transformation in one of his characters equal to that of Sally Beauchamp. Shakespeare had the whole race in him and all its personalized gradations; moreover he possessed in his own right the gift of projecting them into living souls which pass before us in a kind of transparent bodies. Shakespeare in his way shows the working of the multiple Self, but not disintegrated. In fact Genius has the power of descending into the sub-conscious Ego, and thence calling up many shapes, which, however, are still held in the unity of self-consciousness. But if they rush asunder, each becoming an independent unit with its own center, the self-conscious Ego flies to pieces, and even Genius will then go crazy, as it has often done.

FEELING — ELEMENTAL.

The dual Self has become a popular proverb in recent years through the little masterpiece of romance known as *Dr. Jekyll and Mr. Hyde*, still kept before us by theatrical representation.

It is manifest that the Upburst of the Under-Self can have a destructive result. It may dissolve the self-conscious Self back in the sub-conscious units of its transcended past. This is the uncentering of the self-centered or self-conscious Ego, its self-division into its own primordial atoms, which can only produce the destruction of personal identity.

If we go back to Cosmical Feeling we observe that the Totality of Nature, the Cosmos, works for the centering of the Ego (see preceding p. 78). But what the All has been long doing for the Ego is (or may be) now reversed, the Ego at its very culmination in self-consciousness can become uncentered, being resolved back into its antecedent sub-conscious states (or atoms). The very intensity of the self-conscious Ego provokes its opposite, incites the rebellion of the old monsters of the Underworld. Also the weakness or even the unguardedness of the self-conscious Ego may be the occasion of an upburst of the Powers from below.

How is the emergency to be met? The creative All, which produced the self-conscious Ego, which gave to it its process of unity, now appears in defense of it — the original parent rushing down to the defense of his child, taking the same again to his bosom. This is the Downburst of the Over-self, which re-absorbs the Ego into its own Totality, making this Ego an unseparated member of the All again.

III. THE DOWNBURST OF THE OVER-SELF. — There is a second threshold or limit bounding the self-conscious Ego, which limit must be conceived as above it, not below it, as we have observed in the sub-conscious Ego. This new world of the Self we may name the Over-Self, since it is a Self, an Ego, with the latter's process. But it is strictly the All, the Universe of which the ordinary self-conscious Ego is only a part or member. Thus the latter is really inside of the Over-Self, though projecting it outside, and regarding it as something supra-conscious. This division, therefore, is only apparent, and exists merely as subjective, for the self-conscious Ego.

Now in the present sphere the Over-Self or supra-conscious Ego will break through this limit made against it by the self-conscious Ego, nullifying the same and asserting itself as the All, or, we may add, as the All-Ego. This will be the essential fact of what we call the Downburst of the Over-Self, primarily into the self-conscious Ego, whereby the latter is taken up into the All and made a part of its process.

Thus we may see that the separation of the preceding sphere (the self-conscious Ego) is now overcome; the disintegration of the Self which was so striking there, is here redintegrated. The Ego is made whole again, healed, it can be affirmed often literally, for a marvelous therapeutical power frequently manifests itself just in the present sphere as the previous sphere frequently shows malady, dissolution, insanity. It is the Totality which totifies the finite self-consciousness, wheeling it into line with the universal process.

The general way of doing this is to take it out of its limitations in Space and Time, which do not exist for the Universe or rather are inside of it, as is all separation. For Space and Time are the primordial separatists of the finite world, separating all individual objects from one another and separative (infinitely divisible) within themselves. Now the Ego can be removed from their control, it can be everywhere and everywhen.

We have, therefore, to conceive of the universal Sensorium, of which each sense of the individual Ego is a particular form or member which connects with total organism or univeral Sensorium. The Universe as Sensorium must be specialized into single senses which still keep their living organic relation, not merely to the human body but to the universal body, to the All as Feeling. What will stimulate a given sense, such as vision, to reach far beyond the

Here and the Now, and to see objects in remote times and places? Evidently the medium must be universal, yet must feel in its parts everywhere the stimulus at a given point, like the human organism made universal.

In its present condition, the Ego can feel and sense at a distance from its periphery, since the Over-Self breaks down its limit, appropriates it, making it a stage or participant in the universal process. In the ordinary sense-perception of the self-conscious Ego, the object must be in some sort of contact with the nerve-ends of the bodily organism. But now a new power appears, a power of seeing, hearing, feeling what is distant in Space and Time.

There are numerous cases in which a person has seen things and events which were many miles away. Evidently there must be some medium between the two extremes, the Ego and its distant object. Also there must have been a stimulus which specially caused the Ego to act. Usually this is found in some personal tie or interest, as when a father sees his son injured in a distant town, or when there is a vague brooding over something which is going to happen to ours.

This brings us to the other and more surprising fact of the present sphere: the Ego can sense (both see and hear) what is distant in Time, the event of the future. And also the occurrence which is distant both in Space and

Time, which is to happen in another place and on another day, has been often described and announced. Is there some such truth in prophecy, and in the oracle?

Space and Time and Motion must be not outside but inside the Determinant in order to produce such results. The Ego is still awake, self-conscious, though dominated and even absorbed by the Over-Self. It largely, though not wholly, loses its exclusiveness, its self-centered individuality. It is no longer isolated, but gets into such complete unity with the All that it shares in the latter's Space, Time, and Motion. The Universe now centers me, I do not center it; it takes me back into itself so that I am everywhere and everywhen. Thus I am again cosmical without wholly losing my self-consciousness which has been won after such a long evolution. Into this evolution the All dips me afresh, often with a great restorative effect, as if I were being made over. Already we have noticed the dissolution to which the self-conscious Ego seems liable by its very nature. The Downburst of the Over-Self makes for its reproduction, its new evolution.

But there are moments in which the sound self-conscious Ego lapses or is overpowered by the Over-Self. Some strong emotion of my friend, or perchance some thought of his impresses itself upon me who am many miles away. As to the transference there is now little doubt, as to the nature of the transferring power there is a good deal of spéculation. A medium of psychical transference may be conceived, a *Pampsychikon* which under certain conditions can bring together every separated *Psyche* in existence. Under what conditions? That is indeed the mystery.

Still we may put together into something like an order the main facts of this most obscure part of Psychology. All the states of the Ego can be taken up into the Over-Self (or *Pampsychikon*), and carried far beyond the natural limits or the periphery of the Ego, which thereby seems to acquire a new and vastly extended periphery. Now the Ego, as already often observed, has three supreme stages or activities—Feeling, Will, and Intellect. Each of these will be found working at a distance through the Over-Self. The whole man as Feeling, Will, and Intellect, is borne beyond his immediate environment, and can produce his influence far away.

Thus we may observe in the present field the following stages: (1) Feeling-transference — *Telepathy;* (2) Will-transference—*Teleboulesis;* (3) Thought-transference — *Telenoesis*. Upon each of these a remark or two.

1. *Telepathy.* There is a communication of Feeling between two (or more) separated Egos, still awake and self-conscious. The conceived medium is now the Over-Self (universal Senso-

rium, or Pampsychikon). The general movement may be grasped as follows: an Ego under the influence usually of some strong emotion stirs this Over-Self to a corresponding vibration which reaches the second and sympathetically connected Ego at a distance. The Ego receives through Telepathy its communication of Feeling.

We may compare this process to that of the individual as related to the Social Whole receiving and giving, whose analogon is here the feeling Whole or Over-Self. Still more striking both in name and thing is the similarity to the telegraph and telephone which operate at a distance through electricity. And yet closer is the suggestion of wireless telegraphy, whose medium is supposed to be currents of a very subtle ether. At a certain point is the stimulus of those ether-waves which reach another point to be stimulated hundreds of miles distant. In fact, the telepathic connection Crookes has supposed to take place by means of ether-waves (or brain-waves) finer than those of the X-ray; "of smaller amplitude and less frequency" they must be than those which communicate between the two distant points in wireless telegraphy.

A special bond of Feeling, as kinship, twinship, friendship, love, finds its other at a distance. Sympathy is telepathic, connecting two not merely in each other's presence, but far apart through the universal Sensorium. The communication may amount to an imaging of the agent by the recipient or of the recipient by the agent, and they may converse. And even another person present may see the projected form, as two or more see the same ghost in Hamlet.

Telepathy shows the Over-Self removing the limits of the self-conscious Ego, particularly those of Space and Time, overcoming the separation of it from the same, and uniting it (the Ego) with the same (the Over-Self) in one process.

2. *Teleboulesis.* Not only Feeling, but also the power of Will can exert itself through distance, quite beyond the limited periphery of the body. Most of us have seen material objects move without any apparent mechanical cause. Often this is done by means of a trick; indeed just here lies a great domain of deception and also delusion. But this delusion is twofold; it may result from excessive credulity or just as well from excessive skepticism.

The general fact, however, cannot be denied in view of the careful evidence which has recently been collected. It has been given a special name, *Telekinesis,* motion at a distance, for which we prefer to use the psychical term above stated, which connects this class of phenomena with the Will, whereby they are coordinated in the science of the Psyche. We accordingly accept the fact that the Ego exerts its power of volition at a distance with effect, and under certain conditions can move and lift things animate and inanimate without bodily contact. The medium is the Over-Self which can be agent as well as recipient, has a motor power of its own as well as sensory, possesses Will as well as Feeling.

Another fact in this connection is that the muscular strength of the individual is often enormously increased, becomes supra-normal, as if the Over-Self imparted itself physically to the man and endowed him with a superhuman power of body.

3. *Telenoesis.* The activities of Intellect as such — sense-perception, representation, and thought — can be transferred to a distance through the medium of the Over-Self, which often bursts down into the limited self-conscious Ego and carries its intellectual powers far beyond their ordinary range. Not only may I sense things far away, as if I were for a time endowed with universal sensation (by what we may call the universal Sensorium), but also I image distant persons and objects. Also an imageless thought may be transferred.

The difficulty is we do not know how to start the Over-Self — it usually starts of its own accord. It is not a machine which acts from our Will, but has its own volition and also intelligence. Really it too is Ego as well as the man.

Hence it has its end, its nature, possibly its caprice, and the self-conscious Ego can only become a stage in its process and subject to the same.

In Telepathy the Ego may still be awake, self-conscious and world-conscious, making the distinction between the Self and the not-Self. But this distinction gets less and less strong, the Over-Self in the telepathic state is the decided Determinant and is canceling the opposition of self-consciousness. Finally all resistance ceases, the Ego unites with the Over-self and becomes one with it, unseparated from it; the division between Ego and non-Ego is wiped out as real, sinking away in the mind as ideal, and man is again asleep as he was once before asleep in the subconscious (embryonic) state. So he returns to Sleep, which, however, is different from the first one, having passed through the stage of self-consciousness, and retaining the stores of experience gained during that time in the memory. That is, the Ego is now full of new material, not empty of all self-conscious life, as it was when the Under-self.

It is at this point, then, that we pass from the Downburst of the Over-Self to the Over-Self proper, or from the self-conscious Ego as such (waking) to the same as supra-conscious (asleep).

C. The Supra-conscious Ego. — The self-conscious Ego, being taken up into the Over-Self, becomes supra-conscious, the distinction between Self and the World (or Ego and non-Ego) being substantially transcended. The inner distinction of the Ego between subject and object remains and is active during its stay in the Over-self (for instance, during a dream). In the preceding stage (the Downburst of the Over-self) the Ego was not only self-conscious internally, but self-centered externally (awake), though integrated in the process of the Over-Self, and thus carried beyond its own natural periphery. But now this external self-centering is to be obliterated in sleep.

Here comes to light an old problem: to distinguish between waking and sleeping. We cannot say that the difference lies in the act of self-consciousness, for the Ego is self-conscious in sleep as well as in a waking state. When sleeping it can still perform its processes of Feeling, Will, and Intellect, with the accompanying self-consciousness. Where, then, lies the distinction? The outer world is shut off now by the closed eyes, the resistance to the terrestrial power ceases through the prostration of the body, the separation between Ego and non-Ego is quite canceled. I give up in sleep my own self-centering in the Cosmos, going back to and becoming one with the cosmical center, from

THE SUPRA-CONSCIOUS EGO.

which I originally unfolded into self-consciousness. Just this process of unfolding or of evolution is to be re-enacted by the Ego that it be re-born every day. Asleep I no longer behold myself the center of the solar or celestial cycles (see preceding pp. 78, 81, etc.) of the outer world; in that respect I am uncentered, unresisting, having gone back to the primal Cosmos in Space, Time and Motion, with which I am now in unity. Herein lies my possible control through the universal medium (the Over-Self or Pampsychikon) of spatial and temporal separation; that is, things and events become no longer separated for my Ego, as it lies sleeping in the Pampsychikon.

The phenomenon of Sleep must, therefore, be carried back primarily to the decentering of the self-conscious Ego, whereby it renounces temporarily its central place in opposition to the cosmical All, giving up for a time its own cycle and passing into that of the All. Its compensation for this self-surrender is that it becomes endowed with the universal power of the latter. It becomes what we here designate as the supra-conscious Ego, wiping out its opponent, the non-Ego, which hitherto has limited it, and asserting mastery over cosmical limitation, that of Space and Time.

The Ego awake has already felt Space and Time in World-Feeling as bounding it on every side outwardly. But in All-Feeling the Ego as supra-conscious, finds these spatial and temporal bounds broken down, or rather put under its control, since they are now internal, a part of it. In its supra-conscious realm, the Ego, being one with the All-Ego, has internalized and appropriated Space and Time and so uses them as its own properties.

In this fashion we conceive the self-conscious Ego to be taken up by the Over-Self, re-absorbed as an element of its process, whereby it loses its separation from and opposition to the world. This is the phenomenon of sleep, the second sleep of man, in distinction from the first embryonic sleep, hence it is a return which, however, takes along with itself the self-consciousness of the Ego. The Over-Self is now triumphant, its antagonist stops resistance, surrenders, and falls into unity with the All, or the universal process. Meanwhile we are not to forget that the activity of the Ego is not lost, but is controlled by a new Determinant, the Totality, with which it is now integrated. The result is we shall find in Sleep what we may call a new kind of self-consciousness which has also its world, namely the dream-world. So we have to put together the two facts: the double Self of Ego and non-Ego is asleep, suspended, yet its doubleness (as subject-object) is preserved, and is manifesting itself in a new way.

Sleep is a kind of re-birth involving a return to the All-mother for a new creation of the Self. Every twenty-four hours in the natural order of things man has to be restored out of his separation from his creative source, which thus shows itself to be an estrangement to be overcome temporarily at least during life. Daily the self-conscious Ego has to re-enact its rise to self-consciousness, to go back to the first Sleep, to pass through the same and to re-awake in the world of finite sensation, of phenomena, of appearances. But these wear him out in a few hours, the struggle to assert his self-conscious Self in opposition to the Over-Self as separated from him, grinds him to utter fatigue; he gives up the conflict, his head droops first, being the seat of opposition, then his body follows dropping prostrate, unable to resist even gravitation toward the common center of the earth. Thus he renounces his own bodily center, after his mental center succumbs. As he lies stretched out and relaxed in slumber, he is the picture of submission to the All, his self-conscious individuality is submerged into the great sea of being, whose healing or rather creative waters must flow through him again ere he can become a man.

Such, however, is the reward: through his renunciation of Self for a while he gets it back recovered, re-born, ready for new effort. He has been refreshed by Sleep, we say; really it is a renewal, a re-creation through the All, through God, who (according to a passage already cited) of old wrought in this way. " And the Lord God caused *a deep sleep* to fall upon man and he slept. And He took one of his ribs " to create a new being. Sleep was considered a divine gift. " He giveth unto his beloved Sleep," and also during Sleep.

Moreover the alternation of waking and sleeping is intimately connected with a cosmical process, the alternation of day and night, which has a terrestrial cause in the diurnal revolution of the earth upon its axis. Thus our globe has its hours of sleeping and waking, for Nature shares in the process. Still further, day and night have their origin in the sun whose steady light is divided into two opposite halves by the rotation of the planet. Thus our sleeping and waking go back to the center not only of the Earth but of the Solar System, and through it to the center of the Cosmos. I resist gravitation when I am awake, being one with the sunlight which also rays out in opposition to gravitation. But I lie down and become one with the earth in darkness, with closed senses as if unborn, till the terrestrial revolution brings me back to light and self-consciousness, as if re-born from the womb of the All-mother. Thus our sleeping and waking have a remote Determinant in the total Cosmos.

It is manifest that the All (the Pampsychosis)

re-bears the Ego (the Psychosis) every day; for what purpose? It imparts to the Ego its own creative power, which the latter is to use ultimately to re-create the All and so be a link in the Process of the Universe. In the waking state, the self-conscious man asserts himself as individual against the All till he in turn goes back and recreates in thought the All which creates him. This is the supreme waking act of man: he, the created by the Universe, being endowed with the latter's creative power, goes back and recreates its source, recreates that which created it. This completes the ring or the cycle of the All, the explicit Pampsychosis in whose Process lies all Being, even Nothing. This cycle embraces God (the All as creative Idea or the Absolute), Nature (the Cosmos), and Man, who is to return to the All and unite the two extremes, bending them around into the ring of the Universe (to continue the metaphor), or better, to complete the Pampsychosis. Not till God has created that which can re-create Him, is He perfect, or is the Universe truly universal.

Man, then, being created in a sleep, must at last wake up and recreate his Creator creating not only him (Man) but the whole Process of the Universe — God, Nature, Man. It may be said that Man is not fully awake till he does this, nor is the Universe fully awake as long as he partially sleeps, he being an essential link thereof.

So man is likewise to wake up the sleeping or somnolescent Universe by his thought, which makes the Pampsychosis explicit, a complete Process by means of the fully awakened Man reproducing its Process in himself (as God, Nature, and Man) through his own psychical Process (Feeling, Will, Intellect).

Still man is finite also, and that he is finite in his creativity, that he is not the creative All, is seen in the fact that he must often stop and go to sleep again in order to be re-created himself by the All ere he can reproduce the world even in sensation. For his external senses wear out every day and have to be re-made in Sleep by that power which first made them, and of which they are properly special manifestations.

In Sleep, accordingly, we have a process, in fact several processes of the Self. It is true that the self-conscious Ego is inhibited in Sleep, but after self-consciousness has been won; this is not the first Sleep, which is before the arising of self-consciousness, but is the second Sleep, and it has three leading stages.

I. NATURAL SLEEP (HYPNOS); along with the process of Nature (earth and sun) the Self-conscious Ego spontaneously drops back into unity with the All.

II. INDUCED SLEEP (HYPNOSIS); another Ego, the agent, brings on Sleep by artificial means employed upon the recipient.

III. SELF-INDUCED SLEEP (SELF-HYPNOSIS), the Ego becomes its own agent as well as recipient, and so in Sleep reaches a kind of self-determination.

It must be remembered that in all these forms of Sleep, the Ego remains Ego and keeps its power of being subject-object. That is, it can still divide within itself and return to itself as pure Ego, and hence it retains a stage of self-consciousness. But it no longer separates itself from the world; it cannot sense external things and so cannot make the separation between Ego and non-Ego. This is the separation which subsides in Sleep, while the Ego as subject-object remains, and in its way is still self-aware in the dream.

I. NATURAL SLEEP. — Nearly one-third of the normal human life is spent in sleep. Such is the command of Nature herself which the self-conscious Ego obeys, and thereby gives up its relation to the outer world of sense. Sometimes in disease the organism refuses to yield to this behest (*insomnia*); the result is that the creative power of the mind is seriously impaired, being quite unable to think and act in any originative way. The return to the All-mother for the new daily birth is cut off; the negation of Sleep ends in the negation of the Ego itself, and the waking state is no longer fully awake. This regeneration takes place periodically along with the alternation of day and night, harmonious with the movement of earth and sun. Natural Sleep thus corresponds to the movement of Nature in its totality. In this harmony the individual Soul communes with the creative Soul of the All, and receives afresh its power of creativity.

There are various degrees of the foregoing unity of the soul with the All-Soul, or of the self with the Over-Self. There may be merely the doze which is still half-awake. But in Sleep proper the activity of Self-consciousness is changed, the relation between Ego and non-Ego drops away, though sensation and vitality be present. Then the feeling Ego can be dimmed or canceled. Finally there may be in Sleep a cataleptic condition, an apparent suspension of vital functions—no breath, no heart-beat, along with rigidity of the limbs. Still, there is not death but a going back to a germinal, pre-natal condition for a renewal of life and mind. Such states often occur in times of religious excitement and change the character of the whole man for the future, often producing in him a regeneration not only physically and mentally, but morally.

1. *Sleep restores*. We are, therefore, to see that Sleep is not a mere absence of waking activities, as this would be quite nothing, a blank negative. On the contrary Sleep has a positive nature, a life and character of its own. Not

only is it not a mere negative, but rather the negation of a negative — the negation of the worry and weariness which result from all waking self-conscious activity. Its destruction is very decidedly reconstruction. Sometimes a momentary nap gives not simply a cessation of the tension of life, but a renewed creative power which solves the problem before which the mind previously sank down hopeless. Here the fact is the impartation of genetic energy in Sleep from the primal generative power of the Universe, which restores the waning individuality to itself.

The Ego has, accordingly, its own peculiar activity in Sleep. It is no longer in Space and Time as when awake; rather Space and Time are in it or one with it through the All. For Space and Time are inside the All, not outside of it, else it would not be the All. Hence the Ego in Sleep senses through Space and Time, feels at a distance and in the future (Telepathy). Sleep makes the Ego a member of the universal Sensorium which may feel with the right stimulus what is happening or indeed what will happen in the most distant parts.

2. *Sleep obliterates.* We have already noted the primary fact that Sleep obliterates the separation between Ego and non-Ego. In Sleep the particular, finite sense-world in which the waking Ego is placed, is supplanted, and a new

world with its own Space and Time, takes us up into itself, and endows us with its qualities. Sleep does away with the centering of the Ego in the cosmical cycles of sun and stars, so that it is absorbed and carried along by the All in a wholly new kind of revolution to points far beyond its ordinary periphery.

Thus Sleep has its negative side as well as positive — in fact it is positive and re-creative through its being negative. It is a fountain of oblivion as well as of renewal. The Ego through Sleep obliterates its old world in order to build its new one, for it is still Ego, self-conscious and a builder.

What is this new world for which the Ego is prepared through Sleep? Evidently the Dream, which has new sensations, and specially new images, and even new thoughts. Out of such materials it constructs its unique architecture. Moreover a new kind of mind-transference or mental activity at a distance takes place in the Dream.

3. *The Dream.* A counterpart of the real waking life of man now weaves itself into his existence. It is still the realm of psychical activity, yea of the purest psychical activity, since it is all Ego, and no non-Ego, or only the slightest. The Dream, therefore, will show the total process of the Ego in Feeling, Willing, and

Thinking, all these stages beng manifested in its activities.

Here we must emphasize the fact that the Ego in order to be at all, must be active; when cut off from the stimulation of the outer world of sense, it still is working, elaborating its stores of laid-up experiences. Being no longer controlled by the external fact, by the non-Ego, it falls to unmeasured caprice; the Ego shows itself to be self-active, without control; it asserts its freedom by license, and manifests the primal spontaneity of the Self stark naked. The so-called laws of association may sometimes be traced in the sudden leaps of a dream, and sometimes not; its obedience to law is as capricious as its disobedience. The Ego as subject-object pure and simple we have in the dream, calling up its stores, specially of images, as it pleases. The natural liberty of man is greater in the Dream than it can be in the waking state, being under no restraint from a sense-world, still less from a moral and institutional world.

(*a*) The dream has, then, *Feeling,* in fact the fundamental Feeling of the Ego, namely self-consciousness, or self-awareness. Otherwise it could not be self-active Ego at all, which has to separate within itself and then return to itself.

The dreaming Ego is on the one side self-stimulated, yet is on the other side in unity with the All. The outer sense is shut, but the inner sense is greatly intensified; in a dream the Ego sees an object as vividly as when awake. It also becomes telepathic, feels things distant in Space and Time. Its organic connection with the Over-Self gives it the universal power of Feeling, so that it often sees and feels the event taking place far away, and forefeels what is to transpire in the future. There are, however, often presentiments which turn out untrue, and thus the Dream can lie, as it did in a famous instance to Agamemnon.

(*b*) In the Dream the Ego also exerts *Will*, which manifests itself in external movements of various kinds. The Dream as mere Feeling, takes place on the inner stage of mind whose already acquired stores it combines in many ways. But it can also move the body; the motor principle too responds to the Dream. The child smiles in sleep, and the grown person can laugh loud enough to be waked up by the noise. Perhaps everybody talks a little now and then in sleep.

But the striking fact of the present sphere is known as sleep-walking (somnambulism). The subject gets up and performs the most difficult feats of skill, which are beyond his ability in his waking state; he runs perilous risks which he would not ordinarily venture. He seems to have new powers directing mind and body, beyond his self-conscious Ego. A new Self has possession of him which has its senses or universal sense, not limited by the waking capacities. The Over-Self determines him as body, and makes him transcend his real self-consciousness. Such a condition is not normal, but supra-normal. The function of Sleep, which is to reproduce the worn-out Ego, is not fulfilled; the Over-Self in a manner usurps what is reserved for the self-conscious Self.

Such is spontaneous somnambulism, springing up through the caprice of the sleeping Ego. Here we note in advance the fact that this state can be brought about through another Ego taking the place of the lapsed Will. And not only this state but most other kinds of Sleep can be induced from the ostside.

(c) In the Dream the Ego also employs *Intellect*, often in a surprising manner, far surpassing the capability of its waking state. Particularly mathematical problems which have baffled the person awake, have been done by the same person asleep. The revelations of the Dream in poetry and even in philosophy are vouched for by many a poet and thinker. Prodigies (like blind Tom) seem to live and work in a kind of Dream. Some peculiar accession of power from which the waking state is excluded, manifests itself often in the Dream — and oftener not.

Here lies the uncertainty of the present sphere. The higher energy — Over-Self, Pampsychikon, the All-Ego — refuses to be controlled so that its working at a given time in a given way cannot be counted upon. We may deem it the supreme object of this phase of psychical science to get hold of, or at least to find the law of the Pampsychikon, into which the Ego enters as a Dream, and which tells to it seemingly at random the profoundest truths or the biggest lies.

From the foregoing account it is evident that we have in the Dream a mind-transference to a distance, similar to what we saw in the Downburst of the Over-Self. Again there are cases of Feeling, Will and Intellect acting beyond their ordinary periphery (cases of Telepathy, Teleboulesis, and Telenoesis, in the terms of the preceding nomenclature). Space and Time seem to be put under the control of the dreaming Ego, as they were before under the control of the waking supra-conscious Ego.

The difference is that the Ego in its first supra-conscious state is still self-conscious, being aware of its activities as supra-normal and as different from their ordinary range; it knows itself telepathic, for instance. But in the Dream, the Ego has lost its relation to the non-Ego, though it be internally self-aware; what it dreams is real to it, is the new non-Ego created by it, and seems normal. There is, however, a half-waking state in which the reality of the Dream begins to get unreal to the dreaming Ego. But in the full Dream the Ego is quite one with the Over-Self, through which as its very Self, it operates at a distance.

In Sleep with its Dream the Ego of its own accord once a day enters this supra-conscious realm, and passes through some of the experiences just mentioned. But next we find that for this spontaneous activity of the Ego falling into Sleep and Dream, the purposed activity of another Ego can be substituted.

II. INDUCED SLEEP.—HYPNOSIS. Here we enter the realm of what is usually called Hypnotism, which in its typical form is Sleep induced in a subject (recipient) by another Ego (agent), with its attendant phenomena. Moreover, between these two Egos (agent and recipient, or hypnotizer and hypnotized) is the medium, which we have already called the Over-Self. Hence the hypnotized Ego belongs still in the realm of the supra-conscious, being no longer self-conscious as Ego and non-Ego, though it is still internally self-conscious, as subject-object. Its own inner activity as Psychosis it still possesses and must possess in order to be Ego at all. But to distinguish itself from the outer world is not now its function, or only in a diminishing degree.

The sleeping Ego is, accordingly, controlled by another Ego, which makes the distinction from the previous state, where the Sleep was spontaneous. Also this controlled Hypnosis is distinct from the self-controlled Hypnosis, which comes later. Two Egos (hence the doubleness of this stage) play the leading parts; yet the medium, the Over-Self, must not be left out, as is too often done. Indeed just in it lies the main problem, which is still to be wrought out by investigators.

The exact relation of the Hypnosis to Sleep is still under discussion, the subject sometimes sleeping and sometimes not. The difficulty lies in the medium, the Over-Self, into which the hypnotized person enters asleep, or, it may be, awake, as we saw where there is a Downburst of the Over-Self. The essence of Hypnotism is in the relation of the Ego to the Over-Self, in whose power it usually sleeps, though not always. The scientific Hypnotists, especially the Suggestionists, neglect this Over-Self, and so fail to give an adequate view of their science, in spite of their great practical expertness.

It is evident that controlled Hypnosis must be ordered according to the nature of the control. The one Ego is the determiner, and the other is the determined, the induced or artificial sleep being the central phenomenon. We see that the first question will be: How does the hypnotizer bring about this state in his subject? What will then be the reaction of this subject, or the interaction between the two Egos? What, finally, will be the reproducing power of the Hypnosis — its ability to go back and bring up former states of the Ego? Hence we shall consider (1) Methods of producing the Hypnosis, (2) Interaction of its elements, (3) its Reproductive Character seen in its evoking previous conditions of the Self, in its health-restoring power, and even in its calling forth hidden talents.

1. *Methods.* The ways of inducing Hypnosis are varied, but they have a common purpose and a common principle.

The purpose is to bring the waking mind which still clings to the distinction between itself and the world, away from this distinction so that it is more or less obliterated. Then the Ego drops back into the Over-Self, becoming a more or less intimate member thereof, though it still retains its inner activity. The problem essentially is to transform the waking self-conscious Ego into the supra-conscious Ego.

The instrumentalities for this purpose, however different they may be, have a common principle. They turn back the mind upon itself, they seek to confine the Ego to its own inner movement, they concentrate it within, cutting it off from outer attention to the world (or to the non-Ego). The recurrence of motion, for instance, in the repeated passes of the mesmerist, or the recurrence of sounds produces sleep by a kind of correspondence, the Ego being thrown into its inner round of activity by these outer manifestations. Such recurrence of sound is in the lullaby for children, in the susurrus of the trees, in the little waterfall of the brook. We cannot say that it is always fatigue which produces Sleep. The general purpose of the hypnotist must be to submerge the self-conscious distinction between the Ego and non-Ego. The waking state involves a continuous reproduction of this distinction, which, being eliminated, causes the Ego and non-Ego to become one in Sleep, be it natural or artificial.

In this connection we must again mention that the inner self-conscious Ego in its first stage, as subject-object, remains in the Hypnosis as in the Dream. Hynotized people know up to a certain point what is going on around them, yet not in the ordinary waking way. It comes rather through the Over-self with which they are now integrated.

(*a*) The first and most external method of inducing the hypnotic state is the Braidian, so-called after a physician by the name of Braid, of Manchester, England, who also introduced the term *Hypnotism*. The subject looks at some bright object, fixing the attention upon it till sleep intervenes. Here the means is an external object with no direct interference of an Ego as agent. The subject, so to speak, hypnotizes himself, though Braid acknowledges the influence of suggestion. Through attending to the one object the Ego cuts off its relation to all other objects, abstracts from the multiplicity of the world and finally from the one given object. Thus it becomes simply its own inner activity, and in this condition cannot help uniting with the Over-self.

The famous school of Charcot at Paris employs essentially the same sort of means for inducing the Hypnosis, which, however, it regards as a disordered condition of the nervous system.

(*b*) The second method for bringing forth the hypnotic state is Suggestion, which has become the triumphant category of the present stage of the science of Hypnotism. The term seems to have been brought into use (though certainly not invented) by the so-called school of Nancy, France, whose founder was Liébault, and whose chief propagator was Bernheim.

An oral suggestion is given to the subject that he is to sleep; really it is a command, autocratic, perchance over-bearing, by which a waking Will, that of the hypnotizer, supplants another Will, that of the hypnotic, who obeys his hypnotizing lord during the Hypnosis, and often afterwards during the waking state. Here we see an outer control through an Ego which keeps awake itself and dominates its sleeping subjects. This school also holds that every man is suggestible, and hence affirms that Hypnotism is not merely a pathological condition; the Ego by its very constitution is capable of Suggestion.

(c) The third method brings about the hypnotization of both Egos, of both the agent and the recipient. The hypnotizer hypnotizes himself, at least in part, in hypnotizing the subject. Both of them from different sides are integrated with the Over-Self, yet without losing their characteristic relation to each other (that of hypnotizer and hypnotized).

This must be deemed the completed method of inducing the Hypnosis. Both the Egos, agent and recipient, are now in full rapport, being in the same supra-conscious state; the hypnotizer is no longer in the self-conscious waking state (or at least not entirely so), autocratically commanding or "suggesting" his behests to the hypnotic Ego from the outside or from above. Both are on an equal footing as far as condition is concerned, though there is still impartation from one to the other. But the most important fact is that the Over-Self, of which both Egos have become integral members, now comes out of its background and demands to be taken into the account. Undoubtedly this Over-Self is the most obscure, the least developed portion of Hypnotism in general, and it is probably the most difficult. Still the future of the science lies largely in its investigation and development.

The third Method here outlined does not exclude external means for starting the hypnotic act. Especially a system of circular movements of the hand oft repeated, of passes so called, starts the Ego on its inner round till it loses its relation to the outer world, to that of the non-Ego. It should be added that the agent, being also an Ego, gets involved, partially at least, in his own process and shares in the hypnotization of the recipient.

In the historic unfolding of Hypnotism this third method was the first to become prominent. It was essentially the method of Mesmer and his disciples, who ascribed the phenomena to a magnetic fluid. Out of Mesmerism grew Braid and Charcot, and after them came the Suggestionists. But the Braidists and the Suggestionists by no means exhaust the phenomena, as they largely leave out the medium, the Over-Self, and thus move in a limited stage of the science. Noticeable is, therefore, the present trend back to Mesmerism without its unnecessary theories, its mystifications, and doubtless its frequent charlatanry.

2. *Interaction*. It has been already noted that there are interacting elements in the hypnotic state — agent, medium (Over-Self) and recipient. In inducing the Hypnosis we have

seen these three elements combining or cooperating in various ways. Often the recipient is passive and yields easily, though there are many degrees of hypnotic susceptibility. There may be, however, a keen struggle between the hypnotizer and the hypnotized. An immoral suggestion may be resented. It is declared that a hypnotized prohibitionist could not be induced to take a drink of water, when he believed it, under the influence of suggestion, to be whiskey. There is a decided opinion notwithstanding, that Hypnotism can be employed to commit crime, and jurisprudence has begun to take cognizance of the fact. If there is resistence at times, there is likewise submission. Nothing is more common than to see the hypnotized person stoutly refuse at first to obey the request of the hypnotizer, but gradually yield to his more insistent commands when repeated. The hypnotic also asserts his individuality, he cannot allow his own Will to be supplanted by another Will without a struggle. Then he too is an Ego and has his own power of suggestion which may counteract the efforts of the hypnotizer. This is known as auto-suggestion and is often cited to account for failures in hypnotic experiments.

On the other hand the hypnotized person is often endowed with a power far beyond his natural Self. He may show abilities in thought and speech, in writing and in drawing, which his friends never suspected. It is declared that his character is often changed and elevated, and his mind may be heightened into genius.

(*a*) The general proposition holds that every Ego has in its normal state some degree of suggestion, suggestibility, and auto-suggestion. Every Ego can hypnotize, be hypnotized, and resist hypnotization.

(*b*) There are various gradations of the hypnotic state. The first is usually called the light Hypnosis, which again may be subdivided. In general this state can be remembered after waking. The Ego may recall its separation from the world and even from its own body. This condition is reported in the following statement of one who had returned to self-consciousness: "I was immeasurably far away," and "the world was escaping from me." Also "my voice" sounded afar off. My legs seemed "not to belong to me" I was no longer myself but "another had taken my form." (Cited by Dr. Sidis in his *Psychology of Suggestion*, p. 65.) It is manifest that the patient has here remembered his hypnotic condition. But in what is called deep Hypnosis there is forgetfulness after waking (known as *amnesia*).

(*c*) This brings us to consider the post-hypnotic condition, which is of considerable importance in Hypnotism. During Hypnosis a suggestion is given which is to be carried out after waking. A hypnotized person will measure time. If he is told to wake up in half an hour and light the lamp, his sleep will conclude on time, and he will perform the act. Yet he thinks he is free in such an act, and scouts the notion of its having been suggested to him. Thus suggéstions are stored away during Hypnosis in the sub-conscious Ego till the time comes for them to burst forth into action. The hypnotizer in this way may determine in part our waking activities.

3. *Reproductive Hypnosis.* It has been indicated that all stages of the supra-conscious Ego are inter-related in a common character. The first of these stages we came upon distinctly in the Downburst of the Over-Self, in which the Ego remained awake and self-conscious, yet was integrated with the Over-Self and became thus supra-conscious in Feeling, Will and Intellect (Telepathy, Teleboulesis, and Telenoesis). But the Hypnosis may extend back even to the sub-conscious realm, if not to the pre-conscious, reproducing and re-instating some form of the submerged Self.

(*a*) It has been repeatedly shown by experiment that the secondary person in the case of the Dual Self (see preceding p. 161) can be restored by Hypnotism. For instance Ansel Bourne, having recovered his natural state or his primary Self, could be hypnotized back into his secondary Self, during which he called himself A. J. Brown. Thus the Upburst of the Under-Self can be brought about hypnotically. This fact may become of importance in education. If the stores of undeveloped traits lying in the sub-conscious Ego from a long ancestry, can be put under command of the hypnotizer who may select and develop certain traits, a vast new field of mental training opens to the view.

(*b*) Much more common is it that the self-conscious Ego is taken up into the Over-Self in a sleeping and also in a waking state. Here on the whole we place the well-known therapeutic effects of Hypnotism. The diseased or defective body is dipped anew into the creative All and is made over. The self-conscious Ego with its separation from the Over-Self is renounced, and the restoration begins. This is often called the power of mind over body, whereof the appearance of the bleeding stigma is a striking example. Hypnotic suggestion has also its negative power: it can produce paralysis, catalepsy, disease. The various kinds of cures, mind-cure, faith-cure, Christian science, and hypnotic suggestion, go back ultimately to the one principle.

(*c*) There is still another phenomenon, which sometimes results from hypnotization. An ordinary man becomes possessed with rare gifts of thought and insight. We seem herein to go back to the All-giver, who presents a new and great endowment to the hypnotized person, reaching beyond the sub-conscious world into what we have above named the pre-conscious realm. It would seem that Hypnotism in rare cases may rouse some form of genius in its patient. A poor shoemaker boy, without education, without exceptional intelligence apparently, is hypnotized, and begins to construct in thought the Universe, writing out in his hypnotic states a vast system of philosophy which has had many followers. Before each revelation it appears that he (A. J. Davis) had to be put into an hypnotic trance by another agent. Swedenborg, who was a learned man, seems to have been self-hypnotized in working out his grand scheme of God, Nature, and Man.

The poetic genius appears often to see and to speak in a state allied to the Hypnosis. Goethe has declared that he wrote when in a kind of somnambulistic condition. The genius may well be supposed to be in some intimate relation to the creative energy of the All. But he too usually hypnotizes himself, to which fact we may next devote some attention.

III. SELF-INDUCED SLEEP. — SELF-HYPNOSIS. The agent is now the recipient also, the second Ego as hypnotizer disappears. The command is a self-command, the hypnotized person is the dominating will over himself. In relation to the preceding forms this may be deemed the self-determined or free Hypnosis, the dualism of two persons having been eliminated. It is a return to Natural Sleep, in so far as this also belongs to the single Ego. Still it is not spontaneous, but induced, hence it has the second stage as an element of its process. Here indeed occurs a difficulty, that of drawing any exact line between spontaneous and self-induced Sleep; the two stages shade off into each other imperceptibly. Indeed we often go to sleep by an effort of will, which inhibits the thought keeping us awake.

Still in Self-Hypnosis occur the peculiar phenomena of Hypnotism. The Over-Self is set to work by the act, and we behold often what is called the trance, into which the subject is said to throw himself by an act of Will. Sometimes, however, it is quite involuntary and unconscious, especially in the case of a person who has been often hypnotized. Moreover in Self-Hypnosis the subject is by no means always asleep, but may be quite awake, though still hypnotized. Nevertheless we call it Hypnosis since there is an element of Sleep or something akin to Sleep weaving through his waking consciousness.

The result is that the single individual contains within himself the cycle of the Hypnosis, not being determined from the outside, but determining himself to produce the phenomena. He brings himself to feel, to will and to know at a distance. He may see and hear from afar (clairvoyance and clairaudience). What we have already come upon and designated as Telepathy, Teleboulesis, and Telenoesis, rise to the surface again, but in a new way and from a new source; not now bursting down from above (from the Over-Self) upon the self-conscious Ego, nor again induced from the outside by another Ego, the hypnotizer, but induced by the one Ego which is both hypnotizer and hypnotized, he having become the total process within itself.

We might, therefore, call Self-Hypnosis the free Hypnosis, in so far as such a state can be free. The Ego freely hypnotizing itself, calls up a master (the Over-Self) just in that act. By its own free act it puts itself under the yoke. Self-Hypnosis must accordingly be transcended in the interest of the freedom of the Self. This rise we shall behold in the coming stage, which is the Feeling of the Free Self. But at present we must consider Self-Hypnosis (less frequently but more correctly called Auto-Hypnosis).

1. The self-hypnotizing power is manifested by the control which the Ego can get over the tissues of the body. It can change them, causing disintegration of them and restoration. The two most famous recent instances of the production of stigmata with bleeding at the wound (Katherine Emmerich, and Louise Lateau) may be taken as forms of Self-Hypnosis, produced

by long and intense concentration of Feeling and Thought, and doubtless Will at the start, upon the crucifixion. The total Ego, not through itself merely, but through the medium of the Over-Self, began changing the organic structure of the body.

Again the peculiar working of the Over-Self forces itself upon our attention. Many have thought long and intensely upon the crucifixion without producing stigmatization. Why just in these cases? Such is verily the problem of the Over-Self, as already noted repeatedly. The medium exists, but is not yet controllable by science. We may compare it with a recent marvel, wireless telegraphy, which is just now getting control of a new medium (apparently physical) hitherto uncontrollable and indeed unknown.

2. This same self-concentration we have noted in all methods of inducing Hypnosis. Both the hypnotizer and the hypnotized inhibits the outer and develops the inner activity of mind through attention to the one object, which finally becomes the simple Psychosis of the Ego. This easily unites itself with the All-Ego or with the Over-Self, which is inherently creative, constructing and also destroying. Undoubtedly, here lies the mystery of the present sphere; the methods by which the Over-Self works have hitherto escaped the law of scientific procedure.

Virchow is reported to have said in regard to the mentioned case of Louise Lateau, that it was either fraud or miracle. But the alternative does not hold. There is another element, the medium called here the Over-Self, which the scientist, in spite of his seeming aversion, must grapple with and formulate.

3. Again we return to the fact that the Ego can and does hypnotize itself through its own Will, doing away with the autocratic suggestion of another Ego, and controlling in a measure the previous accidental descent of the Over-Self. Thus the Ego even in the realm of the Hypnosis is transcending Fate and Chance, and rising toward Freedom. Mind-transference in the forms of Feeling, Will and Intellect is not now thrust upon the Ego from outside, but the mind transfers itself through its own process and can show itself transcending its ordinary self-conscious periphery through Telepathy, Teleboulesis, and Telenoesis, as already observed in cognate states.

At this point one may well ask the question, Is Sleep trainable? Can we get possession of it so completely that we can employ its states and its powers for the purposes of life? We mean of course Sleep in its widest sense, including the Hypnosis and the Self-Hypnosis — the spontaneous, the directed and the self-directed Sleep. It is highly probable that the Ego asleep is educable as well as awake. Hitherto we have only trained our waking life, the sleeping strand of existence lies undeveloped. Can we cultivate the two kinds of sensation, the two kinds of memory, in general the two kinds of Feeling, Willing and Knowing — the distant and the present? Is every human being finally to be endowed with Telepathy, Teleboulesis, and Telenoesis as a portion of his educational outfit? The culture of Sleep with its supra-conscious Self may well be a part of the future programme of the School of Life. We still throw away Sleep as an educative means, quite as we once threw away the play of children, which is now organized into the system of their most fruitful instruction.

With the conclusion of Self-Hypnosis we finish the sphere of what we have called the supra-conscious Ego with its peculiar problems of the Over-Self, in which center the strange phenomena of mind-transference — Telepathy, Teleboulesis and Telenoesis. Each of the three kinds of Sleep, natural, induced, and self-induced, manifest these phenomena, which already began to appear in the realm of the self-conscious Ego with the Downburst of the Over-Self. Moreover, the Feeling of the Conscious Self, has run through its three stages, sub-conscious, self-conscious, and supra-conscious. There remains one other division of All-Feeling, the Feeling of the Free Self, whose turn has now come. In it the Ego breaks loose from the

Over-Self whose peculiar manifestations henceforth disappear.

Observation. Hypnotism and its allied phenomena are beginning to creep into modern Psychology, though on the whole they are not very heartily received. Their place in the science is uncertain, they seem recalcitrant to any order, being mostly put off into a little corner by themselves.

The London Society for Psychic Research deserves the most credit for its careful and elaborate work in this new field, as well as for its valiant battle against excessive credulity on the one side and excessive skepticism on the other. Its vast materials are, however, of different values, and must be sifted. Then they have no order, could not have in the nature of the case. The attempt of Myers in his two large volumes on *Human Personality*, cannot be deemed a success in organizing the present subject, though otherwise very suggestive, and specially fascinating on account of the unusual excellence of the author's literary presentation.

The subject, being of such an undefined and problematical character, has been afflicted with a very hypertrophy of theorizing. To account for the unique working of the Over-Self there have been invoked the act of God, the act of disembodied spirits, as well as physical forces and fluids. Indeed this is the very region of mystification, with its army of votaries made up of the deceived, the deceivers, and self-deceived.

Our purpose has been to put the phenomena into their psychical order so that they explain themselves without theory. For instance Sense-perception, Representation and Thought as the psychical process of the Intellect need no theory for their explanation when once duly formulated and ordered. There was a time, however, when Sense-perception (the Ego sensing the object) had its theory which invoked for its accomplishment the assistance of God (*assistentia Dei* in the Cartesianism of the Seventeenth Century). Psychology banishes such a theory by defining and ordering the fact. Sometimes it happens that the fact is called a theory by mistake. Mind-transference, for instance, seeks to state a fact, not a theory. If the transfer is supposed to take place through the medium of a disembodied spirit, we have a theory. And the Overself in the preceding account is not given as a theory but seeks to express a fact or at least to give some glimpse of a fact, which has been as yet by no means fully explored.

Out of this dreamy, unfree, often abnormal, yet very real realm of the sleeping Ego, we pass to its awakening to a new consciousness, which is the feeling of its self-determining power against its previous Determinant.

III. Feeling of the Free Self.

The Free Self of Feeling, at which we have now arrived, is self-conscious again but in a new way. Previously (see p. 147) the self-conscious Ego sought to separate and to isolate itself from the All, and so was really determined to its isolation through the latter. But at present the feeling Self as free starts to determining the All and thus asserting its freedom.

A phase of the feeling Self seeking to determine the All as Over-Self we have just witnessed in Self-Hypnosis, in which the Ego may be said to invoke the Over-Self to take control and to put it to sleep, voluntarily subjecting itself, as it were, to the despot, using its freedom to give up freedom. But the truly Free Self tackles the despot and seeks to subject him to itself, though it can grasp him only piece by piece. That is, the Free Self begins to divide up the All outside of it, getting possession of the same through division. It is evident that the elemental relation between the Ego and the All is now broken; the Ego no longer feels itself a member of the Great Totality, but distinct from it; nay, it proceds to dismember that Totality and to appropriate its parts.

In the movement of All-Feeling, or of the All-feeling Ego, the third stage has now been reached, in which the Ego goes back and starts to determining its previous Determinant (the All in the First Stage). In the Second or Conscious Stage (just finished), the Ego is in a state of struggle with its Determinant (the All), striving to determine itself apart from and even in opposition to the same — wherein it was defeated and put to sleep or hypnotized. But in the present stage the Ego wakes up and begins to assert its new freedom, whose universal Feeling is that the Ego must determine that which determines it.

In Self-Hypnosis we saw the Ego assert its power by controlling the All which produces Sleep. Thus the Determinant which originally quenched the self-conscious Ego begins to be determined itself by that Ego, not, however, to conscious, but to supra-conscious action.

The Free Self of the present sphere goes back to the Endowed Self, which was gifted by the All directly with its varied attainments — Disposition, Character, Talent, Genius. But now the individual Self is to control the All and is not to be controlled by it, transforming it and not transformed by it. Thus we see the cycle of All-Feeling: What at first determined the All-feeling Ego, is now determined by it.

Such is a general statement of the stage before

us, in which we may mark a movement through the following steps.

1. When the Ego wakes up after its renewal through Sleep, it has a feeling of freedom, of activity untrammeled. We may call this a feeling of triumph rising with the triumph of day and the flight of darkness, and running parallel with the cosmical appearance of light. But the deeper feeling of triumph is that the self-conscious Ego defeats its former antagonist, the Over-Self, who in the last stage overwhelmed it, absorbed it and submerged it into the Tartarean realm of Sleep and Dream. Such is the second great awakening of the Self, not the first, which is birth, or the first unconscious plunge into light. To be sure, this second awakening of the Self must repeat itself every twenty-four hours, inasmuch as it is succeeded by a second Sleep with its renewal. Thus there is the continuous battle between waking and sleeping, between whose alternations the river of Life rises and falls.

The Ego, having been renewed through Sleep in its supra-conscious State, comes back to Self-consciousness, having recovered the difference between Ego and non-Ego or Self and the World. But this second awakening is not a mere relapse to the first one, as self-conscious Ego; it has brought with it not simply the feeling of separation, but also the feeling of positive freedom which asserts itself against the previous Determinant.

2. The All-feeling Ego in its inner freedom finds that it is limited by an outer world and thrown back upon itself. Such is the contradiction which it has now to overcome if it be really free. We saw in the preceding sphere the self-conscious Ego asserting itself as separate from the All, in which conflict it was vanquished and re-submerged. But the present struggle is a deeper one: the self-conscious Ego must be not simply separate, but free; the separation, the dualism must be overcome. The external world which now appears to it, stands in its way, limits it, resists it, obstructs its feeling of freedom, which, accordingly, proceeds to assert itself anew.

So we conceive for a moment the present Ego feeling free internally, yet feeling unfree externally, and then starting to make itself free externally by creating a free world.

3. The self-conscious Ego, in order to liberate itself from the sway of an external Determinant, the world, feels that it must transform that world, making the same over into an image of and also into a means of its freedom, changing the same into things beautiful as well as useful for its end. Such is the feeling which propels the Ego to re-make external Nature into its own forms. The great industrial transformation which we see going on around us everywhere, springs from this feeling of freedom. The works of man proceed ultimately from his aspira-
for a lib rated Self.

Thus we find the Ego striving to determine that outer world which has determined it. In general, [the self-determined All has created a member as Ego which is self-determined and free as it is. It has imparted to the created Self its own creative process within itself and thus presented it with an individuality which ideally reflects the Universe, and which must, therefore, subsume whatever limits it externally.

On the one hand this individual Ego while determining the world, finds that the world still determines it, stimulates it to its free process, to its assertion of itself. Both sides are separate, and the separation has become explicit. The Ego on its part determines the world, yet is determined by it to such free determination. On the other hand the world is determined by the Ego, yet determines the same to make it determined. That is, each side has its own distinct process as separate and works upon the other externally.

Now follows the main result of this formulation. The elemental stage of the feeling Ego has come to its end in the complete separation and mutual opposition of its elements. The feeling Ego no longer feels itself to be an organic part of the Totality; it is divided from the same and has its own distinct process, which is determined by the All, not from the inside, but from the outside. To be sure this separated All is not the true one but an All which appears yet is not, since it is now limited, finite, not the whole but a part. The Ego in Feeling is no longer a member of the All, in immediate unity with it like the limb of the total organism, but has become an independent individuality in its own right and with its own work.

Such is then the dissolution of Elemental Feeling, which we have followed so long through its many devious passages, above ground and under ground, requiring no small degree of patience, and calling forth at times a skeptical amazement at its labyrinthine circuits, large and little. But we have clung to the basic Norm throughout and have found it with us still at the conclusion. Feeling as belonging to the Ego, as being its primordial stage, must manifest the process of the same, the Psychosis, and thereby get its order and organization.

But, having passed through Elemental Feeling, whither shall we go next? The two realms, the Ego and the outer world, hitherto united and having their separation as yet only implicit, have become explicitly disconnected, and yet mutually determined through their external relations. The feeling Ego still feels the world, but not as a whole within itself, but as divided, specialized, cut up into an infinite number of particulars. Each of these is to stimulate its special Feeling, making the whole into a realm of limited, finite Feeling. The latter term is the one which we shall employ.

Part Second.

FINITE FEELING.

In the preceding Feeling, that of the Free Self, the Ego has come to feel itself as the determinant of what is outside of itself. We see it not only separating from the Universe which created it, but also determining the same as something distinct from itself. Thus the elemental relation between the Ego and the All is broken up, and at the same time the All is broken up within, divided, dismembered, particularized by the Ego, its product or offspring. We recollect that in consciousness the Universe imparted to its child, the Ego, its own process, thus endowing this child with its own gift of a separate, independent individuality, which also must be creative in accord with the innermost nature of the parent. So the Ego, having been endowed with the feeling of freedom, turns against the All which gave just this endowment of freedom, and asserts itself as free against its former Determinant, which limits it, seeking freely to reproduce in Feeling what produced it. For such purpose it divides up and particularizes the All as its outer world, in accord with its nature, since it sprang from a dividing of the All.

The feeling Ego as free having reduced the Universe to parts or particulars, a new movement begins. Each of these particulars becomes or may become a Determinant of the Ego (which is itself now a particular) to Feeling. That is, the Universe, no longer as Totality (as in Elemental Feeling) but as Particularity, determines the Ego to Feeling, so that we enter the realm of particular Feelings, which we shall call Finite Feeling. Again, therefore, the world stimulates the feeling Self, but it is the world particularized.

We have accordingly come to a stage of Feeling which embraces a much greater diversity than the last (Elemental Feeling), in fact the present is just the sphere of diversity, separation, multiplicity in Feeling. The Determinant becomes specially many Determinants, and the implicit All of which the feeling Ego is a member, is explicit in a vast manifoldness of forms which more or less externally stimulate the Ego to its

Feeling. In other words, the finite world is now to be the determining principle of Feeling.

We might call this entire stage by the name of *Passion*, though the latter term is of varied usage. Passions are properly what the Ego suffers, and the word puts stress upon its recipient character. But the more common significance of Passion is at present the violent outburst — which meaning is quite opposite to its etymological sense. Descartes means all Feelings by what he calls *Passions of the Soul*, and this is the better usage.

Going back to our formula of Feeling *as the process of the Ego within itself turned inward* by some Determinant, we mark that this Determinant is not *immediately* connected with its object as in the previous stage. Nature or the All stimulating the Ego as a member of its own organism, is now separated into many determining objects moving the Ego which is likewise separated from the All. A new world of Determinants is thus interjected between the two extremes, Ego and the All. This is of necessity a world of finite Determinants, each of which stimulates the primal Norm of Feeling and so produces its own distinct act of Feeling. Or, better, the All is itself divided, particularized, finitized into a world of Determinants.

If we look closely into the relation between these two stages, Elemental Feeling and Finite or Determinate Feeling, we shall find that the former is stimulated directly from within — the Ego feels itself feeling the Whole, though this Feeling also has various forms. Strictly, Elemental Feeling has no external Determinant, being really inside the All in whose organic movement it shares as a member of the organism of the Universe. But Finite Feeling is conceived as having the distinct external Determinant which is separated from itself and lies outside of itself. Thus it too is finite and becomes a particular member of the finite world which is composed of a multiplicity of particulars, each of which may be a Determinant of the Ego to some finite or special form of Feeling.

In this way the Determinant is seen to come from the outside and is taken up by the primal Psychosis or Norm of Feeling, whereby it receives its special character. We may conceive the Universe divided up into Determinants which produce every variety of Feeling. The sight of the flag of my country rouses in me the Feeling of patriotism — a particular Feeling excited by a particular object. The Norm of Feeling as universal is thus particularized by some special occurrence, which comes upon the Ego from the bosom of the Great All lying back of particularity, and stimulates it to that process within itself called Feeling.

There is another fact about this sphere which

must be brought out in the exposition: The particular determinant does not directly pass to its particular Feeling, but stirs the whole man with his associated store of Feeling. In order that the flag of my country may rouse my patriotism, I must have had many experiences, and quite a little bit of knowledge. For the insignificant piece of bunting has to be transformed by me into a symbol of what my country means to me and to the world.

The next question is, How shall we order this large and diversified sphere of Finite Feelings? As usual, by the kind of Determinants, which we may see to have the following classes.

I. IMPRESSION: The outer sense-world is the Determinant coming to the Ego through the senses associated in the physical body.

II. EMOTION: The inner mind-world is the Determinant coming to the Ego through images, thoughts, impressions, in fine the associated stores of mental concepts.

III. SYMPATHY: The inner mind-world of one Ego is the Determinant coming to the inner mind-world of another Ego or other Egos, which are thereby associated in a common Feeling (Sympathy). Or, the Emotion of one person stirs a like Emotion in another or in many persons, who are then said to sympathize, or feel together in common bond.

Thus Sympathy associates separate individuals who are capable of Emotion which goes back still further to Impression. In general we shall find that every being which has Pain and Pleasure, will rise to associate with other similar beings through Sympathy. Such is indeed the movement of Finite Feeling, which, starting with a separate world full of separated Egos, brings them to union and association through Sympathy.

We shall find, accordingly, that the end and purpose of Finite Feeling is to overcome the state of division with which this stage begins, and to bring the separated units into an inner emotional association, which renders possible the external organization of men in institutions. The natural bond or the subjective fusion from which the institutional world springs, is Sympathy. Such is the conclusion of Finite Feeling, whose starting-point we must first consider under the head of Impression, which is its most external form.

Here it may be stated that we use the term *Impression* also in Intellect under Sense-perception (see *Psychology and Psychosis*, p. 126), where it designates a form of particularized Sensation. But in the present case it is regarded as a form of particularized Feeling accompanying Sensation. Or, there is an intellectual Impression and a feeling Impression.

SECTION FIRST.—IMPRESSION.

Impression, as here used, means the Feeling or group of Feelings which are stimulated into activity by the external world reaching the Ego through the Senses. The external world thus specialized produces a corresponding specialized Feeling. These are frequently called sensuous Feelings, or the Feelings of the Sense-world.

The particular Determinant impinges upon the totality of organized Sensation as found in the human body, out of which proceeds the partienlar Feeling. The so-called Five Senses constitute this organic Whole, which we may, from the present point of view, call associated Sensation. The different organs of associated Sensation (the five Senses) are the product of a long heredity, and contain a store of Sensations which were developed in the past but can be stimulated to activity in the present.

But Sensation is not what we call Feeling, though the latter is its concomitant. An Impression is that form of Feeling immediately connected with and springing from Sensation, when the latter is felt to be agreeable or disagreeable. In a burn of the hand, there is a Sensation, also a Feeling, or what we call here an Impression. This distinction we shall illustrate more fully.

If a pin sticks you, there is a peculiar internal movement involving your body, which both recoils from and reacts against the intrusion. Your organism asserts itself, and you are said to feel. It does not yield or resist simply at a given spot, like so much matter, as when the pin is stuck into a piece of wood, but the total body responds with an inner self-assertion. In this case we observe that there is first a special stimulus at a special point of the organism; then the total organism is affected and proceeds to posit or localize the disturbing stimulus at the special point whence the latter originated. Thus a cycle of organic activity takes place, from the stimulated spot, through the totality of the body, back to the starting-point. This is the primitive process which underlies all Sensation.

The pin does not stick into the spinal cord or

the brain, it touches only the bodily periphery, still this stimulus is taken to the central organs by the molecular movement of the afferent nerve and is returned by the efferent nerve to the point affected. If the pin actually went to the center, that would be the end of you; still it gets there ideally, with its material extension canceled, and you feel the prick of the pin only in that way. The one spot must be made over into the total organism, must be annulled as particular, then ideally reproduced and localized. Moreover, in the case of the prick of the pin, there is an interference with the organic totality as process, which stoppage gives the color or form of the Feeling as Pain. All Pain, therefore, has an ideal element, as well as a physical; the inhibition of the organic rhythm must be ideally reproduced in order to be painful, or become Impression.

The total Organism is sensitive, capable of Sentience. Any part of the bodily surface can be touched and will create a sensitive reponse. To be sure there is a great difference in various parts of the body; a few excrescences — hair, nails — have no feeling. The nervous system is the instrument of Sentience.

Any obstruction of this fundamental process of Sentience brings forth Pain, which is the negation of the free process of the Organism, the inhibition, in some form, of the primal self-activity of the somatic Ego. Thus a negative power enters the regular organic activity, disturbs it, and may destroy it. Still the organism is to overcome this negation, and transform it into Pleasure. With Pain and Pleasure we have Feeling.

One may as well ask: What is the meaning or purpose of this companion to Sensation called Feeling? Sensation has two relations: the sensing of the object and the sensing of the Ego at the same time. The sensing of the object gives simply knowledge of a certain kind; but this knowledge calls forth Feeling also. Does the act of sensing the object promote or retard the process of the Self? In the first case the response is Pleasure, in the second case the response is Pain. Here Feeling enters Sensation and in its way judges the same as favorable or unfavorable to itself. Now Feeling is usually said to be of the Soul whose voice it is, yea whose judgment it is, uttered in the form of Pleasure and Pain. The Soul feels, or the Ego as Soul is Feeling. The Ego is present in every act of Sensation and approves or disapproves of that act by Feeling.

The present sphere of Feeling as Impression is next to be brought into order. We must keep in mind that Impression is stimulated by some particular form of the external world (as the point of a pin in the preceding illustration), and is itself the particular counterpart (in Pleasure or Pain) of a special Sensation which is also produced by the foregoing stimulation. So we shall have to consider (I) *Sensibility*, or the capacity of the Ego to receive Sensation and therewith Impression; (II) *The Special Senses*, through which the outer world is particularized and received by the Ego; III. *Impression* in general, as separated from Sensation, which being stored away becomes the material for Emotion in the coming stage.

I. *Sensibility*. Here we must again grasp the receptive or pathic principle of the Ego, along with its reaction against the external Determinant. Thus it is capable of receiving Sensations and Impressions, of adopting and unifying with its own immediate process this external Determinant. The Ego is ever ready to be at one with the world in Feeling. This world may come to it and determine it in every shape of external multiplicity, each shape as stimulus producing its own special Feeling. In this sphere all externality has as its destiny to become an Impression, reducing its outer separation and finitude to the inner unity of Feeling. Yet having attained such unity, Feeling too will diversify itself into multitudinous forms in accord with the Determinant.

Passing through the woods on a warm day, I observe a breeze springing up and stirring the tree-tops, producing a movement of their curves which is pleasing to the eye, as well as an undulation of sound gratifying to the ear. Also an invigorating coolness is brought to my cheek, and draughts of fresh air fill my lungs. What a receptive being is man! All the diversities of external nature stimulate him and produce an activity within him called Feeling which in the above cases is grateful. But the same breeze may be the last little thrust which loosens the dead branch above my head; down falls the new stimulus of the external world and calls forth a new Impression from my bruised scalp, which may be the beginning of a painful line of Impressions indefinitely extended.

In this illustration we have the two factors of the present sphere; the outer world in its vast diversity with a process all its own of which the breeze, the tree, the limb, are elements, and on the other hand the Ego with its process, here that of Feeling, and specially that of Impression. This Ego is capable of Sensation and Impression, has Sensibility, is a kind of individual Sensorium, which takes up and transforms into its own inner process whatever comes upon it from the outside. Such is the two-sided relation or dualism of the present sphere.

But Sensibility, in order to be capable of sensing anything, must have its process which may be more definitely set forth as follows.

1. *Organic Rhythm.* This is the state of the Organism in its free, natural, undisturbed process, as it is in complete health. We might conceive of it as the happy equilibrium of the bodily energies, except that this equilibrium is not a stand-still, not passive. The perfect adjustment and co-operation of all the corporeal parts make this rhythm, not indifferent, not excessive, showing the happy mean, the proportion suggestive of the Greek moderation.

Yet this rhythm is the result of activity. The Organism gives many external manifestations of it, inspiration and expiration of the lungs, systole and diastole of the heart, recurrence and cessation in many forms. The appetites have this rhythm or oscillation, as hunger and satiety, thirst and its slaking. It is the undertone throughout the realm of Feeling, and thus images the Ego, which is rhythmical, alternating between unity and separation.

2. *The Disturbance (Determinant).* The inner rhythmical movement of the Organism is disturbed by the environing world, primarily through Sensation. Our bodies have to receive; if we look up with open eyes, we have to see yonder tree; if we brush against a hot stove, we have to accept its heat, though it burn up the recipient organ. There is an inflowing stream of sensed objects from all our environment, a

vast current of Sensation is always sweeping inward to the central Ego.

But if there is an inflow, there is a corresponding outflow from the Ego to the environment, making the cycle of Sensation. Even the Organism has the corresponding sets of nerves, afferent and efferent, which are the roads upon which the Ego travels from and to the sensed object, and thus in turn to and from the central Ego. The human body may be likened to a sphere, whose periphery, netted over and over with the recipient organs of Sensation, takes up the external Universe part by part and conveys these parts along the afore-mentioned roads as radii to the center, whose grand capacity is to turn the Sensation around and send it back again to its starting point over new radiating roads outward (the efferent nerves).

Such is the round or cycle of Sensation which the Disturbance from the environing world has introduced. It is very different from that quiet inner round of Life which we noted as Organic Rhythm. But now the round gets outside the body and connects with the external world, which is wheeled into this new cycle through the Ego within. So we may conceive a series of eyeles reaching out from the Ego and picking up every outside thing in the environment, and then returning with it to the center which is Ego. Moreover each of these cycles of Sensation bears with it a Feeling or specially an Impression as we shall see later.

But this Disturbance of the organic equilibrium is going on continually, and has been going on for indefinite ages — what is the result?

3. *The Store.* The Organism is a vast store of these Sensations, which are united with it and indeed change it, giving to it new capacities of sensing the outer world. Every fresh Sensation is a new potentiality, and has in a manner made or remade an organ for itself, which falls back into the Organic Rhythm of the body awaiting another stimulus. Every day our physical Organism is being re-created by exercise in the struggle with externality. The Disturbance from environment is a call for a new adaptation of our corporeal system to meet the emergency. Hence we are to conceive our Organism as an immense reservoir containing organs which have been evolved in the past, are now evolving, and will be evolved still further in the future.

The development of the organ has been studied a good deal since Darwin set the pace. The hand, for instance, with its keen tactile sense at the tips of the fingers has been traced back through a long series of analogues to the fins of the fish. By use it has grown through ever-renewed struggle for life with environment, till we reach the Bimana. Now all these transcended stages still lie in the hand, and sometimes it may relapse to one of them, showing the potentiality of the past as still existent. And the whole human organism is simply full of organs like the hand, with a history in them which we can read in the ascending order of the organic world.

The Evolution through the struggle for Existence it has been called, and this is certainly present. But there is something more than Life involved. Unless the organ can improve, unless it has within itself a limit-transcending power, it can give no guaranty of safety to Life. That organism which can unfold out of itself in the briefest time to meet the emergency of environment will survive. Here we catch a glimpse of something at work above Life, of something beyond the mere vital activity of the Organism, of that realm of Feeling which is not simple Sensation, but which is often identified as Soul.

At present, however, we are to behold the Ego meeting the multiplicity of the world half-way as it were, on the surface of the body. The corporeal unity separates into the Senses which are to take up all the diversity of the macrocosm; the body particularized has now to sense the world particularized.

II. SENTIENCE. — THE FIVE SENSES. Here we come to the active principle (*sentiens*) which stirs the previous passive element (*sensibile*), Sensibility. The result is the Ego, the inner and non-extended, takes up the outer and extended in a sensation. How this is done, is indeed the first and probably greatest *crux* of Philosophy and also of Psychology.

The realm of Sentience — the Five Senses — is to be regarded as an organized Whole for transforming the outer material world into the inner mental world, both sides being differentiated into a multiplicity of parts. Thus the part of the great external All is taken up by the part (organ) of the corporeal totality in a multitude of ways. It belongs properly to natural science to treat of the physical media (light, sound, etc.); to physiological science to treat of the organs in themselves; but to Psychology it belongs to consider how they stimulate the Ego to Feeling, Will, and Intellect.

In the activity of all the Senses we shall find lurking some form of Feeling, something agreeable or disagreeable. This is the fact for which we here bring to notice the Senses, in a very brief survey. The Five Senses are associated in the corporeal totality, and are ordered as follows: —

(1) *Touch* is the most general sense, being distributed over the corporeal periphery in varying degrees of intensity. It senses immediate contact with matter, reporting weight, warmth and form to a degree, and cohesion.

(2) *Taste and Smell* are often called the

chemical Senses, since they report the dissolution of the external body. Connected with their Sensation is a very decided Feeling, agreeable and disagreeable, so that these Senses are often stimulated artificially.

(3) *Sight and Hearing* do not sense the dissolution of the object (as do Taste and Smell), but leave it in its integrity while sensing its vibrations, which convey its message from a distance. Artistic Feeling as pleasurable and painful is specially connected with these two senses, which have been accordingly called the Art Senses.

The sphere of Sentience is, in general, the stimulating or determining element of Sensation which has its echo in Feeling as Impression. With the activity of each of the Senses there is an accompaniment of Pain or Pleasure, which is the primal characteristic of Feeling as distinct from Sensation and gives the general form of Impression.

In this connection we may cite a statement of Weber. He declares that by plunging his hand into very cold or very hot water (intense enough to produce Pain in both cases), he had the Sensation of cold or heat before feeling the consequent Pain. The re-action of the organism is immediate in Sensation, after which comes Feeling as the counterpart or resonance, separate in time and in consciousness. This

Feeling is Impression, springing from a specialized Sensation, yet endowed with a universal element. To this we pass.

III. IMPRESSION AS UNIVERSAL. That is, the Sensation is transformed into Feeling through the universal attribute of the latter, namely Pain-and-Pleasure, which we have already seen to be in itself a process, a Psychosis (see pp. 36-38). This Feeling in its present form, as finite and particularized, receives its basic characteristic, namely Pain-and-Pleasure, in which the Ego may be said to have its first real Feeling as distinct from its abstract Norm (p. 30).

The distinction between Sensation and Feeling in general often recurs in the Psychology of Feeling, and has been already stated several times. When I say that the column before me is round, I affirm a fact of Sensation, which belongs to the Intellect; when I say that the same object is agreeable to me, I am in the realm of Feeling. In relation to the object Sensation gives some kind of knowledge; but in relation to me Sensation either promotes or disturbs my inner harmony, and causes like or dislike. Here again we observe the two extremes, the Ego and the outer world; Sensation (with the five Senses) stands between the two and has a reference to both. On the one side it is a knowing, and on the other it is a feeling, or specially an impression. These two sides of Sensation are twinned indissolubly, yet they are also distinct. Likewise the phraseology is double; Sensation is applied to Feeling, as a Sensation of Pain, or to an act of knowledge, as a Sensation of the round column. Sometimes the two sides are called its subjective and objective aspects, or better, its affective and presentative characters.

Such is the doubleness which comes from the Five Senses; each Sense and every act of each has its own echo in Feeling, which is primarily an Impression. This must now be separated and looked at by itself. The Sensation must arouse or disturb the inner harmony of the Ego, must excite Pain or Pleasure, ere its counterpart of Feeling appears.

In this connection we shall again have to consider Pain and Pleasure. Already (under Elemental Feeling) we have looked at them by themselves, as elemental. But we have to renew our acquaintance with them in connection with Sensation, which in a manner begets them, or has them as an accompaniment, sometimes quite unobserved, but sometimes overwhelming. It is through Pain and Pleasure that Sensation is transformed into Impression, which is the first stage of Finite Feeling and runs through all its stages.

1. *Pleasure stimu ated.* What the First Pleasure is in itself, as an element of Self-Feeling, belongs to the elemental stage, and has already

been considered (p. 38). At present we must regard it as specialized, particularized, stimulated through the senses from the outside world. The First Pleasure is inherent in all unobstructed activity even the most simple; also it can lurk in the Organic Rhythm which keeps the Organism in equilibrium unless disturbed. Such an activity may be called pleasurable though not intense, not rising to consciousness. It is a kind of middle lying between stagnation and excess, and has what we may call a mean stimulus whose presence we shall note in three different relations.

(*a*) There must be the mean in the strength of the stimulus — which is to be not too strong nor too weak. The direct ray of the sun and complete darkness disturb the equability of the rhythm; the noise may be too loud, or too low, if you are eager to hear.

(*b*) There must be a mean in the duration of the stimulus. The dulcet sound may become monotonous and tiresome; the golden tint is charming at first, but may last too long. Even novelty gets to be no longer novel by too much of it, and the love of change transforms itself by a surfeit into the hate of change.

(*c*) Stimulation has also a qualitative element, as well as a quantitative; the bitter taste disturbs its rhythm, also the discordant sound, and often certain kinds of color. The Organism selects divers qualities of objects as harmonious with it, or agreeable; it manifests a mean not only as to strength and duration but also as to kind of stimulus.

It is evident that this finely balanced equilibrium is perpetually exposed to disturbance, **in** fact life itself is such a disturbance.

2. *Pain stimulated.* The world of externality in some form comes into contact with the Organism and interferes with this rhythm of it, which is its primal immediate activity. Such is the appearance of Pain, an inhibition of the native organic energy, the struggle of the corporeal totality with a foreign interference.

Pain is the negation of Pleasure, that is, of that first unconscious Pleasure, which is the undisturbed Organic Rhythm already mentioned. But of this Pleasure we are hardly conscious, we come to know it when it is gone. Pain wakes up the Soul, is the grand stimulus to self-knowledge and self-activity; it has its very important place in the Universe.

The Organism itself will manifest this interference in a variety of ways. The rhythm is thrown into disorder, the breathing is irregular, restrained, spasmodic; the heart beats faster, out of order; in general, the orderly rhythmic movement is ajar, the body responds to the disturbance, often very emphatically.

We observe the following process in Pain: —

(*a*) The outside interference is taken up by

the Organism and internalized, becoming a constitutent part of the organic movement.

(*b*) This makes an inner contradiction between alien and native elements, a struggle between the disturber and the rhythm.

(*c*) This inner conflict is what produces the Pain, which is a Feeling separating itself from Sensation. It is as if an enemy manifests his hostility by a blow which goes inward and sets the body into hostility with itself — whereof the indication is Pain. Corporal punishment seeks to make the doer feel his outer act against order by transferring it to his own organism which experiences thereby Pain. The dissonance of the deed is made over into a dissonance of the body.

The general aspects of Pain as well as its process have been already set forth under Elemental Feeling (pp. 41–46). Here we repeat that Pain as activity has in itself its own opposite, if all activity be pleasurable. Thus it has the tendency to undo itself as being not only negative but self-negative. Completely seen, Pain is not merely a destroyer but a destroyer of something which is itself destructive, a negation of a negative. Whereby it mediates a new Pleasure, which is not the First Pleasure above given, but a restoration.

3. *Pleasure restored*. This is, in its present form, the restoration of the Organic Rhythm

which has been disturbed; it is the triumph of the total body over its alien intruder, the overcoming of Pain.

It is not intended to affirm that all Pleasure is through the mastery of its opposite. The present is a mediated Pleasure brought about through its negative, Pain, which is now negated in turn. But there is an immediate Pleasure in the Organic Rhythm, in the normal, uninterrupted activity of the bodily functions. There is also a Pleasure in intensifying this activity up to a certain point. Increased muscular activity is often pleasant, nay, necessary to health; the organism does not like to stay in its old round, is limit-transcending. What Pleasure play gives to children! Yet, here, too, the negative in the milder form of fatigue rises in opposition, and has to be overcome, like Pain, when a new Pleasure sets in.

Thus the whole organism asserts itself as master of Pain, but is also the source thereof. Pleasure too has its process, it can lapse into Pain through its own excess.

(*a*) We feel a restored Pleasure in the recovery from illness, in the new upbuilding of the organism; also in the gratification of hunger, thirst or other appetite, which implies a want, vacuity, chasm, the filling which gives pleasure, by restoring the Organic Rhythm.

(*b*) Equally certain is it that Pleasure in this

last case can fall back into its negative character and can become a disturber, through the excess of gratification. Appetite is a void, but the filling of the void can produce Pain. Pleasure as the indulgence of the appetites is self-destroying.

(*c*) Thus the void and the fullness, the want and the excess are equally inhibitive of the Organic Rhythm, which is the process of the totality, to which we again return.

Pain has a mission, which is to interrupt the uniform, identical movement of the organism and make it master its opposite, which is the external, the other side of it in some shape. The infant starts with Pain, Hunger and Thirst, through which it is driven to take possession of the outer world and assimilate it to its own organism. Pain is thus a great trainer of the organism into a mastery over what is outside of itself, and also over itself. The immediate Organic Rhythm, or First Pleasure, has to be broken into, and to get out of its little self-satisfied round, if there is to be any development. In fact Feeling to a degree pivots upon Pain, upon that interruption of mere Sensation which produces the echo characteristic of the feeling Self. Pain in some form is the primal stimulus, which rouses the quiescent organism; but it may in its negative intensity bring on death.

We have now brought the sphere of Impression to the point at which it is stored up in the Ego and becomes a past experience. Sensation with its affective counterpart in Feeling is internalized by the Ego; thus the Impressions arising from the outer sense-world are laid away in the inner mind-world, from whose depths they may be recalled by Memory, and become the Determinants to a new kind of Feeling.

SECTION SECOND. — EMOTION.

From the outer particularized world of Sense-perception as Determinant to the inner particularized world of Representation and Thought as Determinant is now the transition. This is still the realm of Finite Feeling, but it is the mind which is finitized and made particular, being divided into numerous activities which determine the Ego to Feeling. *The process of the Ego within itself* is *turned inward* at present by special forms of mentation.

Instead of the sensuous Determinant of Impression we have the mental Determinant of Emotion. Impression springing from Sensation is internalized by the Ego and stored up; Emotion in its turn springs on the whole from this internalized Impression, and may be regarded from the present point of view as the Impression of Impression. A man does me a favor in an emergency, this act taken by itself remains with me as an Impression with its Pleasures. But when I recall this Impression afterwards, it stirs within me a new Feeling, that of gratitude to my benefactor, which is an Emotion, as we are using the term. Every Impression, or Feeling with its Pain or Pleasure, stored up in my memory, starts some Emotion when recalled. It is the second echo or duplication of Feeling, of which we noted the first in Pain-and-Pleasure. A remembered impression reverberates, often very powerfully, in Emotion.

It is evident that Memory has a very important place in the present sphere. Also Imagination rouses Emotion, as when an imagined wrong brings on a fit of anger. But not merely our own stored-up experiences are Determinants to Emotion; our instincts and impulses coming down through a long heredity have their influence, and at least pre-dispose us to certain Emotions, which may thus be deemed natural endowments.

So it comes that our Ego is a vast magazine of Emotion, quite inflammable, ready to be lit by a spark. Etymologically Emotion is conceived as a moving outwards on the part of Feeling, an outburst in a particular direction from the great reservoir of the Ego which includes man's subconscious and even pre-conscious states. These we may take as forming the inner society of the Self, composed of many members, some very old and some very young. As we saw in the last sphere a body of associated Senses, so now we behold an associated inner world of the feeling Ego, from which our Emotion in all its variety is to be unfolded.

Accordingly we shall set forth first *the Process of Emotion* in general, then *the particular Emotions*, winding up with *the universal Emotion*.

I. THE PROCESS OF EMOTION. — The main attainment of the preceding sphere was the store of Impressions laid up in the mind and body to be called forth by a proper stimulus. The Sensation with its attendant Pain or Pleasure has gone from present to past, and has become quiescent, a matter of memory. In such a state it is no longer real but ideal, and can be recalled only as image or representation. The Impression of a burnt hand with its Pain is a sensuous Feeling, which is stored away in Memory; but the presence of a hot stove may produce the Emotion of terror through recalling the former painful experience. Thus it comes (as already noted) that a second Feeling (Emotion) springs out of that first Feeling (Impression) recalled from the store-house.

1. *The Store stimulated.* We start, then, with our store of Impressions, each of which is a Feeling capable of being recalled by a stimulus. But this recalled Feeling, we must observe, is not merely the old Impression, but it is a new one with its own peculiar Pleasure or Pain, not sensuous and corporeal, but ideal and mental. I recall the severe blow inflicted by a windlass; the Pain then was real and of the body, while the Pain now, that of fear and avoidance, is of the mind, coming from memory. In one sense this may be said to be no actual Pain, being brought about so completely through the mind. Still my body reacts in the latter case also; the representation of my past experience has its echo in the body, which makes a movement in correspondence with the event recalled.

The Stimulus is what starts the image or idea recalled, being outside of it, yet connected with it externally or internally.

(*a*) First is the sensuous Stimulus, the presented object, which excites the image directly, causing to be represented the former similar object along with the experience connected with it. A child leaning on a window sill in the upper story of a house, may cause great discomfort to the passing stranger who has seen a child fall to its death from a similar position.

(*b*) But the Stimulus may be also internal. The stream of ideas may run along smooth, till a thought rises in the chain which stimulates an outburst of tears. There may have been originally some sensuous Stimulus starting the chain, but the intervening links are internal, till they call up the given Stimulus. Revery is full of such instances.

(*c*) The Stimulus may be conscious and purposed, being evoked by an act of Will. It is the actor's business to rouse these emotional states in himself, which pre-suppose the stimulating image or representation, in order to manifest themselves in bodily action. For the organic response in Emotion cannot come of itself, but must be an answer to an imaged condition whose visible outburst in the body reveals the inner workings of the soul. We may read the play of King Lear with its mass of emotional imagery seething in the mind with almost no corporeal outlet; but histrionic art is to restore to this imagery its counterpart in the organism, to reproduce along with the spoken word (which conveys the image) its corresponding world of action.

2. *Impressions represented.* Already the place of Representation in the genesis of Emotion has been passingly indicated. It is the representing mentally of that which was once presented sensuously. It is the separation of the stored-up Impression from its store in the mind by means of the Stimulus. It is, therefore, in the form of image, idea, an inner copy

of the total Impression; in general we call it Representation versus Presentation, since it corresponds to the Representative function in Intellect.

Here it must be grasped specially as a medium or Mean, since it mediates what goes before with what comes after: the Stimulus and the Emotion proper. The Stimulus presented starts it, calling it up from the deep cave of Retention, where all past Impressions lie sleeping till they be awakened by the right call. It is the second stage of the total Ego (as Psychosis) which makes this separation, and sets forth the represented object or image, making ideally present what is really past.

This representative Mean is, accordingly, an axis of the entire sphere of Emotion, being roused by the Stimulus and bringing the whole Ego to a new kind of Feeling. We shall, therefore, give a little study to the ways in which the Stimulus may excite this Mean preparatory to its going over into Emotion. These ways we may designate in advance as instinctive or unconscious, conscious, and automatic. The Impressions which they call forth may be the inheritance of a long line of ancestry, historic and pre-historic, or they may be the fruit of our own life's experience past and present.

(*a*) The connection between Stimulus and Mean may be immediate in the sense of being an inherited instinct, which works without apparent cause. The fear of a child for certain animals seems to be transmitted; even grown people are not free from unaccountable emotions of this kind. A woman sees a harmless little pussy on the walk just before her; she gives a shriek, leaps to one side and runs away from it in abject terror. Yet she cannot recollect of any cat ever harming her. Many of these instinctive stimuli coming to us by inheritance course through our daily life darkly and vaguely, and sometimes can rise to sudden overmastering prominence. Yet the tendency of culture is to suppress them.

(*b*) Some past experience injects into our life a Mean of which we are conscious, and which we can remember. We may recall the time when a cow scared us in childhood; the mere presence of a cow thereafter may be sufficient to rouse the dormant terror. The image of possible harm will come in spite of all reason, and the cousequent organic response will take place. Not only this, but association plays in variously; the locality where the fright took place may be forever afterwards an uncanny spot; the house near by may be a forbidden abode; the person who had some hand in the matter, or who laughed at us, may be held in secret execration. The Stimulus prods the memory which recalls the experience; the emotional act repeats itself, you ideally go through that same disagreeable process every time you see the object.

In teaching, the nature of this ideal Mean plays an important part. The school-house yonder which you see — what emotive reactions does it rouse within you? Those of tortures, of tasks, of whippings? Or of festival, of triumph, of knowledge gained? Many a strand of the career of the child depends upon his school experience. How do you feel at hearing the school bell in the distance? You are never too old to be without some emotive re-action at its sound. When the call is heard: " come to the class in Psychology "— what is your inner echo? " There! another roasting! once more to be ground in the mill! when will this desolation cease! " Effort there must be, but what is the association and its echo in Feeling?

(c) The Mean itself with its own immediate reflex in Emotion becomes the Stimulus for another Mean with its reflex in Emotion; thus it propagates itself and there is the chain of Emotions. The fright from a cat may be transferred to any animal, similar to it or dissimilar; the child which is afraid of a dog is likely to receive a Stimulus of a similar sort from a swine or a calf. Association again links the original stimulating object with others; not only the barn where the fright first took place, but all barns may become disagreeable. Each vivid Emotion — with its Stimulus, mean, and response — has a tendency to become a center from which many circles of Feeling are roused in the sea of the Soul; as the stone flung into calm water produces a series of concentric ripples more and more remote from the central disturbance.

Still further, a different Emotion may be excited by the same Mean, the one stone produces many separate ripples, which may be broken in upon by others from the outside. I hear the croak of a raven; it recalls a country scene of my childhood with attendant pleasant emotion; the image of this scene brings up a descriptive passage in a poem, and so on through a chain of Emotions. But in a different mood or place, that croak of the raven may stimulate an uncanny Emotion, may suggest death (as it did to Macbeth). So the Mean stimulates diversely the Feeling which becomes specially Emotion.

3. *Emotion specialized.* Repeatedly we have had to speak of Emotion in the preceding account. But it properly follows the Mean, or Representation, which mediates it by transforming Impression. That is, the represented Impression also throws out its fringe of Pain or Pleasure not now immediate but represented, imaged, ideated, and produces Emotion. The outer Impression being made internal as image, has a new character, non-sensuous, ideal. A real Pain ideated is likely to rouse some form of

fear, which seeks to avoid the real Pain. But this fear is disagreeable, is a kind of Pain.

(*a*) It is evident that the great variety of Impressions stored up in the Ego will produce a corresponding variety of Emotions. These in their turn are stored up and become a constituent of the inner life of the Ego. There is also a continuous transition of Impressions into Emotions going on within us, a perpetual metamorphosis of stages of Feeling into one another. Memory calls up former Pains and Pleasures connected with things remembered. Every reminiscence has its peculiar tinge of Emotion. It is not necessary that the original Impression be painful in order to have some regret or sorrow in its remembrance. My intercourse with a friend gave the greatest Pleasure at the time, but the recalling of that fact may be colored by many intervening occurrences which change that Pleasure to melancholy. The play of Emotion is like shot-silk which throws a different sheen with every ripple of the material. The total Ego is involved in this dramatic interplay of Impressions and Emotions, which chase one another on the inner stage with panoramic fullness and variety.

(*b*) Thus each special Emotion has a tendency to stir the total emotional man by a kind of sympathy. On the other hand the Ego, in accord with it deepest character, is inclined to totify the single object represented, whose image thereby becomes the center of a whole world of connected images. Yonder real bell-stroke on top of the old school-house becomes an ideal bell-stroke, in its sphere universal and creative, summoning into existence a world of events, persons, actions with their accompanying Emotions. We separate and specialize the Feelings, but in reality they arise in multitudinous groups or flocks from the sea of the soul. In this way we see that Emotion is of a social nature, associating its kindred in retinues which people the inner world in lines of vanishing forms.

(c) Finally we are to note the return to the organism from which the Stimulus to Emotion first started. As my body once responded to the sensuous Impression, so now it gives a similar response to the memory of it, the Emotion. As I once jerked my burnt hand from the hot stove, so now I withdraw it when I sense the heat and thus am reminded of my former experience. In the second instance I have a fear of the hot object which I did not have in the first instance. But that fear causes a movement of the organism corresponding to the movement caused by the burn. This is the outer corporeal resonance of the inner Emotion with its ideal Pain which is the concomitant of the remembrance of the real Pain. Thus we behold the corporeal expression of the Emotions, anger, fear, love.

There is also echoed in the body the movement of Emotion — its rise, culmination and subsidence. For Emotion is not an even thing in its progress, upon its waves there are wavelets and upon its wavelets there are ripples. Particularly anger is subject to rises and falls; when seemingly quiescent it suddenly flashes out anew, calls up the original cause even when this has been withdrawn, and no longer properly exists. Still the image of it returns and with it comes a fresh paroxysm, producing reverberation upon reverberation. Herein the eternal example is the wrath of Achilles depicted by Homer with such psychological truth. When the atonement for the insult has been made, he keeps going back to the original cause, repeating it over and over again and totally unable to hear the voice of reconciliation from his own friends.

Thus we have completed the general Process of Emotion, showing how it starts with an outer Stimulus of bodily Sensation (for instance the sight of an object) which stirs the memory of some former experience and produces a Representation with its peculiar fringe of Feeling constituting it an Emotion, the latter having its final echo in the physical body. It is, however, evident that there are many kinds of Emotion; the diversified world passing through the Senses diversifies Emotion thousandfold. Whereat rises a new stage of our present subject.

II. The Particular Emotions. — The general process of Emotion has been unfolded; what we are next to designate is its special manifestations in the particular Emotions. We found that in Impression the Ego was to a great extent externally determined through the Senses to which it spontaneously responded. But in Emotion the Ego rallies upon itself as center, and asserts itself as individual primarily, against the determination from without. So we see its characteristic to be determination from within, and it proceeds from within outwards; hence its name (Emotion). If a person treads on my toes, there is the sensation and the pain, or the Impression which comes from the world outside of me. But if the act is intentional and insulting, I am likely to have an additional Feeling, that of indignation, the latter coming from within, from my Ego, which asserts itself at least to that extent, and may proceed further.

Evidently Emotion is a form of Self-feeling, in distinction from a Sense-feeling (Impression), and it may become selfish. It asserts the individual side, and may become individualistic (which is the excess). Here, then, rises the question, in what bounds is it allowable, and in what is it to be suppressed? It can be pushed to a point at which it is contradictory of itself and becomes destructive of the end for which it exists, namely, the preservation and furtherance of the individual.

In the present sphere the difficulty is to bring some kind of order into the vast diversity of Emotion. It specializes itself almost to infinity, still we may be able to see certain organizing lines running through the apparently capricious mass. The particular Emotion we shall observe gradually transcending its limit by getting rid of its particularity and reaching out for universality. Still in form Emotion remains particular (otherwise it would not be Emotion), but in content it becomes universal through Recognition, as we shall see later.

The term or category by which one may best see the movement of the particular Emotions, is, in our judgment, Self-love. It is the Ego turned back upon itself and asserting itself with no small regard for itself, which is a form of love. Any conflict with the outer world provokes it to take its own part, to feel with itself, to have special Self-feeling. Yet it will have to deal with another Self or Selves having the same quality of Self-love, or Self-assertion against all else. Now the particular Emotion is to affirm particularity, yet is also on the other hand to get rid of it and to be universal. The leading stages of this process we may designate in the following captions: (1) Self-love as immediate,

(2) Self-love as mediated through another Self,
(3) Self-love reciprocally mediated.

1. *Self-love as immediate.* The Ego in Emotion asserts itself immediately, without regard to other Egos or to external circumstances. This is the primal affirmation of individuality, of the right of self-preservation against all opposition. The Ego feels that it must first secure itself in a world of contingency. Undoubtedly this form of Self-feeling has its negative side, but at the beginning it is positive, preservative of the individual. It may be said that every object with which I come in contact stimulates me primarily to Self-love or the assertion of my existence in the world against other existence. Says Spinoza: Every particular thing must persist in its own being, and that is the foundation of virtue (though not by any means its superstructure).

Self-love as immediate has many forms. The reaction of the Ego against the world in favor of itself deversifies itself in a multitude of ways, according to the outer stimulus as well as the inner mood and character.

(*a*) Self-love shows itself in the direct satisfaction of bodily want, as hunger, thirst, etc. The animal shows little restraint upon its immediate impulse to gratification, civilized man puts many a limit upon himself in this regard.

(*b*) Fear in its primal form is an Emotion

which seeks to preserve the Ego. Its end is the safety of the Self in the presence of some real or supposed danger, which usually causes a recoil from the peril. Hope has the same regard for the welfare of the Ego, though it does not recoil (like Fear) but advances with, look upon the future.

(*c*) But the chief Emotions in this sphere are known as Pride, Envy, and Anger. These all involve the other Ego or Egos, and have, therefore, a social substrate. They have, likewise, a decided double character, positive and negative, preservative and destructive, like the whole realm of Emotion, like individuality itself.

Pride may be regarded as the basic Emotion of human existence, the primordial Self-feeling, which cannot be separated from the very nature of the individual. In this sense it affirms the infinite worth of the Self and is positive. Yet it also has a corresponding negative side which is perchance more striking, since it seems to have attracted more attention, particularly from the religious mind. Pride is declared to be the primordial sin of man (or of individuality) by which Satan fell from Heaven and thus came down into our world. In Pride the Ego turns away from the other Ego into itself ignoring all association. The two Prides may be described as follows: The first or positive Pride asserts the infinite worth of the individual; the second or negative

Pride asserts the infinite worthlessness of all other individuals. In which statement the inner contradiction of Pride becomes apparent.

Envy is likewise an Emotion turned toward the Ego and affirming its validity when this is supposed to be jeoparded. It also goes out toward the other Ego whose excellence it must first recognize and then belittle or deny. Thus Envy seeks to destroy the very worth which it cannot help seeing (hence called *invidia*, a refusing to see what it sees). Here too the inner contradiction is apparent. We can trace in Envy the same double character, positive and negative, which we noted in Pride.

Anger is also a self-asserting Emotion, but proceeds to action against the other Ego or Egos who may antagonize it. Thus it differs from Pride and Envy which stayed inside the Ego and brooded there. To be sure there are many kinds of Anger, from a mere superficial ebullience to the wrath of Achilles. Properly it has an element of revenge which pays back the supposed wrong or meanness which it has received. Of Anger we may also say that it has a good and bad side, a positive and a negative manifestation as in the preceding cases.

It is to be noted that the Church has taken hold of these three Emotions and formulated them as the three fundamental Sins of the entire system of the seven mortal Sins, on account of their negative character. (For a full discussion of Pride, Envy, and Anger both in their psychical and religious aspects see our *Commentary on Dante's Purgatorio*, pp. 196-263.)

It has been already observed that the individual who through Self-love falls into conflict with another individuality, has a decided tendency to undo himself; really he is in conflict with himself, with his own self-hood. His next Emotion will, accordingly, assume a new attitude toward the other Self.

2. *Self-Love as mediated through another Self.* This form of Self-love shows itself in the love of approbation, love of praise, and, still further down the scale, in the love of flattery. The individual now loves himself by a reflected light, loves his image as thrown back to him with new radiance from another Ego or from a multitude of Egos. In the previous stage the individual loved himself immediately, against the world, but now he loves himself mediately, through an alternate. It is a new gratification of our Self-love to have our own good opinion of ourselves confirmed by an Ego different from ours and also having its own quota of Self-love, which is doubtless seeking a similar gratification. We seem then to have first gained a complete right to our Self-love, when such right is so completely acknowledged by others. Thus it becomes explicit, existent in the world, no longer

merely implicit and subjective in ourselves. Not merely a potential but an actual possession does it become in such a case.

It is evident that this form of Self-love, like the previous one, has its positive and negative sides. Not only legitimate, but indispensable is it within its due limits. The worth of the individual must not only assert itself, but must be acknowledged by other individuals. The recognition of merit is necessary not merely to its possessor; those who see it must recognize it or lose their ability to see it. And yet the present sphere has its excess in adulation, tuft-hunting, insincere praise for gaining private ends. Thus the love of approbation is a two-edged sword for both the seeker and the giver. It is capable of breeding vanity on the one side and hypocrisy on the other.

The following points may be specially noticed in the present connection: —

(*a*) The emotion of Self-love mediated through another has primarily to subordinate Self-love as immediate on its negative side. That is, Pride, Envy, and Anger may turn against the other Ego which is the means of Self-love in the present sphere. There had to be, accordingly, the overcoming of that Self-love which excludes the other Self from co-operation.

(*b*) The Emotion of Self-love through another Self is, therefore, associative in its character, not exclusive. The other Self or Selves are united in a common bond of appreciating one and the same Self. It may be his deed which is admired and which is deemed heroic. Thus people will appreciate their heroes, and become one with them in the act. Or it may be his doctrine, his view of God, his philosophy. In this way religions, sects, schools are founded. The strong man is not lacking in the assertion of himself, which rests upon Self-love. Whatever binds many souls together is holy, says Goethe. Such is the positive side of the love of appreciation: it is social, uniting men into societies, great and small.

(c) That this form of Self-love has a negative side has been already noted. To see yourself reflected caressingly in the regard of a multitude of people is an intoxicating sight. Many seek to get it without duly paying for it through merit. Love of popularity is an emotion of Self-love which often leads to demagoguery in the State, and to a lowering or suppression of conviction in word and deed generally.

In the foregoing instance we have taken Self-love as reflected through another Self. But this second Self has likewise Self-love which requires reflection in another Self, and thus demands back what it gives. This is a new stage.

3. *Self-love reciprocally mediated.* The mediation has now come to be mutual; my Self-

love mediated through another Self is one-sided till this other Self has its Self-love mediated through me. As Ego it too must have Self-love, or be without individuality; and I must grant to another that which I demand for myself. Thus it comes that I not only assert my Self-love through another, but he also asserts his Self-love through me. In this reciprocal mediation, the cycle of Self-love rounds itself out to completion.

Moreover Self-love now recognizes Self-love in the other Self, which is no longer merely a reflector of the first Self, but demands a like office for itself. Thus both are on an equality, whereas in the first stage the second Self was in a kind of servitude to the first.

In this sphere we may note some leading manifestations which also show an inner connection.

(*a*) The Emotion of Justice springs from this mutuality of Self-love. I am in possession of a piece of property, and I request that others recognize my ownership. But they too have their possessions, and demand from me the same recognition for theirs which I demand from them for mine. In fact my Emotion of Justice grants in advance their right to theirs, since it is the same as my right to mine. Even among animals we can find a certain degree of recognizing ownership. *Suum cuique* is the adage of Justice, which renders peace possible among clashing individuals, each with his own Self-love and Self-assertion.

This mutuality of Self-love associates men and produces law, which is to define and administer Justice. For law is primarily to settle what belongs to me and what to the other man. Both the conflicting sides in a lawsuit appeal to the common Emotion of Justice, saying not only *I want mine*, but also *I want you to have yours.* The individual litigant may not always feel this Emotion of Justice in the heat of the contest, but the Law and Institution have only this standpoint and compel him to submit to the decision.

(*b*) Friendship is based on the mutuality of Self-love in two individuals, each of whom gains himself through the other. Friendship expects to receive back what it gives, namely itself; if one-sided, it is not likely to last very long. Why should it? It is an emotion of Self-love, therefore, but also of Self-love sacrificed as immediate; it is a process of the Ego which gets itself by giving up itself. Friendship implies equality, if not an outer equality (of rank, age, ability, etc.), at least an inner equality of Selves.

The Emotion of Friendship belongs largely to youth and middle-age; with time the Ego becomes self-centered and self-sufficient, and is its own Friendship. Moreover it exists chiefly between two persons of the same sex; but when a difference of sex enters in, the mutual Emotion undergoes usually a great change.

(c) Sexual Emotion is or may be, and perhaps ought to be, the strongest, deepest and most lasting of the Emotions. The grand separation of Nature into male and female individuals is the source of an Emotion which drives each individual to sacrifice himself or herself for and through the other, and therein to recover and even to reproduce the Self.

There may be, however, the sacrifice without the return; the mutuality of the Emotion may be cut in twain. Then follows the pang of Emotion unreciprocated; the mediation through the other being left out throws the individual back upon himself to recover his lost Self as best he can. Such a negative condition is possible in the present sphere. Literature has not failed to celebrate unreciprocated love in a great diversity of forms in poetry, drama, and novel.

But the true mediation of the sexual emotion lies in the Institution of the Family. The mutual Emotion of the sexes is thus made permanent, and becomes the basis and creative source of other Institutions. Also it is the central principle of many varieties of reciprocal Emotion. Gratitude is a feeling of requital for kindness said or done. Independence of character will not take favors without reciprocation. Honesty will not take something for nothing, but demands a mutuality of service. In education a similar principle holds. The rational mother trains her child not only to receive, but to give, yea, to make some return to her for what it gets from her. A one-sided maternal devotion makes the child selfish and anti-social.

Still there is a love which is defiant of the reciprocity, which can fall back upon itself and enjoy itself without seeming to care for the return through the other. In Goethe's *Meister* the light-hearted Philina can say: *Ich liebe dich; was geht das dich an?* Her love claims not to need any requital from the one whom she loves, being sufficient unto itself.

This suggests an Emotion which rises out of the present sphere of love proper, and does without the reciprocity, reposing upon the pure recognition of the Self without the return, without the individual mediation. This brings us to a new field which we shall look at next.

III. EMOTION AS UNIVERSAL. — The particular Emotion is to evolve more and more till it has Self as universal for its content. When I no longer demand of the other Self that it give back to me what I give to it, but regard it in its own absolute right of Selfhood, I have attained the stage of recognitive Emotion which is universal as far as Emotion can be. Self-love has become the love of the Self; the individual previously loved himself individually even when mediated through another; now he loves himself universally, as Selfhood which embraces all Selves. This means that I recognize the Self in the other whether he recognize me or not. I regard the worth of the man in his manhood, even if he personally disregards me. I am no longer to be determined in my feeling or conduct by his feeling or conduct toward me.

In such case we say that the individual Self in its Emotion has attained a universal content, namely the Self as such, regardless of any personal attitude friendly or unfriendly. The supreme value of the Ego has thus become the content of the Emotion which is stirred by every stimulus. Or the Self as universal is the object of my individual Self in Emotion.

This is the true intellectual Emotion, since it requires Intellect, Thought, the faculty of the Universal, to attain it. The Self now seizes itself as universal and possesses the same not only in Thought but also in Emotion. Herein also man has become emotionally free, though he may not be legally free.

Emotion as universal has a process through which the emotional Self passes in order to attain this supreme stage of itself. The Self must be suppressed in its individual form, yet affirmed in its universal form in and through another, and finally affirmed as universal through itself. Three phases: —

1. *Self-suppressing Emotion.* The forms of particular Emotion which assert the Ego immediately, must now be subordinated in the presence of the higher end. The stages of Self-love, such as pride and also approbation, cannot now be allowed to dominate in their own right.

2. *Self-affirming Emotion.* Not the special Self in any form, but the universal Self must be affirmed. The negative act of suppressing Self-love is transformed into the positive love of the Self as such, as Selfhood in general, which, however, at first goes out toward another Self manifesting this love. The rise to universality is primarily through two Egos mutually affirming not simply each other's Self-love, but each other's Love of the Self.

3. *Self-determining Emotion.* But the Ego in its completeness is not to be determined by another Self to the Love of the Self, but by its own Self. The friend may turn out disloyal, you are not to follow him therein, or to requite him in kind; thus you become what he is, disloyal. Even his negative act is not to determine you to a similar act which undoes the Love of the Self. Rather you are to affirm it anew through yourself, showing that you are self-contained, self-determined, a free being even in Emotion. You feel the worth of the Self as such and are devoted to that, whatever may be the conduct of the individual toward you.

Thus you have attained universality, as far as this is possible to Emotion, which is still finite, being manifested in the single, separate Ego. You have also attained freedom in Emotion, since this is here determined, not by something or somebody external to you, but by the Self as such which is now yours. It may be said that you have attained the love of Humanity, of the Self as universal.

And yet this love in Emotion remains individual, cooped up in the Ego of which it is a subjective state. So it is not rightly universal and cannot be; it must go forth and manifest itself. The emotional Ego finds itself limited from its lowest to its highest stage and yet (as Ego) endowed with an impulse and aspiration to rise out of its limits of mere Emotion.

Accordingly the Emotion of one Ego, getting outside of itself, stirs the Emotion of another Ego, which thus responds to the first. Here we enter a new stage of Finite Feeling, that of Sympathy, in whose sphere Feeling will again show both its resonance and its harmony.

SECTION THIRD — SYMPATHY.

Emotion, being roused or stimulated, becomes itself a stimulant of Emotion, reproducing itself in the Ego or Egos. Such an echo or response of one Emotion to another is Sympathy, which is Emotion associating itself and thereby bringing together the whole man with other men. Sympathy is the welding principle of society. Emotion taken by itself is individual, belonging to the one Self. But when Self-love rises to love of the Self as such, this love (which is an Emotion) goes out toward the other Self and unites with it in one process of Sympathy or Fellow-feeling, since Emotion has roused and taken a fellow or comrade in order to make itself complete and a reality.

It will be observed that Emotion now makes

itself twofold, with the end of becoming threefold in the process of Sympathy. Starting from one Ego, it sounds back or reverberates from a second Ego, and the two Egos unite in a mutual resonance which forms a new totality of Feeling, and this is just the mentioned process or round of Sympathy.

Already we have noted that Feeling in its very nature is twofold and self-echoing, or self-separating and self-returning. It duplicates itself within itself in order to be its own inner act, as was observed in the case of Pain-and-Pleasure (see p. 36). But in Sympathy this duplication is manifested not merely in the one Ego subjectively, but it shows itself objective, involving in its round two Egos, and possibly many.

In the present sphere of Sympathy, Emotion has become an external Determinant since it stimulates externally Emotion in another Ego. From this point of view we may consider Sympathy to be a return to Impression, which had as its stimulus the outer world of Sensation. But now the inner world of Emotion has become an outer stimulus, which stirs a similar Emotion in a separate person. Thus the internal Emotion, preserving its internality, becomes an external Determinant, moving the Ego from the outside, as did the five Senses in Impression. That is, the inner Ego moves the inner Ego externally, and the two Egos are one in Sympathy.

So the twain (or more) are fused in the common Feeling of unity. Primordially they cannot help themselves, they naturally answer each other's Feeling, though they may and often must learn to inhibit or to control such response. Sympathy melts the hard limits of individuality, and associates men, canceling for the nonce their separation and joining them spontaneously in a common humanity. All diversity of Selves has the tendency through Sympathy to become one Self, or to manifest the All-Self (Pampsychosis) in Feeling. Sympathy as universal we may, therefore, define to be the Feeling of the All-Self in each individual.

Here we catch a glimpse of the purpose and end of this whole sphere of Finite Feeling pushing forward to its conclusion in universal Sympathy: it is to unite the separated, invidualized man into Society. Sympathy is the primal associative principle of the individual which thus feels the All-Self as the unitary bond of humanity. "One touch of nature makes the whole world kin," and Sympathy is just this natural touch.

What we have stated in a general discursive way, we shall now seek to formulate more exactly. Sympathy has its movement, which we shall set forth under the following heads: first, the Process of Sympathy; second, the Particular Sympathies; third, Universal Sympathy.

I. THE PROCESS OF SYMPATHY. — The fact which is to be grasped at the start is that Sympathy means the second Feeling which is roused by the first Feeling; it not only feels but feels *with*, it is a Feeling which feels *with* another Feeling so that the two are in one process together. Sympathy, accordingly, implies two Feelings, an antecedent and a consequent, with a copula or connective which forms them into one round of Feeling mutually causative and sympathetic.

Feeling thus as Sympathy echoes itself or rather causes a vibration of itself. This may take place in one and the same Ego which, being a reservoir of stored-up Feelings, can be thrilled by Sympathy wholly within itself. One Emotion of the soul may internally set to throbbing many Emotions or perchance the entire Self. But Emotion is able to stimulate to response not only its own Ego, but another different Ego. And not merely one other but many Egos it can rouse to activity, which we may note in the Sympathy of a herd of animals, or in a multitude of men, who mutually intensify the passions of one another.

In general we find the following factors in the Process of Feeling: there must be first the stimulating, suffering Ego, which we may call the pathic element; secondly there must be the stimulated, responsive Ego which we may call the sympathetic element; third is the return of the second to the first which thus becomes the recipient Ego, wherewith the cycle of Sympathy is completed.

1. *The Pathic Element.* Let us take the human being in some state of Emotion, as joy or sorrow, which is usually expressed by it in such a way that others are reached and stimulated by this expression to a similar state. The Ego is an immense emotional storehouse, upon which some occurrence may fall from the outside, rousing one or more of its quiescent Emotions into action. Such is the pathic element of the Ego, being the possibility of all Emotions, whose nature and order have been already considered.

Now this Pathic Ego is conceived as stirred or struck by some Determinant, which has the power of evoking its laid-up Emotion. The result is a concomitant Emotion or a companion of like sort which feels with it and which is expressed linguistically in many words with the Latin prefix *con* (*cum*) such as *compassion, commiseration, condolence.* All of these are forms of Sympathy.

2. *The Sympathetic Element.* Here again we must bring before ourselves the Ego with its store of Emotions, implicit, inherited, and preserved from the past. Then comes the roused Emotion, explicit, active, throbbing; this is now the Determinant, is really the suffering or Pathic

Ego, which breaks in upon the primal or dormant Ego and starts it to vibrating in accord. Thus the latter becomes the Sympathetic Ego.

Sympathizable more or less is every person and indeed every animal. Primarily the Ego sympathizes with itself, containing in its depths many Emotions, each of which, being stirred to a thrill, will start others to thrilling in response, or perchance the whole mass. Sometimes, indeed, we are too intent upon our own Emotions and excite them artificially or indulge in them excessively. Self-Emotion is inclined to degenerate into selfishness of Emotion, and in a manner to tyrannize over the whole Ego. The best cure for these self-occupied states of Feeling is to give them an outlet upon another Ego.

On the other hand the one Emotion may stimulate not only many Emotions within the one Ego, but also many Egos outside of it, in the multitude or the flock. Both are societies or associations of Emotion, the one inner, the other outer; both can be started to vibrating by a pathic Determinant. The inner association of Emotions in the single Ego is the prototype and the germ of the outer association of many Egos, the latter being a realization of the former. We may well regard the chief object and the essential movement of Sympathy to be the outer association of many individuals through the inner association of Emotion. That is, man, having

Emotion within himself, must realize outwardly this Emotion, and so associate with his fellow-man through Fellow-feeling (Sympathy.)

3. *The Recipient Element.* Two sides have now appeared, or, let us say, two Egos, the Pathic and the Sympathetic, the suffering and the responsive, the antecedent and the consequent in Emotion, or the Feeling in the first Ego, and its Fellow-feeling in the second Ego. Of this second Ego we distinctly predicate Sympathy, which is a responding to and also a going back to the first Ego with its roused Emotion, in which act takes place a fusion or union of the two Egos in Feeling. Such is the round of Sympathy, composed of the pathic, sympathetic and recipient elements, the latter of which is a return to the first, yet through the second. Thus Sympathy reveals a self-returning cycle in its process, in which two Egos primarily unite into a ring of Emotions, through which ring not merely two but many Egos can be interlinked into a society. In this way we can again see Sympathy as the basic social bond of men, as they unfold into institutions.

Moreover through this process of Sympathy individual Emotion finds a vent, passing from within outward through the aid of others. Sympathy gives relief and brings restoration. It was characteristic of Emotion that it went outward (in accord with its etymology) toward the other Ego in love, hate, anger, etc. But in Sympathy the Ego as sympathetic moves the other way, responding to the Emotion of the first person or pathic Ego, which returns the response, wherein we see the Ego's nature to be that of fellowship, that of the responsive comrade.

And yet we must not fail to mention the opposite trend. In certain cases the pathic Ego rouses Antipathy instead of Sympathy, driving asunder the two or more Egos instead of associating them. Between these two opposites lie many kinds and degrees of their intermingling, which gives manifold phases of the Particular Sympathies.

This manifoldness of Sympathy lies already in the manifoldness of Emotion. When the outer Determinant is another Ego with its associated store of Emotions, we have two inner emotional societies which become an outer society of Sympathies, being fused together by their common Feeling.

II. PARTICULAR SYMPATHIES.—In the preceding account we have given the general movement or Norm of Sympathy. The next step is that this Norm specializes itself and becomes the Particular Sympathies. But what is it that specializes the previous round of Sympathy, or the abstract Norm of it, making it truly Feeling which has to be particular? Pain-and-Pleasure now enters the Process of Sympathy and gives to it the required particularity. Feeling is not real Feeling till it has some strain of the agreeable or disagreeable, till it has its concomitant of Pain or Pleasure (see under Elemental Feeling, p. 36).

In the present case the elements of Sympathy — the pathic, the sympathetic, and the recipient — must each become pleasurable or painful, and manifest the process of Pain-and-Pleasure along with their own process. For instance, the Pathic Ego is stimulated to an Emotion pleasant or painful, which then stirs in another Ego a corresponding Emotion, which is Sympathy. And this Sympathy being thus endowed with Pain or Pleasure, is a particular, real one — we may call it specialized.

1. *The First Sympathy.* We have already noted the First Pleasure (p. 38) as the primal stage of the process of Pleasure-and-Pain, as the unalloyed agreement of the Ego with itself. It was also observed (p. 39) that Pleasure is by its very nature a kind of Fellow-feeling of the man for himself, and thus may be deemed the inner source of all other sorts of feeling. That is, the Ego is first sympathetic with itself, and then becomes sympathetic with others.

All joy is contagious, we say; it reproduces itself in every soul within the sphere of its influence. The innocent delight of children has a peculiar power of starting the echo of itself in grown people. The sympathetic vibration of laughter may become irresistible, and the panic cannot be withstood.

2. *Compassion.* If the First Pleasure of the Pathic Ego sends off its ripples of joy, which stirs in response the Sympathetic Ego, Pain in its turn produces a similar effect. Indeed Pain has almost monopolized Sympathy, since this word suggests a Fellow-feeling with Pain rather than with Pleasure. Pain needs Sympathy, being an interruption of the rhythm of life, which calls for the help of another. The one that suffers or lacks must receive from those who can give and so restore.

Pleasure, accordingly, is more self-sufficing than Pain, and is not especially in want of Sympathy. Hence Pain binds man to man more than Pleasure. In joy the primal rhythm of existence is unbroken and runs of itself; Pain breaks into this paradisaical happiness, while Sympathy seeks to restore the original process of Pleasure. Pain is, therefore, more deeply associative than Pleasure.

There is also a form of Pleasure in Pain, which designates a particular kind of Sympathy, in which the sympathizer finds delight in Pain — not in causing it, but in sharing it and assuming it when found in another. Perhaps all truly sympathetic natures find an inborn delight in condolence which means fellow-suffering. Compassion comes to mean not merely the feeling of sorrow for the Pathic Ego, but a feeling of self-satisfaction in such sorrow.

At this point rises an excess. Sympathy becomes a dissipation, a self-indulgence which can only be compared to the destructive effects of any other appetite in excess. The emotive nature is disordered and gets to be deeply negative, as in all intemperance, be it that of eating and drinking, or that of inebriated Sympathy. People may be pain-intoxicated and seek their stimulant as the drunkard seeks alcohol. In fact there are epochs of history which show this trait. A person of this sort often attracts an army of cormorants, who retail their little ills and feast off the roused Sympathy, to the undoing of the sympathizer.

3. *Self-undoing Sympathy.* It is evident from the preceding stage, that Sympathy driven beyond a certain point becomes negative, assailing and perchance destroying the sympathizer specially, and even the object of such Sympathy. You may choose to suffer for another that he escape suffering for his deeds; you may bear the burden that he have none to bear. You take the doer's place and put him into yours; you accept the consequences of another's wrongful act, in order that he may go free. Thus the Ego quite reaches the point of self-undoing through its Sympathy, substituting for itself another Self,

even unto death. This is the height of altruism, or self-sacrificing Sympathy, but it bears within itself a tremendous contradiction, since the Ego destroys itself in order to save another Ego, which has no such self-sacrificing spirit.

(*a*) Through Sympathy unselfishness may cause itself to perish in keeping alive selfishness. The sympathetic man may go hungry in order that the unsympathetic man may be filled.

(*b*) Sympathy is often so unregulated that it is not only ready to take the burden of the little ills of others, but it easily passes into assuming the enmities of others, with a whole line of lies, prejudices, misconceptions. Thus Sympathy starting with love, passes into hate, its concord turns to dissonance. In this way it is transformed into a negative force against the other instead of a preservative.

But the person who receives this intemperate Sympathy is in the long run not improved. It destroys self-help, makes him a kind of parasite, pensioner, beggar, or at least generates selfishness. The ill effects of indiscriminate public charity are now very generally acknowledged.

(*c*) Sympathy has also a tendency to turn anti-social, assailing secretly the bed-rock of society which rests upon the individual giving of his own for what he receives. When a man seeks to live from the bounty of others, he is at least a dead weight, and has the tendency to become actively hostile to order, anarchic. Sympathy gets to hating any order in which misery is possible, little attending to the conduct of the individual which has caused, in many cases, his own misery. Commiseration is not supposed to ask questions. Hence Sympathy can and often does issue in the hate of the other, and mounts up to the hate of all institutions, culminating in the anarchistic tendency of our age.

Thus Sympathy has touched the point of self-annihilation, it has become anything but sympathetic, is rather the most hardened inhuman feeling. Yet anarchism may certainly start with Sympathy. Still Sympathy is not for this reason to be destroyed, but rather purified; it is to get rid of its negative element, or to subordinate the same. So now we are to see a new Sympathy, that which feels its own negative power and negates it in its own act. This is based upon the complete recognition of the other as Self and your Self likewise; as you recognize him, so he must return the deed and recognize you in just requital.

III. UNIVERSAL SYMPATHY.—We have seen that Sympathy can become destructive to both sides, to the Pathic and the Sympathetic Egos, which can only mean destruction to the Self as such. In this extreme result Sympathy has shown itself to be self-destructive. Consequently the problem arises: How shall we preserve the positive and avoid the negative power of Sympathy?

The sympathetic person is not to allow his Sympathy to undo himself, and so undo Self as such. If his Sympathy be truly universal, it includes his own Ego, as well as the other. So he must reach the point of sympathizing with Self, even his own. In this way he starts to universalizing his Sympathy. If in universal Emotion man attains the love of the Self as such, which includes all, not excluding his own, so in universal Sympathy he sympathizes with the Self as such, which includes all not excluding his own.

·1. If Sympathy be truly universal, both sides, the Pathic and the Sympathetic Egos, receive back what they give; if there is the sacrifice, there is also the recovery. If all feel for others, each who feels for his fellow-man is felt for in return, being also a fellow-man. If all, imitating the great Exemplar, perform the Christian sacrifice, each must get back in essence what he has immolated. Through all is restored to the individual what he imparts.

2. Sympathy must not relieve the man so that he is not responsible for his deeds, his place is not to be taken by another, nor is the consequence of his act to be withheld. True mercy supplements justice, not supplanting it, nor destroying it. Universal Sympathy will help,

but not undermine your self-activity; it will insist that you the helped be also helper, be what I am in helping you and others. It will refuse generally to help you to be an idler, a pauper, a pensioner, for that is just what it is not. I shall give you myself, but you must not leave out just this giving of Self to others.

The foundations patterned after Toynbee Hall, are a two-edged weapon, capable of good and evil. If they simply help, their benefit is dubious; but if they help the other to help himself and others, and insist upon that, then they can do much good. In such societies too, Sympathy may develop its negative, anti-institutional side, and lead some ardent members quite a little distance on the road toward anarchism.

3. But even Universal Sympathy belongs still to Finite Feeling, and so reveals a limit which makes it not truly universal, and hence contradictory and self-annulling. It remains subjective, in the individual, even when manifesting itself in its process. Universal Sympathy with its responsiveness unites many Egos in a common bond, but this bond is still internal or subjective. It is the associative principle, or, perchance, the associative protoplasm of man, formable but not yet formed, not yet actualized in an institutional world but the possibility thereof.

Thus all Egos through Universal Sympathy become one feeling Ego as it were, a kind of All-

Ego, which, however, manifests itself in each individual. Such is, indeed, the highest outcome of Sympathy, and of the entire sphere of Finite Feeling: the All-Ego is felt in each Ego, which Feeling sympathetically unites it with its fellows. This is not the All-Feeling which we had back in the elemental stage, and which was the conscious Ego as direct product of the Universe (see p. 132). Keeping up the analogy in expression we may call the present stage All-Fellow-feeling, which presupposes the conscious Ego as already existent and separated, but which is to overcome this separation and to transform the many individual Egos into unity through Sympathy. Thus the People feel a common Self, an All-Ego (God); each Self has such a Feeling, and is moved by it to transcend the bounds of his individual Self and to rise into an universal Self through which he associates with other Selves.

Still we are to mark just here the limitation. Though the Many, the People, have this Universal Sympathy, it stays in the manifestation of their Egos, it is not objectively existent, not truly universal. Hence comes the call to take the next great step: the All-Ego stirring each person in Universal Sympathy must be made actual, existent in the world, institutional. Or the internal totality of social Sympathy is to become the external totality of associated man, his social institutions, which will rouse in their turn a wholly new order of Feeling. These institutions, however, have to be organized, have to be formed out of the original protoplasmic Sympathy of Human Nature, ere they can stimulate afresh the feeling Ego.

Man is and ought to be sympathetic, but he should also rise out of Sympathy, making it a means for something higher. Through it the bond of association between man and man is to unfold from the more or less fluctuating inner Self into an established outer Self, an actualized Will, an Institution, round which his Feelings will cluster anew as a permanent anchorage.

Herewith, however, the realm of Finite Feeling is brought to its conclusion. It started, we recollect, with the Ego separating from the World or the All, throwing it outside and seeking to determine it by manifold division. But now the feeling Ego, having passed through its finite, particularized forms, has come back to the Feeling of the All (or of the All-Self) in Sympathy. Thus the All is mediated by the Ego, is brought to manifestation by it through the sympathetic process. Formerly we saw the All (or Universe) create the feeling Ego as conscious (in All-Feeling), but now the feeling Ego re-creates the All which once created it, evoking the same subjectively in Universal Sympathy. We see, too, that the whole movement of Finite Feeling through Impression, Emotion, and Sympathy, has been to overcome the present separative condition of the feeling Ego, and to restore it to harmony with the All by means of its own inner activity of Feeling. Moreover it has become evident that underneath these varied phenomena of finite particularized Feeling the All was lurking and working toward its own self-manifestation, yet as developed and organized through the individual Ego. But with this organized All rises into our horizon a wholly new realm of Feeling which is next to be considered.

OBSERVATIONS.

1. The present stage of Finite Feeling, as the second of the total Psychosis of Feeling must have a separative character as compared with the previous stage of Elemental Feeling. This is primarily seen in the fact that the Ego and its determining All are no longer taken as organically united (as in Elemental Feeling) but are divided into distinct parts, opposed yet interacting. Still further the organic All is in itself divided and dismembered, as well as the Ego.

2. But this second stage, which is Finite Feeling as a whole, must be grasped as having its own movement within itself. It too is a Psychosis with its triple process — Impression, Emotion, Sympathy. The first (Impression or Sense-impression) is the Feeling which accompanies immediately every act of Sensation.

But the second (Emotion) springs from the image or mental state separated from the Sensation and internalized, and moreover is individual (as in Self-love) over against other individuals. But these separated individuals begin to become one in the third stage (Sympathy), in which Finite Feeling starts to return into itself, and to become one with itself in the sympathetic round. We can also observe that the one Emotion (pathic) in Sympathy stirs another (sympathetic) externally, as the sensuous object stirs the Ego in Impression. Thus the third stage is a return to the first, and still keeps up the separation of the two sides, though both are now Egos.

Moreover it may be here noted that the non-Ego, which is in general the Determinant in Impression, becomes an Ego, the other Ego, in Sympathy, which internally cancels their difference.

3. So we are to see that in this stage, which is Sympathy, the separation is for the time overcome, and the two Egos are united in Finite Feeling which has therein attained its conclusion. The disjointed is now jointed, at least subjectively and temporarily. Whereat the question must come up: Cannot this union felt in Sympathy be made objective and permanent? The answer carries us out of Finite Feeling into the next higher part, Absolute Feeling.

4. It is, however, well to remember that each of the foregoing stages of Finite Feeling had its process, which ended by calling for something beyond itself, beyond its Finite nature. Sense-impression showed a universal element in its Pain-and-Pleasure. Particularly Pain means a struggle against, a breach with, finitude, in which that which is beyond the Finite begins to make itself felt. Hence Finite Feeling is full of suffering,

which intimates something transcending its limitation. Emotion also, as Self-love, universalized itself as love of Self, in which the All-Self begins to peer forth. Likewise Sympathy, becoming universal, manifests a universal Self in all individual Selves.

5. This last point we shall unfold a little. Sympathy reveals in the individual Ego the All-Ego as Feeling. Or what we may name the All-feeling All comes to light in each person through the manifestation of Sympathy, which unites souls, being the medium of fusion between all Egos, and indicating the common Self of all Selves. We often speak of being stirred by a common humanity, or a common selfhood in which all Egos share through Sympathy. This universally feeling principle we may call the God in us, the universal Ego as Feeling. It is what makes every sort of human community possible, and must be seized and organized in order that it may keep alive and render permanent the community-making element of man, his association. Such is primarily the work of Religion, that which binds many souls together. So this common bond is not to remain subjective and individual, but is to become objective and universal.

We have above noted that Sympathy has a powerful negative side, it may turn dissevering and anti-social if left simply to itself. The personal element must rise into the institutional in order to save itself. The All-Self in Sympathy must be separated from the special person, and organized in its own right, which new organization gives a universal content to Sympathy, making it over into a new kind of Feeling (here called absolute).

In the transition from Finite to Absolute Feeling it is not too much to say that we rise from the Fellow-feeling with man to the Fellow-feeling with God.

6. There is a connection between the appearance of the Over-Self in Elemental Feeling and the All-feeling Self in Sympathy. Both may be deemed to be phases or manifestations of the universal Self as a medium between individual Egos which feel it and are determined by such Feeling. We saw the Over-Self as a means of communication between Egos far apart in Space and Time, uniting them autocratically from the outside as it were. But in Sympathy the Over-Self has become inside the separated Egos, who are, however, in each other's presence, but who are united by the common Feeling or medium existing within both. Thus the Over-Self is individualized in Sympathy, yet is working to free itself from its individual prison, and to manifest itself again as the All-Ego, which it will do next.

7. In Finite Feeling through all its stages — Impression, Emotion, Sympathy — the Ego has

this universal element (the All-Ego) lurking in it, but not separated from it or separable, not freed from the pain of finitude, like the sighing Ariel pegged up in the cleft log. And yet the movement of Finite Feeling is the aspiration, the grand search for the All-feeling Self organized, the bringing forth of the new-membered from the dismembered Whole. Sympathy begins to break down the hard limits of individuality with its separativeness, and to reveal what is common to all individual Egos, a universal selfhood which can only be of the universal Self, the All-feeling All as Ego. Such is the object which has now evolved for our consideration.

Part Third.

ABSOLUTE FEELING.

We have now reached the third stage in the total development of Feeling, in which the feeling Ego again has as its Determinant the All, the Universe, the Great Totality. The latter, however, is in the present field ordered, organized, formulated, and that too by an Ego, by a finite individual, whom in general we shall call the Genius. Such is the great new sphere of Feeling which is stimulated in man by the process of the Universe, not directly now (as in Elemental Feeling) but mediately, through its order, this order being the work of man.

Absolute Feeling is, accordingly, the Feeling

ABSOLUTE FEELING. 295

of the Absolute ordered. Such a Feeling we may call a Sentiment, though the word in its common usage does not adequately express the present sphere; so the reader will have to reconstruct it, partially at least. The suggestion for its employment is that modern Psychology speaks of the moral Sentiment, of the aesthetic Sentiment, and sometimes of the religious Sentiment, though with small interconnection, and with insufficient grasp of their meaning. These are properly stages or forms of Absolute Feeling, which, however, has many others, all of which should finally be seen as members of one great Whole organized.

We are to keep in mind that we have returned to All-Feeling or Consciousness, which is the product of the All or of the Universe as Ego (see pp. 113–5). Consciousness must, therefore, have within itself the process of the Ego as Feeling, Will and Intellect, though as yet undeveloped. Now it is the process of the All-Ego which is to be developed and organized in Absolute Feeling. Thus it is made absolute in the sense here employed, after having been finitized in Finite Feeling.

Sentiment as now used is the Feeling of the Universe, and indeed of the Universe psychically organized, or as Ego. Sentiment is the Feeling of the All as the explicit process of the Self universal. The individual Ego feels not merely in a dumb and instinctive way this universal Ego — as a limb feels the whole organism — but feels it as Ego, as a psychical Totality, which has likewise Feeling, Will, and Intellect, and is perpetually creating itself as the Universe. The created Ego or Psychosis, by the very fact of being created, feels the All which has created it and continues to stimulate it to Feeling in the form of Sentiment or Feeling of the Absolute. Every human Ego feels the Divine All of which it is a spark endowed with the creativity of its source, being a created Self creating, and destined to recreate its own creative origin. Thus man begins to reveal himself as the image of his Creator, namely by creating the Universe which created him. The creative impulse from its lowest to its highest manifestation in re-creating the original All, is the Feeling of the Absolute as its own essential process. The individual Ego is indeed but a link of the total process, yet a link which bears in it this process in order to exist as a link of the same.

Thus in Absolute Feeling the Ego has to take its place within the Whole (which is the Universe), of which it is a part or member, and feel that. Its Feeling is no longer finite, as in the preceding stage, or a part feeling a part; the part must now feel the Totality of which it is a part, and whose process it bears within itself as its essential nature.

ABSOLUTE FEELING. 297

Moreover we shall find Pain-and-Pleasure as the concomitant of Absolute Feeling. In this sense it too is double and has its echo, like every form of Feeling. Sentiments are agreeable and disagreeable; sometimes there is a commingling of the two sides. Still the Pleasures and the Pains of the Feeling of the Absolute have their own distinct character and hence their own special classification.

We are again to mark that the Ego in the present sphere is inside of that which stimulates it to Feeling. Such was also the case in the first or elemental sphere, as already noted. But that primal Feeling of the All (or All-Feeling) did not have the All organized as a Self by a Self. The Universe determined every Ego as an organic part or member directly, without being ordered anew. But the Ego returns to the great All and reconstructs it, is in fact stimulated by it to such reconstruction, since it is likewise Ego. This of course takes place after the individual has had the experience of Finite Feeling, in which the Ego feels itself outside of its stimulating world, and really determines the same. Finally the Ego moves forward through the particulars of Finite Feeling to what embraces them all, namely the All, and begins to determine it, organizing its various stages.

We have repeatedly stated that the All must be organized in the present sphere of Absolute

Feeling, and that in this organization consists its fundamental distinction from Elemental Feeling. But by whom is it to be organized and in what way? Such a question calls for the man who possesses supremely creative power — the power to re-create the All, precipitating it into forms through which it can be appropriated by other minds. Such is the Genius, the unique Ego specially endowed by Nature or rather by the All with its own creative energy. He belongs in every department of this Absolute Feeling, since he is the one who organizes the Absolute so that it can be felt by his people. Thus he is a mediator, bringing the Divine and the Human together in a common act of participation through Feeling, as well as through Will and Intellect.

Already we have seen the Genius as the one endowed of the All-Giver, and have briefly designated his character (see preceding p. 129). He has primordially an elemental power, being gifted with an elemental Feeling of the Great Totality of which he is the product and whose immediate creative nature he is endowed with in his sphere. So he, though a finite individual, proceeds to re-create the All and its order, according to his special gift (as poet, philosopher, founder of a religion, etc.). The Genius may be said to have an immediate Feeling of the Universe in its self-generative process, which he possesses the ability to form anew in his special field for finite minds, that these too may share in the Absolute through Feeling, and thus be brought to be participators in Absolute Feeling.

It is evident that we here pre-suppose two different kinds of Egos, the one gifted with Genius, the other not. The one is the unique man of his time and people, perchance of his whole race. Then come the Many, the multitude, the mass of Egos who are nevertheless to be made members of the organized All.

There is no doubt that both the Genius and the Many have a common Elemental Feeling, both being conscious Egos and children of the same Universe, which has imparted to them the one general consciousness of Humanity (see preceding pp. 121, 132). But the Many do not and cannot at first organize this primal Elemental Feeling, though they certainly feel it as Egos. Then rises the Genius who also has this same Elemental Feeling, but with the additional ability of organizing it in its divinely creative character for the Many, who thereby are enabled to advance out of their immediate elemental stage into Absolute Feeling.

If we go back to Sympathy (in Finite Feeling), we find that all individuals are similar in it, a mass of Egos on quite the same level. But now behold the one individual, the Genius, rising out of this common prostrate mass through possessing the power of putting this Feeling of the All-Ego into a form for the innumerable finite Egos, and thereby elevating them into communion with the ordered All as Ego, or with the Pampsychosis. Sympathy is the grand potentiality of the Feeling of the Absolute organized; it is the associative protoplasm in which the Genius works and which he forms into Religions, Institutions, Philosophies, all of which are his organizations of the Self universal.

If we look into the history of the past, we find that the Genius takes his place at the important turning points of human development. The Great Men of the world have been its spiritual architects who have possessed the divinely creative gift; for this reason they have been often regarded as gods, demi-gods, and heroes. Evidently in tracing the Psychology of Man they are not to be left out, but must be assigned their true position in the universal Order. The Great Man we meet at every turn building the edifice of his age or some part of it, according to his special endowment. The race moves on a line through its mighty individuals, who for their time are the vicegerents of the All-Ego.

It is manifest, however, that the Genius as he has hitherto appeared in our world, is autocratic through his endowment. The Many are to receive gratefully and submissively what he has to give, namely his law, his scheme, his formulation. His is the Absolute Gift, which is just the Gift of the Absolute, and nothing further is to be said. He rules by a God-granted power, the original unlimited monarch. To him, however, there is a limited, finite, mortal side, though a Heaven-descended Genius. He dominates and also domineers, he is absolute and also absolutistic; he runs the eternal danger of mixing up the universal Self with his individual Self. How can he separate the divine decree of which he is the mouth-piece from his personal whim or passion? Moreover, how can he impart freedom to the Many who receive his doctrine as the law and the truth? For as long as they take the truth from the outside, at the instance of another, it is not truth, at least not the highest, and they are not truly free.

The Genius must rise to an even more exalted position than he has hitherto held. He also must evolve. To the Many, to the recipient mass he is to impart not so much his dogmatic doctrine, as his Genius, his creative power. Thus the protoplasmic multitude of Egos is individualized, no longer a mass or simply the Many (Hoi Polloi), but each is a Genius for himself through the training of this new king of Genius in the World's History. Every man is brought to partake of the creative energy of the All, which he re-creates for his own behoof, having been unfolded thereto by the new educative Genius, who, still endowed by Nature, is to train the world out of the uncertainty of Nature. For Nature showers her gifts, even the rain and sunshine, in a rather desultory fashion upon her beneficiaries, who must in some way get control of her and direct her supply. So the birth of a Genius has been and will remain an accident of Nature till some Genius will train every born Ego to be a Genius.

The supreme act of Genius is, then, to impart its own creative Self, not merely its own formula or its own special view of the Divine Order. Such a formula is, indeed, necessary, but simply as a stepping-stone leading up to that excellence by which each Ego can make his own formula or his own philosophy. Genius is a sign of degeneration only to degenerates, even if we grant that it has its negative side. It has yet something to do; we think its greatest manifestation lies in the Future. For the Genius of the Past has transmitted his deed and not his power of doing, his song and not his power of singing, his thought and not his power of thinking. He has not imparted his creativity but his creation, for which indeed we are very thankful, since it has given us our start. When Genius can educate the mass to be Genius, then it is beginning to reach its true destiny.

Genius hitherto autocratic or at least aristocratic, is henceforth to be democratized. This, however, must be done in the right way. The

Many are not to drag down the Genius to their natural level, but he is to lift them up to his creative level. His problem is, Can I make all men my equals? For they are not certainly so by nature, or only in a limited sense, hardly more than that of mere consciousness. In this way the Genius shares his original birthright with all men; he becomes a leveler, not downward but upward. Moreover he calls forth and trains the free man, who is certainly not born free according to any high view of freedom. When Genius can unfold men into creativity, then they can be free, determining the order which determines them, and so being self-determined.

We are still in the realm of Feeling, which has been already often defined as *the process of the Ego within itself turned inward*, of course by some Determinant inner or outer or both. In the present sphere this Determinant we call absolute, which here signifies that the determining All is organized by the Ego and is no longer merely elemental.

Already in Sympathy we noticed that this Determinant of Feeling has a triple movement, going inward, then outward, then inward again. That is, the first or Pathic Ego was stirred to some Emotion inward, which then passed outward and became itself a stimulus stirring the second or Sympathetic Ego to a corresponding

Emotion inward, which was the act of Sympathy. Now this triple movement — inward, outward, inward — is kept up in Absolute Feeling. Inward the Genius is stimulated by the ever-present All to organize the same, which is thereby thrown outward into a form as deed, word, system; then this form is taken up and made inward by the multitude of Egos to whom it appeals, whereby they share in and make their own the work of Genius. Note that the unorganized Feeling which is the medium between two Egos in Sympathy, is now organized, and becomes in Absolute Feeling an existent object from which a wholly new order of Feelings spring, and round which they cluster. For instance, religious or political Feelings arise from a Church or a State as an organized institution, through which the process of the Ego within itself is turned back upon itself and so feels.

We can, therefore, say that the organized All (Pampsychosis) is the Determinant of the present sphere, determining the Ego (Psychosis) through all its stages to Feeling. That is, the Ego as Feeling, Will, and Intellect must be stirred to Absolute Feeling, which will accordingly manifest these distinctions of the Ego, and be divided by them. The Universe in its total self-creating movement is to reach the individual man, and to fill the forms of his Feeling with a supreme content, so that he has the Feeling of the Absolute. And this is to rise within him through the various channels of his Ego, and thereby to assume various shapes and degrees, which constitute the order of the present sphere.

In this connection we may look back for a moment at the Over-Self, which we noticed as a peculiar indeterminate medium in the movement of All-Feeling (see preceding p. 169 *et seq.*). It would burst down upon the Ego awake in a fleeting, intangible manner; then it would put the Ego to sleep in a variety of ways. Here, however, we may note that this indeterminate Over-Self has become determined and ordered by the Genius who feels it and its process, and formulates the same. The unorganized All of All-Feeling has become the organized All of Absolute Feeling. Through the discipline of Finite Feeling, which drives the Ego to determine the world for the sake of freedom, it (the Ego) has attained the Over-Self determined, ordered, realized in institutions and in religion. This we designate by a new name, the Absolute.

If we look back still further to World-Feeling, we find that its external cycles, which were the primeval training of man to a presentiment if not to a knowledge of his Ego, have become internal. We recollect that the orbital and the axial movements were everywhere thrust upon his vision from the physical Universe, and called forth the first Feeling of the process of his own Self.

306   FEELING — PART THIRD.

But now this Self has produced and organized its own world, in which we find a profound correspondence with the orbital and axial movements of the Cosmos. Moreover the view of this new world rouses its own characteristic set of Feelings, different from yet related to World-Feelings.

We shall now endeavor to put into order this domain of Absolute Feeling, seeking to set forth its total process and then its subordinate processes, each of which must ultimately find its unitary principle in the process of the Ego itself, the Psychosis. If we connect together the main points in the foregoing remarks, we shall observe the following movement.

The Absolute (organized) stimulates the Ego (recipient) to oneness with itself (the Absolute) in three main ways.

(I.) To that oneness with itself which is to be attained first through Feeling.

The Absolute as the All stirs some Ego (prophet, founder of a religion) to express and to organize itself in an order which the recipient Ego may commune with directly through Feeling. Thus the latter feels God, gets the God-consciousness ordered — the sphere of Religious Feeling.

(II.) To that oneness with itself (the Absolute), which is to be attained secondly through Will.

The Absolute as the All stirs some Ego (moralist, lawgiver of a State) to express and organize itself in an order which the recipient Ego may make real in himself and in the world, in conduct and in institutions. The act of making real is that of the Will.

(III.) To that oneness with itself (the Absolute), which is to be attained thirdly through Intellect, that is, through vision, contemplation, knowledge.

The Absolute as the All stirs some Ego (artist, poet, scientist, philosopher) to express and to organize itself in an order which the recipient Ego can behold and know, and therein be moved to Feeling.

Such may be deemed the three grand divisions of Absolute Feeling, following the stages of the Ego itself — Feeling, Will, and Intellect. Employing for Absolute Feeling the term *Sentiment*, we can name these divisions as follows: —

(I.) *Religious Sentiment.*
(II.) *Practical Sentiment.*
(III.) *Theoretic Sentiment.*

Primarily this division is to be referred to the individual Ego as its source. For every person has the triune process of the Self—Feeling, Will, and Intellect. But the All-Ego likewise has the same process within itself, which at first creates and then continues to stimulate the individual Ego. That is, we have (1) an All-feeling All,

(2) an All-willing All (3) an All-knowing All as Determinants of the present sphere, determining the finite Ego to feel primarily these three activities of the All-Ego or God. The transmitted conception of the divine attributes as psychological embraces these three stages of deity as omnipresence (omnisentience), omnipotence, and omniscience, representing Divine Feeling, Will, and Intellect.

Thus the individual Ego rises out of its finite realm of Feeling, in which it feels a part, to the Feeling of the All, and that too of the All as organized. Still this All as Ego has its process which impresses itself upon the feeling Ego. I feel the All-feeling All immediately, in the form of Feeling; I feel the All-willing All in my Feeling of Freedom; I feel the All-knowing All in my Feeling of Knowledge. Upon these primordial Feelings of the Ego giving the first impress of the All, the religous, ethical and intellectual worlds are built.

The whole realm of Absolute Feeling is essentially religious, since it springs from the All-Ego felt in me, or my God-consciousness. I feel the Divine, feel it as Feeling (omnisentient), as Will (omnipotent), as Intellect (omniscient). I feel God in Religion proper, I will God in Ethics, I know God in Art, Poetry, and Philosophy. All these may be Religion in the wide sense. We shall, however, confine the term *religious* to the first sphere, which is now to be considered.

SECTION FIRST.— RELIGIOUS SENTIMENT.

Such is the first stage in the total sweep of what we call Absolute Feeling, or the Feeling of the All ordered. It is not the Feeling of the All such as we have previously noted in Elemental Feeling, in which the Ego feels as an organic part or limb of the total cosmos, giving its response in Feeling to daylight and darkness, for instance. Now the Ego is separated, individualized, and it gives its response in Feeling to the All as Ego. Using our terms, we may say that the Psychosis is determined by the Pampsychosis, the latter being what is felt by the former. Yet on the other hand we are not to forget that this All has been determined, formulated, organized by an Ego whom we distinctively call the Genius.

Religious Sentiment, however, shows a peculiar form of this Determinant, which therein stimulates or moves the Ego to Feeling *immediately;* the Absolute (or the **Pampsychosis**) stirs the Ego to unity with itself directly as Feeling, not as Will or Intellect. Or we may say that the Absolute Self is felt by the finite Self, in Religious Sentiment, to be one with itself as recipient — this unity being felt, not necessarily willed or known. Thus the finite Self feels God immediately as its own, and enjoys its Feeling of Him. This is the first Sentiment, indeed primordial, the source of all other Sentiments, which must have this divine content. The All in Religious Sentiment is taken as Ego, Person, God, who likewise feels; the human Ego feeling feels the divine Ego feeling, and becomes therein one with the same. Thus there are two Feelings in the present sphere, manifested in the two extremes, God and Man, who are by them fused together so to speak. The Absolute of Religious Sentiment must feel and stimulate us to a Feeling of its Feeling. God has a heart, we say; by it Man's heart is stirred to a throbbing in concordance.

At the same time Religion must have an organization or formula of some sort, even if this be nothing more than mumbo-jumbo. Around such an ordering principle Religious Sentiment clings and generates itself afresh, getting therefrom its chief nourishment. The humblest tribe of savages has a religious organization of some sort, which becomes more complex with advancing culture. The simple Feeling of God or the Absolute is not the whole content of Religious Sentiment, which demands an order for its content, with rite, offerings, ceremonies. Through these the recipient Ego (the people) comes into communion with the Divine Self and is made to feel its presence, or its Feeling, is made to feel God feeling.

Hence the question comes up: Who establishes this religious order? It grows in a sense with the growth of the popular mind. Still it is often the product of men, or of a man, the prophet, the founder. There rises the religious genius who gives expression to his nation's or his race's view of God in rite, symbol, word. He orders the Absolute as the Determinant for his people, who thus are brought to share in their creative source, which they in their way feel afresh every day. In fact through worship they are in a manner to be re-made by their God or Gods with every diurnal round of the sun, quite as often as they sleep.

Thus the recipient Ego by means of Religious Sentiment feels the universal order through an order which the religious hero creates. The object of the sacred rite and word is to stir in the man the Religious Sentiment and to keep it active — his Feeling of harmony with the All, whence he sprang and whence he receives his creative power. He is brought through religious Sentiment to take his place in the grand process of the Universe, of which he is a part and whose process he is to reproduce in every act of his conscious Ego.

On the other hand the individual can become estranged from the All and its order, can become hostile to the divine origin of himself. Feeling of alienation in connection with the Religious Institutions is not uncommon in all countries. This negative attitude is a phase of the total process and is not to be left out.

Certainly the Universe is an ever-present fact to every born individual, who is its offspring. This offspring has as its deepest character that of the parent whose process (the Pampsychosis) is to be taken up and felt by its descendant, the human Self (the Psychosis). Thus man, though created, communes with what created him, and he makes it his own, namely the creative power of the Universe. Through the Religious Sentiment he shares in divine creation, turning it into his own soul as Feeling. There is a renewal of yourself in thinking God, and in contemplating his manifestations in the Beautiful, the Good and the True. You, the created, must recreate yourself in Feeling through feeling the creative All.

And now into this vast and complex realm of Religious Sentiment we are to bring something akin to order. This will be like what we have seen in other spheres of Feeling. There are the following stages which also form a movement: (I) *The Process of Religious Sentiment*, its inner character which makes it religious; (II) *The Particular Religions;* the unireligious Sentiment necessarily (that is, psychically) splits up and becomes multireligious; (III) *The Sentiment of Universal Religion;* the multiplicity has in it the one, though implicit, which, however, drives foward to become explicit and organized in the one Universal Religion which exists as a Feeling in every particular Religion.

Of all the Feelings that move the human soul, Religion probably produces the deepest, strongest, most universal. Along with Self-consciousness arose in the primitive mind God-consciousness, the two were born together and they have remained twinned in some form ever since. To be sure they may be and have been separated by an act of abstraction; but sooner or later they reunite themselves with increased power begotten of their separation. It is a curious fact that modern Psychology has almost nothing to say of the Religious Sentiments, when it comes to treat of the Feelings. A cursory survey of the works of our leading psychologists will show that the present sphere does not enter their horizon; at least such is generally the case. Thus the fundamental Feeling of humanity is left out of the account — that Feeling which has roused a greater activity in the history of the human race than any other, and still exercises its potency around us everywhere. We might call it the genetic Feeling, that which creates all others, the Feeling of the Absolute as creative of the Universe, the Feeling of that which creates all Feeling as well as everything else.

It shall be our attempt, therefore, to put the Religious Sentiment as the Feeling of the Absolute into its proper place in the World of Feeling, and to organize its most distinctive elements into some kind of an order.

I. THE PROCESS OF RELIGIOUS SENTIMENT. — Here we have to bring before us the Self as human and the Self as absolute. These two Selves are distinct and influence each other, yet they are one, belonging to one process, and to one and the same Universe. The human Ego must have within it potentially that which created it, namely the absolute Ego. It could not feel the All-Self (Pampsychosis), unless it were a Self (Psychosis). Feeling is the process of the Ego within itself turned inward and made to function by the Determinant; in the present case this Determinant is the Absolute as process which stirs the Ego to an immediate oneness with itself, and this oneness is Feeling, the direct Feeling of the Absolute or God. I feel the Universe creating me, of which I am a member not only feeling the Whole, but reproducing its process in Feeling.

But this process is usually prepared for me, being already formulated and established as a special Religion. Some man or men have to put into form for me (as recipient Ego) the Divine Process in order that I may truly share it, in order that my implicit Feeling of God may become explicit, and present to me in outer shape my inner aspiration for the All-Self (*Urselbst* of Schelling) whence came my very Self.

At this point, then, we have to see that man is primordially God-conscious, that the Ego in order to be Ego must have God-consciousness. Such may be well regarded as the fundamental fact of the human Ego: as created by the absolute process of the Universe, and internally endowed with that process, it must become conscious of it. The starting-point of Religion is not to be located in some special faculty of mind, but is itself the mind starting to become aware of itself. Self-consciousness and God-consciousness are counterparts, belong together, and develop together. The first self-knowing of the Ego is the first knowing of the divine or absolute Ego, who is also person and self-knowing. Cognizing myself I recognize God who has imparted to me the process of his Self. Given the self-conscious man, he is in the same act God-conscious primordially; his inner process of self-consciousnsss is one with that of his creator.

This is the first Absolute Feeling and the basis of all the rest. For the Absolute Self is the Determinant and determines me to feel itself in my self-conscious act. It imparts to me creatively its own process, so that I have to reproduce it in self-consciousness. When I begin to know myself, I begin to feel God, performing the process which is his; and conversely, when I begin to feel God, I begin to know myself truly, as participant in the divine act. Now this immediate unity between the human and divine Egos in man we call his Feeling of God, of the absolute Ego. Such is the basic fact of all Religion: the total Ego in its first self-conscious act feels the absolute Ego as the ground of its being as Ego, for that self-consciousness is man re-enacting the divine process, which lies implicitly therein.

But this implicit state of the absolute Self in the human Ego is to be made explicit. In the primal condition of God-consciousness the Ego does not yet know God, but feels him in his own self-knowing. Or we may say that the absolute process is as yet potential in the human Ego, a mere Feeling accompanying it, subjective, unconscious, personal.

The next stage is evidently that of making actual this potential state, of putting into objective and permanent form this fleeting subjective Feeling, of uniting in a religious society these God-conscious individuals. Accordingly we must first ask, Who is the doer, and then more definitely, What is the work done, and finally, For whom is it done.

1. *The Religious Genius.* — Such we must call the founder of a Religion, who unfolds or creates the forms which hold together vast portions of humanity in Feeling, like Mahomet or Buddha. It is true that the earliest stages of Religion seem to be an evolution of the tribe or people; still we have to regard such a work as done by persons, though these be nameless. But the most important and lasting Religions of the world have not only a known founder but are usually named after him.

The unique man appears when the great work is to be done. We call him the Religious Genius, who possesses the original power to represent the absolute Ego in a form which keeps it ever-present to his people. He reproduces in his way the divine process which has been hitherto a vague Feeling, and establishes it objectively in rite, ceremony, creed. The Absolute stirs him also to God-consciousness; but his Genius lies in making the implicit God of a self-conscious Ego into an explicit God whose process is given in a realized Religion. All have the former, he alone the latter. He as Genius can by his creative power organize the Pampsychosis into a new order whereby all can participate in what he has by divine insight.

Thus he unites his people — tribe, nation, even race — in a common faith and worship. They all share in his peculiar way of looking at the divinely creative process of the Universe. Hence Religion associates men up to a certain point, for it also separates them. Persian, Egyptian, Greek — each had a national Religion, which unified and nationalized these peoples as nothing else did, yet also separated them.

Such is, then, the prophet, the religious lawgiver, the founder of a Faith. A curious fact is that he belongs quite exclusively to one part of the globe, to one grade of mind, to the original home of the civilized race, to Asia.

2. *Religion organized.* — The God-consciousness is not to remain implicit in the Ego, unseparated from the self-consciousness with which it is twinned by the creative act of the Universe. On the contrary it is to have its special organization and institution through which man becomes conscious of it and its source. This, as already stated, is the work of the religious Genius, who rises up from the mass of God-conscious Egos, and constructs for them their Religion.

In the earlier appearances of religious organization the Prophet (or Founder) and the God are not yet separated with distinctness. He at first is the very incarnation of the deity, and utters divine decrees and makes the divine revelations in person. Among Orientals the monarch was often deemed the God, and the Roman Emperors also asserted their divinity. Christ, the Founder of Christianity, is a person of the Trinity and as such is worshiped throughout Christendom. The Religious Sentiment of the people longs to see the real God as personally present, to see the All as Ego, or the universal as individual. A Theophany in some form underlies all Religion, and the Genius himself is literally a divine appearance, whether he be taken as the God Himself or the God's vicegerent and inspired mouthpiece. To organized Religion belong also the priest, the ritual, the creed, all of them being means for calling up and keeping alive the Religious Sentiment in man through worship.

When the founder dies, the organized Religion continues, in some cases has continued thousands of years.

3. *The worshipers.*—The vast mass of mankind obtain their formula for holding communion with the Divine Order from some transmitted religious institution. They could hardly of themselves make any such formula; that is the

work of the religious Genius, or perchance of many of them. Were it not for the established ritual, man could hardly rise out of the mere Feeling of God, quite unconscious and purely individual. But the formulated Religion, through its rites, creed and organization enables every human soul, however humble, to participate directly and consciously in the creative process of the Universe. To be sure, the formula which suits the savage, does not suit the civilized man. Still both are seeking the same end.

It has been already noted that the Religious Institution associates men, who would otherwise be mere individuals, through objectifying their Feeling of God. But this Feeling still remains, though now it has a known content, around which it clusters with the greatest intensity. The strongest Feeling seems to be that which clings to the rites of a given Religion. It has often suffered without swerving banishment, torture, death.

Moreover through the Religious Institution every participant is trained to a continuous harmony with the Divine Order. This is truly the salvation of the soul from its own negative condition into which it is whelmed by the very fact of being an individual.

Such we may regard as the Process of Religious Sentiment as it has appeared and still appears upon our globe. There is first the original God-consciousness, born with the Ego and inherent in it as Feeling; then this subjective Feeling of God is made objective in the Religious Institution by the Genius who is here the founder of the Religion; finally through this Religious Institution all the people participate in the absolute Process which created them.

It is evident that with these external forms of the Religious Institution, a great diversity sets in corresponding to tribe, nation, race; even a continental division can be noted, as Asiatic Religion differs from European.

II. PARTICULAR RELIGIONS. — This is not the place to give any account of the vast diversity of Religions on our globe. Hardly more than the fact that Religion has the tendency to an infinite divisibility of sects, forms, creeds, can here be noted. It is such a personal matter that every individual seems to move toward having his own special Religion. And yet there is the one common God-consciousness out of which all this multiplicity springs. The unity of Religion comes from the unity of man, the oneness of consciousness which is the distinctive mark of the human Ego. If Religion has been a great unifier, it has been an equally great separator, drawing its lines of separation around race, nation, tribe, city, and also individual.

1. The primal act of particularizing the original God-consciousness is seen in the religious

reformer who begins a new religion. The old forms have grown inadequate or corrupt, the religious Genius arises who is to reconstruct them. At every such event — a religious reformation or revolution — there leaps forth a mighty display of the Religious Sentiment, both constructive and destructive, both for and against the new order. The religious heroes of the race appear at such turning-points, and arouse a fierce persecution and equally fierce devotion. Buddha, Socrates, Christ, are the most famous examples. All wars in the Orient have had a decided religious substrate, though the European has recently introduced there his political domination, warily leaving Religion untouched.

Religion dividing itself and making itself particular calls forth the most intense Feeling. Yet Races seem to differ in this regard. It is usually stated that the Semitic Race is capable of the deepest and most abiding Religious Sentiment, and hence is most susceptible of fanaticism. The Arabian Mahometans are still easily stirred to a holy war by the preaching of some enthusiast, and the Jew clings to his faith amid alien institutions.

Religious Sentiment progresses and forms new Religions, or new sects and varieties of the old Religions. But there is also a pronounced a counter tendency, a going back from the new to the old, from the existent to the past.

RELIGIOUS SENTIMENT — PARTICULAR. 323

2. If there is religious progress, there is also religious reversion. We are indeed to return to former Religions and study them for the purpose of broadening our Religious Sentiment. But we are not to return to these former creeds and stay there. It may be laid down as a general rule that the present has no decisive call to rehabilitate a past Religion.

Still the thing is done and has to be allowed within given limits. Especially in America we give, among our other freedoms great and small, the freedom of religious reversion. Particularly in the Christian world exists the tendency to go back to forms and states depicted in the Hebrew Bible. We have witnessed in our day the Theocracy revived, with the leader proclaiming himself both priest and king in one, both being absolute functions of the one autocrat who is wholly irresponsible to his people. These people have likewise the principle of reversion, having honestly gone back to an ancient and transcended stage of Religion. Even the old Hebrew polygamy has been revived, as well as the communistic ideas of the New Testament.

Thus reversion plays a very important part in Religious Sentiment. The ideal of the Holy Books lies rearward, not frontward; to it Religious Sentiment longs to assimilate itself, transforming the wicked world by a headlong retreat to the past. To be sure the roads of this retreat are exceedingly diverse, each of which is traveled by a flock of reversionists under their leader.

3. And yet this prodigious diversity of Religions has in it everywhere a reaching out for the one Religion which lies in the very nature of the God-consciousness of man. These manifold forms of Faith show a tendency to come together in classes and groups from one point of view or other, and thus to unite or at least to federate under some common arrangement. For Religious Sentiment shows a unifying power just through its separative tendency which must at last undo itself.

In this connection we shall only note the three great World-Religions, Mahometanism, Buddhism and Christianity. All these have shown themselves able to transcend Nativism, they have not been confined to the people and race of their respective founders, but have been adopted by other peoples and races, who have cast away their own native or racial Religion. Of the three the Mahometan is perhaps the most violent in his Religious Sentiment, being famous specially for his fanaticism, though this term is applied by each to the others. Mahometanism seems the most immediate, spontaneous Religion of the three, if we judge by the fact that it holds together in Religious Sentiment a greater diversity of race and of culture than either of the other two (see our *Social Institutions*, p. 449, *et seq.*).

These three World-Religions begin to touch the boundaries of one another on many sides. The result is a world-process of Religions, especially in Asia, the great religious home of the human race. A new Religious Sentiment seems to be slowly evolving in the very source of all Religions, which Sentiment can only be called universal.

III. THE SENTIMENT OF UNIVERSAL RELIGION.—This is not the primal Feeling of God which has been already considered, and which accompanies the self-conscious act of the Ego, yet we may regard it as a return to that stage through all the diversity of Religions, which have some underlying unity, some universal principle or process. That primal Feeling of God may be taken as the first germ or creative cell out of which develop the particular Religions. But these now seek for the one all-embracing religious process which can be made institutional in a Universal Religion. Such is the Feeling everywhere existent at present, though as yet but a Feeling, subjective, individual, unorganized.

A profound religious Sentiment of unity animates the best souls of all the most different Religions. Can we find its inner moving principle, its process? That such exists is evident, else there would not be this common aspiration of such diverse peoples and indeed diverse races.

Every Religion must formulate the movement of the Universe and man's relation to it in some way. So they all have deep down a common process which makes them religious; this process we shall try to bring to light in a few outlines.

1. *The Conception of God.* — Such is the matter of deepest import in a Religion: What is its view of God? Of course the answer is exceedingly diversified and complicated, when we take into account the lowest and highest and all intervening forms of faith. Still in this variety runs a common thought. Is the creator of the world outside or inside of it? And is the creative act personal or impersonal? And is it capricious or rational? Here again we we shall do well to mark the process if we would escape the contradictions which are involved in the present subject.

(*a*) God's Transcendence is the most direct and immediate way of conceiving Him. He is outside of the world which he creates by the fiat of his Will. Moreover the creation of the All depends entirely upon his pleasure, his caprice. He was the perfect and self-sufficient from the start, without the world or without creating anything. He is not pure self-activity, but rather self-contemplation (*noesis noeseos*). And still he creates the world and Man who are quite external to his process. Man is the poor finite creature, a worm in the sight of God, yet made in the divine image.

The difficulties which beset the conception of God's Transcendence causes a protest both of Thought and Feeling. If He is so completely outside the world, then He is limited by it, and becomes finite. Hence the opposite doctrine.

(*b*) God's Immanence becomes at times the prevailing conception of Him. It is the view that dominates most of the thinkers and scientists of the present age. It is essentially the basis of all kinds of Pantheism from the ancient Hindoo form to recent monism. God becomes one with the world and loses his distinct personal character. Or he may be divided into many persons who appear with consciousness, which, however, is to be re-absorbed into the one above consciousness (Plotinus). Or He may be regarded as the one Substance without Intellect and Will (Spinoza). Thus, however, there is no psychical process in·God, he is not Ego which is a mere appearance, a mode of Substance. Such is the general result of the pantheistic view: the extinction of the Self in God and man.

In such a conception great difficulties arise. Immanence finitizes God by putting Self outside of Him as Transcendence finitized God by putting the world outside of Him. It is evident that both Transcendence and Immanence are two phases or stages of one complete conception of God which beholds Him as the universal process embracing both.

(c) This is what we have to designate by a new name, the **Pampsychosis**, which has the process of God, World and Man: of God as transcendent and creating; of the World as His creation and immanently containing Him; and also of Man, the Ego who has to re-create Him creating the All. Both the preceding views really leave out the third stage of the cycle of the Universe, namely Man, the created who is to recreate the All and thus unite creator and creature in one process of the Absolute. Such is the Pampsychosis, which puts me inside the process of the Universe which both Transcendence and Immanence were inclined to leave outside.

2. *The breach.* — Having thus taken up the human Ego into the process of the All, we must now add the other side, the negative one: it can refuse to perform its part of the process, it can stand out against God and the Religious Sentiment. Being free, as God is free, the Ego can use its freedom by destroying the harmony of the Universe in deed, and by denying it in thought. Man, the created, is a part of Nature, but that part which can overcome its separation and return to God, completing the grand cycle of the Universe. On the other hand he can stay with Nature and decline his universal function asserting the purely individual side of his existence,

with which his birth into Nature has endowed him. He can refuse the return and thereby break the round of the All, at least as far as he is concerned. Man is the turning-point at which Nature remains in separation from its divine source or is restored to the same.

At this point of division between Man and God rise up the strongest Feelings of which the human soul is capable. It is the grand breach between creator and creature, giving origin to internal struggles which shake the Universe. The absolute Process stimulates the Ego to a harmony with itself, but the latter resists and seeks to be for itself. And yet from this profoundest of estrangements Religion has made a way of return and restoration. This we may briefly note, as it is and always has been a controlling part of Religious Sentiment.

(a) That which is called Wrong, Sin, Evil reaches back ultimately to a Feeling of defiance of the providential order, which is the process of the All. The Ego in its negative state refuses compliance, and may assail the divine supremacy. All the passions of individualism, Pride, Hate, Anger, may be directed against the Supreme Person as well as against a human Self. One thinks that the Pessimism which regards this world of ours as the worst of all possible worlds, is the deepest abyss of spiritual estrangement and utters the Feeling of strongest hatred for the Process of the Universe. The pessimist has dug a new circle in Dante's Inferno and put himself into it, far down toward the bottom, possibly among "the violent toward God."

(*b*) Such a Feeling has a tendency to nag itself to death. There can be no rest for it till the Nirvana. Hence it begins to feel its own negativity, its own slow-consuming fire. A conviction rises that such an attitude is not only destructive, but self-destructive, and this conviction also has its element of Feeling which gnaws back at the soul (remorse), bringing home to it its own self-negation.

At this stage is found a vast variety of Feelings which must be deemed religious, such as tribulation, heart's sorrow, contrition. The Scriptures express this agony with vivid and harrowing metaphors which for certain cases can hardly be too strong. The process of Repentance in its various stages becomes often an immense generating reservoir of Religious Sentiments which we need not follow out in the present connection.

(*c*) The positive outcome is a transformation of the Self, and with it necessarily a transformation of Feeling, which now becomes that of harmony with order of the Universe. The Self as limit-transcending must master its own negative condition and reconcile itself with the process of the All against which it formerly stood out. The result is the positive Religious Sentiment, that of reconciliation with God, as contrasted with the foregoing negative Religious Sentiment.

But this is not merely an individual matter. The return of the estranged Ego to the divine fountain-head rounds out the grand cycle of the Universe — which fact also reflects itself in religious Feeling.

3. *The Return to God.* — Such is the statement often made concerning the end and aim of Religion: to bring man back to God. This presupposes that by the divine act of creation man has been separated, ejected, and made alien by his Creator. Thus man is a part of Nature, or the created; but he is also to reach out of the created back to the creating, and interlink the disrupted ring of the All.

Nature we may regard as the emanation of God, His overflow into something different from Himself. Man shares in this difference in so far as he belongs to Nature, and has a body. But his function is to change emanation into restoration; he is to turn back to the divine source, and his Ego is the turning-point of the Universe. We may express the same thought thus: without the Psychosis the Pampsychosis would never get back to itself, and complete its cycle of God, Nature, and Man.

In this way we grasp the place of Man in the Universe, giving him his axial position in the process of the Absolute. He must thereby come to feel his infinite value; without him there could be no process of the All.

(*a*) We may conceive the return to God to be an immediate one; the individual returns to a transcendent God in Heaven, in whose blessedness he participates after death with many a foretaste of bliss in this life. Religious Feelings of untold strength have clustered around this view, giving comfort and sustaining power against suffering down the ages to milliards of human beings.

Or the Ego may be conceived to be re-absorbed in God pantheistically, and thus the separation involved in all individuality is canceled. In this life such a state might be temporarily reached through ecstasy, according to the Neo Platonists.

It is evident that each of these Returns is but to a part or stage of the total process of the Absolute. Hence the following: —

(*b*) The Return is now conceived to be to God as the complete movement of the Universe, as both transcendent and immanent, or as the Pampsychosis. The ordinary formula of the grand Totality, God, Nature, Man, implies a transcendent deity as first, from whom Nature and then Man are separated. Thus, however, God is finitized, with the world as such outside of Him. But as truly universal he must be the total process of the Universe, which by way of distinction we call the Pampsychosis.

With this thought a new Feeling of the harmony of the All enters the Soul, being relieved of the contradiction between Transcendence and Immanence, which causes a profound dissonance, not only in the thinking mind, but also in Religious Feeling.

(c) The return to God is not completed in the last stage, in which the Ego feels or grasps the Pampsychosis or the Universe as process. I am not only to take up the divine movement of the All, but also to take up myself reproducing this movement. That is, I am to include myself in my own universal act, and not stand outside of it, looking at it so to speak. For it is I who am functioning this process of the Absolute, and I must feel myself as a link in the chain.

Religious Sentiment now feels God creating man who recreates God creative. Let each of these words be duly weighed. Thus the Psychosis (my Ego) feels its place in the eternal process of the Universe, or in the Pampsychosis. Religious Sentiment has herein attained its height. The Pampsychosis or the divine Totality (God, Nature, Man) stirs the Ego as Feeling to take up this Divine Totality as the process of the Universe, to recreate it, and to live its life. Such is the ultimate training of the heart. We are not only to dwell in harmony with God, but

but we, each individual, are to help recreate Him who has created us.

But there is a still more personal attainment in the foregoing process; it is a renewal of the Self, a daily regeneration of the Ego. We recreate ourselves, make ourselves over by re-creating our Creator. A perpetual rejuvenescence of Selfhood is won by this intimate daily communion with its source, the process of the All-Self.

Such is the Sentiment of Universal Religion in its supreme attainment. I in my highest worth, in my strongest individuality, am to recreate perpetually the Creater who created me, and thus am to be perpetually recreated myself. The process of creation spiritually must never stop, my Ego is pure self-activity, which it inherits from its Creator the Universe, the All-Ego, whose process must ever be the re-creating one; and I as Psychosis, am always re-creating it as Pampsychosis. Thus the universal Religious Sentiment has risen to what we may call the Sentiment of the Pampsychosis.

Another great phenomenon of Religious Sentiment in the past is that of Religious Bibles, which have usually been produced by the Religious Genius, and have remained the great promoters and preservers of instituted Religions. After the death of their authors they remain and bring the believing people into harmony with their conception of God, becoming in their turn the center of a vast and very active body of Religious Sentiment.

And yet the fact remains which came strikingly to light in negative Religious Sentiment; the individual can refuse to dwell in harmony with God; my Ego can hold aloof from the positive process of the All-Ego, declining to make the grand Return, and rejecting its restorative power. The ability to do thus lies in my Will. I can take sides, and go one way or the other; I am free, as the saying runs, to do or not to do. This Freedom, implicit though secretly active in the feeling Ego, must now be made explicit, and be looked at it as in itself.

Already the Feeling of Freedom has been noticed under the head of All-Feeling as elemental (see p. 212). The conscious Ego as product of the free Universe, must also be free internally, and thus manifest Will, which is the power of self-separating within itself and of uttering itself in the object. This elemental Feeling of Freedom is now to be organized, and thereafter to become the source of a new set of Feelings, which are still absolute, not as religious but as practical. The individual Ego is not simply moved by the Absolute to feel the All-Ego immediately and rest there (as it were, in the bosom of God), but also to make it real in conduct and in institutions. This is what comes next.

SECTION SECOND. — PRACTICAL SENTIMENT.

We must again conceive of an All-Ego having Feeling, Will, and Intellect, each of which has its manifestation in Absolute Sentiment. That is, one of these activities is dominantly present as the Determinant, though the other two are by no means absent or even quiescent. The All-Ego organized or the Absolute stimulates the recipient Ego to a Feeling of oneness with itself — which oneness is now to be attained through Will (not through Feeling merely, as in the previous stage of Religion). We call this sphere practical (*praxis*, doing) as it drives forward to the Deed out of Feeling. Accordingly I am primarily stirred to the Feeling of Will (practical) by the All-Ego as Will, or more completely stated, by the All-willing All. This primordial practical Feeling (that of Will) is the first Feeling of Freedom, not yet strictly the Sentiment of Freedom.

Taking up the general proposition that Sentiment is the Feeling of the All or of the Universe organized, we pass from its first or immediate form (religious) to its second or separative form corresponding to that of Will. This Sentiment embraces the large area of Feeling known as the Sentiments of Freedom. What a part it has played in the History of World, the records of the Past tell very fully. We are still stirred by the account of the struggle for liberty on part of the Athenians against the Orient. This Feeling lies at the root of Universal History, which has been the movement into a more complete Freedom. Endowed with Will man has this Practical Sentiment as his original endowment for Freedom, the end and fulfillment of Will being Freedom. The mere Feeling of Freedom is often called an instinct, and so it is, being also unconscious in the Human Race, and even in animals it is found.

The first matter, then, is to grasp the universal Will, or the Will of the Universe. Psychically the All-Ego is (as Ego) self-separating within itself, and externalizes itself as its own other, or object, which is still itself. Such is the movement of the All in its freedom. By a direct glance we can see that the Universe must be free, as there is nothing outside of it to determine it, otherwise it would not be the Universe. It must be self-determined, its very necessity is its freedom. Conceived as Will, the Universe has to divide its own Self and yet come back to that same Self in such a division. Its activity must, therefore, be an eternal process, cyclical, that of the All-Ego.

Now just this process is also that of the human, recipient, finite Ego, created by the All-Ego, the child of the Universe. This Ego of mine has also for its primordial heritage the Feeling of Freedom as my own, or as subjective, which is verily my endowment from my father, the All-Ego. Every conscious act of mine has in it the Feeling of Freedom, self-separating and then self-returning within itself, like the Universe. In this sense I am universal, having such a process within me, as my consciousness. (See preceding pp. 113-5, 132-4.) From this point of view I am born free, subjectively not objectively free; objective freedom I am to get through myself by making institutions. In my conscious Self and in its free process as Will lies the germ of all actualized freedom; having consciousness inside, I am to make my world free outside. Such a great work, nothing less than the building of man's institutions, unfolds out of human consciousness with its Feeling of Freedom. And

PRACTICAL SENTIMENT.

these institutions will in their turn beget new Feelings, all of which spring primordially from this inner Free-Will of consciousness.

But in order to produce the institutional world of Freedom from this mere aspiration or Feeling of Freedom, the Genius must again appear, endowed with his divinely creative power in this field. Of him we shall again speak.

Freedom may then be deemed the ultimate purpose, the moving end of the Universe as Will, or as active, as process purely. My most insignificant deed carries out and reflects the All-Will, which is really the final design of every movement of man and even of the animal. Such a movement in itself is free or is self-moving, and usually struggles for greater Freedom.

In the present sphere we have to grasp two Wills, that of the Universe and that of the individual, co-operating to produce a Feeling, this Practical Sentiment. The All-Ego as Will, or the All-willing All (omnipotence) stirs the human Ego to feel it as Will. As conscious I feel Will, yea, the All-Will, which is my primal Feeling of Freedom.

We may note a separation, and to a certain degree an opposition between Religious and Practical Sentiment. The All-feeling Ego stimulates the recipient Ego to be one with itself as the Feeling of All. But the All-willing Ego stimulates in the recipient Ego the Feeling of

Will, of Freedom, against even the All as Determinant. Religious Sentiment makes the recipient Ego submissive, yielding to the All in Feeling. But Practical Sentiment has its root in the Ego as endowed with Freedom, with the very Freedom of the All. So the Ego having received such a gift, must feel self-determining, self-assertive even against the donor.

Still in Practical Sentiment we shall find the same general movement which belongs to Absolute Feeling in all its stages: (I) the Process of Practical Sentiment; (II) its particularization in Moral Sentiment; (III) finally it will be made universal in Institutional Sentiment. The whole sphere may be regarded as an unfolding of the Feeling of Freedom.

I. THE PROCESS OF PRACTICAL SENTIMENT. — The Sentiment of Freedom is what is here called practical; active Feeling or the Feeling of action means that the Ego has internally at least the capacity to act. Indeed the Ego is activity itself and must act in order to be; such is its primal Freedom. Not stagnant, not crystallized, but ever moving and self-moving; thus it is the child of the All-Ego, which is eternally process or Will. My Ego can never stop without passing into non-existence. This is its heritage from its Creator, who has made it like unto Himself. The Universe is free and man as universal has primarily the Feeling of Freedom.

Thus we seek to bring before ourselves that original, spontaneous Freedom which belongs to the soul itself antecedent to moral and institutional forms of liberty, that is, before it realizes itself in Morals or actualizes itself in Institutions. The Ego is primordially free, has an inner Freedom of its own. Ere it can be free in personal conduct, or make a free world for its own security, it must be psychically free. Under the most galling despotism the Ego can have its own internal Freedom, or as the Stoic said, can be free in chains. But it may have to suppress Freedom in the deed and do without the same in the government.

In some such manner we seek to grasp the Sentiment of Freedom as purely psychical, the original endowment of Free-Will which seems to be given by nature itself. Still we have to ask whence it came. Undoubtedly it has evolved and is still evolving; it is working out its own salvation. But whence this power of self-evolution? Here we have to invoke the creative process of the Universe which is the first Freedom and is generative of all other manifestations of Freedom. The Pampsychosis is absolute Free-Will and so must create Free-Will in order to be itself. The Sentiment of Freedom as psychical is a reflection of its origin as pampsychical. If God is free, He must make man free or give up His divinity.

The Sentiment of Freedom as psychical will also have its process (like the Universe) whose main stages we may note by way of explanatory preface to what follows. It is well known that men have very diverse conceptions about Freedom; in fact Freedom itself is a changeful, diversified thing. The different historic ages give different definitions of Freedom. Probably Time will continue to evolve our free inheritance.

Of this inner or psychical Freedom the following forms are to be looked at with care in order to understand fully the present sphere.

(*a*) There is first the *spontaneous* Freedom of the Ego, its primal Freedom, which can also be named *capricious*, as having no motive or content but itself. The earliest consciousness of the free Self is that simple subjective activity of the Will which knows as yet no limit within itself. It acts of itself, it cannot yet accept any determination but its own, is without rule or law. Such is the primordial free-acting individual, showing the original power of initiative in every Ego, which thus is able to make itself a center of deeds. We call it caprice or capricious Freedom, the germ of all higher forms of Freedom, which develop out of it through the addition of external materials of growth.

To recognize this germ is a very important point in education, but it must be recognized as the germ. It is to be unfolded into and filled with the moral and institutional ere it become truly free. The child is largely a creature of caprice, which is but the possibility or the condition of rational Freedom. The main duty of education is to train this capricious Freedom into a Freedom through law and institution. It is a great mistake of some recent educators to think that we must go back to the caprice of the child and be guided by it in building a system of education.

Still this first spontaneity of the human Self is by no means to be ignored or even rudely suppressed. It is, indeed, the original Freedom of man which conditions all other forms of its development. In a profound sense it is the God-given, yet this gift of God must be made over by man, else he is not free. Freedom is given to man that he may make himself free.

(*b*) But Freedom finds limits, hence we have *determined Freedom*. The twofold and indeed contradictory nature of this expression is what our reader must first grasp. In the stage of psychical Freedom which we are now considering the Ego is moved to be self-moved, is determined to be self-determined or free. Your body has self-movement; when you dodge a stone thrown at you, you move yourself through an external cause or determinant. An object which has no power of self-movement, like a piece of wood could not be so influenced. This is an outer cause, but there are also inner causes. For instance, my desire for an apple moves me to a self-movement, namely to extend my hand. Still more complex is my choice between two or more motives for action.

In all these cases we see our first unconditioned Freedom or Caprice is conditioned or determined by something outside of itself. This is the sphere of what is known as Determinism. It is in this sphere that there arises the much-discussed question: Is man a free agent? Or is he always determined by some impulse, desire, or motive? The answer, if we confine our view of Freedom to the present sphere, can only be that man is both, he is moved to be self-moved or is determined to be self-determined. Hence both Determinist and the Libertarian may prove their distinctive points, but each cannot disprove the position of his opponent.

But there is another sphere of Freedom in which it is possible to escape from this dualistic see-saw.

(*c*) This we shall call in contrast with the last, *self-determined Freedom*. The Sentiment of Freedom as psychical reaches its culmination in the fact that man is to make an outer world in order to be wholly free, not only subjectively but also objectively free. In the preceding sphere he had a determined Freedom; but his instinct for complete Freedom impels him forth to that which determines him and which he is to transform into a means of Freedom. For instance, before man lies the vast Ocean which he cannot cross, and which, therefore, puts a limit upon his Freedom. He proceeds to build a raft (like Ulysses) or finally a steamboat (like Fulton) in order to overcome this obstacle to his Free-Will. In the final view every blow struck by a workman in making and putting together a locomotive is a blow for Freedom in the supreme sense. That is, his Free-Will in his work is willing Freedom, is transmuting material nature into an implement of Freedom for man, who thereby is able to transcend greatly the limitation through Space and also Time. The Sentiment of Freedom underlies the colossal industrial development of our age, which is seeking the transformation of the physical world into the habitation of the free man. Of course other ends play in, such as the making of money and the acquisition of power. But ultimately it is the Sentiment of Freedom which drives the human being to free himself from the trammels of external nature.

If we wish to express the present fact psychically, we can formulate it as follows: The Free Will of man wills Free-Will, has itself as its own end, motive, content. Man reaches true Free-Will only when he wills Free Will. Or we may also say he determines himself to be self-determined. Every Marathonian soldier went out to fight against the Persian for Freedom, his Free Will willed Freedom, while his enemy's Free-Will (for the Persian doubtless acted freely) willed slavery. So during the Revolutionary War, our fathers determined themselves to be self-determined, their free activity had freedom as its content. This was their persistent Sentiment of Freedom, not a transitory Caprice of Freedom, which Sentiment would be likely to vanish at the first serious obstacle.

But man is not only to transform physical nature into a realm of Freedom; he is also to construct an entirely new world of Freedom through Law and Institutions. In these the Sentiment of Freedom finds its highest realization; it is no longer a subjective Caprice, as we saw it at the start, but has evolved an objective Order whose purpose is to secure Freedom. Having thus realized itself, the Sentiment of Freedom as psychical and subjective has reached its conclusion. It has manifested its great purpose, which is in the widest sense of the word to make man ethical. But this cannot be done without an order or process which is briefly indicated as follows.

1. *The Ethical Genius.* — The creative man again appears, rising up from the mass of humanity, all of whom have the foregoing primordial Sentiment of Freedom, since they possess

Wills. But the Genius organizes this Sentiment, so that it is a new objective order in the World, a moral or institutional system whose great end is to make Freedom real, and to safeguard it against its foes. This system in turn becomes the source of Sentiment, which has likewise its absolute character, being derived from a form of Freedom organized.

In the Orient the Ethical and the Religious Genius is usually one and the same man, as we see in the case of Moses, of Zoroaster, and Buddha. But in Europe the two are quite differentiated, as in the example of Socrates, who cannot be deemed the founder of a Religion, though he makes an epoch in the development of Morals.

Under the head of Ethical Genius we class two different kinds of men, the Moral and the Institutional. The strictly Moral Genius is he who unfolds the Moral Law for the individual, the latter taking it for guidance in conduct. The Institutional Genius is the man who makes the objective Law over all, in the State for instance. Plato and Aristotle had both elements, moral and institutional, while Epicurus and Zeno seem to have developed the moral spirit, each in his own way.

2. *The Ethical Order.* — The Sentiment of Freedom is to be organized into an Ethical Order that it may exist and do its work in the

world. The mere subjective Feeling of Freedom is indeed the germ, and yet but a germ which is to be unfolded. It springs from the All-Ego as Will, which cannot be hindered or determined by anything outside of itself. Conscious man, created of the All-Ego, must likewise have Will, or the self-determining act of the Ego within, which, however, is to become an object, an entity in the world. Thus natural Freedom is *ethicised*, filled with the All-Ego (its original) ordered. This, as before stated, is the work of the Ethical Genius.

The moral life and the institutional life are now possible, having their presupposition in the psychical element already given — that of Freedom.

3. *The Recipients.* — These are the people, the mass of Egos, who are also born with the Feeling of Freedom, but are not able of themselves to rise into an ordered Freedom either inner (moral) or outer (institutional). Hence they are to be brought into participation with the Divine Will not only immediately, but also mediately through the Ethical World of Morals and Institutions. Every man is to be ethicised, yea every deed of every man. The Sentiment of Freedom in this way gets to have a universal content, that of the Universe or All-Ego as Will organized by the Genius, whose work is thereby

not simply for himself, but also for his people or race.

II. PRACTICAL SENTIMENT PARTICULARIZED. — That is, the Sentiment of Freedom ordered is to be made particular in each individual and is to determine his conduct. The All-Ego organized as Will universal is to be taken up by the particular Ego which is thereby moralized. The Moral Sentiment is, accordingly, God or the Universe in the feeling individual, who acts universally in his relations to others.

Such is the Sentiment of Freedom as moral, or what is often called the Moral Sentiment, whose nature has always attracted much attention. How shall we formulate it so that we may really get at it? And what is its origin? It too has been often called the God-given; specially the Moral Conscience has been identified with the voice of God Himself.

Free-Will certainly plays an important part in this field, or at least a supposed Free-Will, since Herbert Spencer and many others deem Free-Will a delusion. Still in every moral act there is an immediate Feeling of Freedom that most men will not allow to be sophisticated out of themselves by the cunning of the philosopher. The Sentiment is there, and is to be accounted for, and rather the shallowest way of accounting for it is to brand it as a delusion. Psychology teaches that the man who sees so much delusion in others, is apt to have a large fragment of it himself.

The Moral Will rests upon the psychical idea of Freedom which it is to realize in conduct. Life is to be moralized through and through, in its great and its small activities, by an ideal end, which is the realization of a complete Free-Will in the personal career. What is this complete Free-Will which hovers before the moral doer? It is the Freedom of the Universe, of the Absolute Process of Spirit. The human individual Ego is to have as ideal end in conduct the Universe which is the original divine Freedom. The Psychosis is to realize on its personal side the Pampsychosis, which created it and gave it a moral character. My Moral Sentiment is ultimately the Feeling that I can and ought to incorporate in my doing the great Totality, though I in my Freedom can refuse to do so.

Such is the attainment of Virtue, and the development of the completely moralized man. Still even he does not wholly get rid of the separation, the two Selves are present and persistently active in his moral consciousness. He is the finite, not the infinite; he is the created Ego who is to realize the process of the Absolute Ego; he is not and never can be that Absolute Ego. Thus the Moral Sentiment must always recognize the chasm between the two Selves, and feel that the Ideal when realized is no longer ideal. God is after all not exactly man, though the latter recreates Him in Feeling, Will, and Thought. We may say, however, that the Universe is not truly moralized till man has done the work. We can add that man is to realize in himself God's Freedom, in order to make the Universe objectively free. This we hold to be the ultimate purpose and aim of the Moral Ego.

1. *The Moral Consciousness.* — The basic fact of the Moral Consciousness is the two Egos, the finite and the infinite, and their interaction through the Will. When I say *I ought*, there are suggested two Selves, one of which may be called my real Self, the other my ideal Self, one of which I am now and here, the other of which I am not, but would be if I truly realized my ideal Self in my daily existence. Such is the twofoldness which gives rise to the Moral Sentiment, the Feeling of an eternal ideal Self to which I must strive to make my real Self conform in all the details of life. There is no exception, even the most trivial of my practical concerns are to be moralized, for every act of Will has in it the double character before mentioned. Will is naturally, that is psychically, free, and Freedom is the own gift of the Universe, of its very process. Every act of mine has in it both myself and the All. My Will is there, but my Will bears the stamp of the one great Totality which is free.

To go to my dinner at a certain time, to go down this street or the other, to buy a pin or not are usually deemed acts morally indifferent, and they may be; but the Moral Sentiment in its universality demands that every act, however small, share in the Moral Ideal or be left undone. If it cannot be moralized, or be made conducive to the realization of Free-Will, let it be dropped. The non-moral element is to be eliminated from human life; not only the positively immoral, but the indifferently non-moral belongs not in the Moral Universe and hence not in the Soul which is moral.

2. *Moral Ends.* — The Moral Sentiment has called forth many theories to account for itself. Whence comes that *ought*ness which so imperiously speaks down to my *is*ness? I am obligated to obey its behest, but if I disobey (which I can in my freedom) there is a peculiar, but very effective punishment. There is the law, the tribunal, the judge, the culprit, the decision, the penalty; the whole process of an inner Judicature takes place within my Self. It often proceeds in direct opposition to my wish; whence its authority? The problem is often stated as a search for the Ground of Moral Obligation, a hunt for the source of that power which imposes upon me Duty, endows me with a Conscience, commands me with its categorical Imperative more coercive and sometimes more crushing than any

external edict of king or emperor. It is a phenomenon which thinking men have been curious about and have speculated upon, especially since the time of the old Greeks.

It is evident that the source of Duty, or of Moral Obligation, and therewith of the Moral Sentiment, is the great object to be attained, to be known and formulated in the Science of Ethics. Such is that ideal End which we seek to realize by moral conduct. What shall it be declared to be?

One of the first ends which man finds himself pursuing is Pleasure. But the great difficulty with this end is that it does not moralize life, it is not an ideal End; it is not really universal but is very particular, since one man's Pleasure is likely to be different from that of another. A variation of the Hedonistic Theory affirms that Happiness, and then that the greatest Happiness of ·the greatest number are the right formulas for moralizing human conduct. But these also show an insufficiency, and even the Theory of Benevolence will not adequately account for the Moral Sentiment in its origin.

There is no doubt that all these Moral Ends have a certain particular validity, each in its limited sphere. But Moral Sentiment must have a universal content, being itself a product of the All-Ego though confined to the individual.

3. *The Universal Moral End.* — The Moral

Sentiment is stirred by the Universe, otherwise it could not be rightly called universal. There comes the Feeling of oneness with the All and its process, which give rise to every form of Absolute Feeling. The moral consciousness hears this All commanding it as individual. The two Selves, the finite and the infinite, are now in the relation of lawgiver and subject.

But we are not to think that every Ego can be its own moral lawgiver. Here the Genius must appear in person and formulate for his people just this moral Law. The Decalogue was an early code of this kind, and shows the process. Moses was the lawgiver of the Hebrews, the ten commandments he received from God, who did not give them directly to each individual of the people. It is true that each individual had potentially the Law within him, his Ego was itself sprung of the Absolute Ego and bore its impress. Still the intermediate Genius was required who could formulate the Divine Will and thus make it possible for every man to share in the Universal.

The early Greek had a similar process, since it is said that the Delphic Oracle gave to certain lawgivers their codes. But Socrates separated the inner Law from the outer, and thus unfolded the distinction between the moral and institutional, which were not differentiated by the early lawgivers. In fact the life and death of Socrates manifest the conflict which may arise between the Law of Conscience and the Law of the State.

It is a great thing for man, the finite individual, to realize Freedom coming from the infinite Ego. Thus he becomes a kind of a God on Earth. Still this inner freedom of the moral Sentiment is to be made objective, actual, truly universal.

III. PRACTICAL SENTIMENT UNIVERSALIZED.— If in the previous stage the Sentiment of Freedom was particularized, now it is to be universalized, rising from its subjective or moral order, to its objective or institutional order. It is true that the universal element is in both stages, but the first shows it in the individual Ego, while the second shows it existent in the world, where it stands forth in its own right. Hence in Institutions Practical Sentiment is truly universalized; Free-Will becomes objective and universal, making a new Universe of Freedom for securing itself. All men are associated in the institutional world which the Genius establishes or helps to establish, being driven to such a work by the Sentiment of Freedom. This Sentiment, being objectified and organized in Institutions, makes thereby a new source of itself, which permeates and unites the multitude, the people.

An institutional Sentiment we find existent and very powerful in the present sphere of Freedom, for Institutions have as their ultimate purpose the securing of man's Free-Will. Our Feelings are stirred by Family, State, Church in a unique way and to a high degree of intensity. Thus we have an institutional Determinant rousing in us a distinct kind of Feeling which is designated institutional Sentiment. Patriotism is such a Sentiment and it moves men to offer life for country. There is a Sentiment for Church which is very distinct from the religious Sentiment as such. Indeed the ecclesiastical and the religious Sentiments may be antagonistic and seek to put down each other.

In this connection it is well to mark the different usage of two words related and sometimes employed as synonyms, *realized* and *actualized*. The Moral Will realizes Freedom in individual conduct directly; the Institutional Will actualizes Freedom in and through Institutions. The Institutional man is, therefore, different from the Moral man. The latter takes up and is ruled by the Pampsychosis immediately; the former is determined by it mediately, through Institutions, which are social forms, or products of associated man. The Universe (or the All-Ego) with its process working through a society of some kind is what stirs the Institutional Sentiment. An Institution is Will actualized, existent in the world, whose end is to secure Freedom. Thus Institutional Sentiment is a Sentiment of Freedom, not immediate or psychical, not moral with an inner law, but institutional with an outer law becoming inner not in one soul but in many souls associated together and forming one nation or one faith.

1. *Institutional Consciousness.* — Every man feels the oneness of his people or of his race. This is the social, or better the institutional consciousness (or Feeling) out of which Institutions spring. We may call it the inborn sense of society, of men associating together for the great ultimate end of securing their Freedom. The individual finds that he can become free not through himself alone, but through others who along with him will his Free-Will. Such a society of Egos organizes itself and becomes an Institution.

Undoubtedly such an inborn tendency to association in the individual is a product of the Pampsychosis which, creating the Ego and endowing the same with its own process, gives to it the power of self-evolution, of rising above the finite limits of nature toward the All. So the individual creates a greater Self in Institutions, combining many Selves into a society which unites them.

Every born person has accordingly this institutional consciousness, which, the germ of Freedom being given, starts on a long career of evolution, manifesting itself in various institutional forms. Aristotle says that man is a "political animal," which we may interpret in its universal sense as "an institution-making animal," making not only the State (political Institution), but many other Institutions.

2. *Particular Institutions.*—With the development of man Institutions become differentiated and diversified. Association reveals itself as the common fact of human activity, man turns organizer of societies, builds them great and small by the thousand. Indeed the greatness of man is now tested by his ability to associate men for a great purpose. The individual is fast approaching the stage where he will do no important thing alone, but organize a society for doing it. The chief function of man will be to organize men. This power will grow more and more a teachable matter, an inheritance of training. At first only the divinely gifted genius could unite his fellow-man in one Institution.

Already we see that a chief end of education is not merely to accumulate stores of knowledge but to learn to organize for important ends, particularly for that most important of all ends, the securing of Freedom. This Institutional Sentiment has, therefore, a great future before it, greater, we think, than the Moral Sentiment, though this of course is not to lapse. The old Greeks had Moral Science, in fact created it and set it moving on lines which it largely keeps to-day. But the Greeks had no complete institutional science, though they had Institutions. Plato's Republic and Aristotle's Politics are very valuable documents of thought pertaining to the State. But they hardly give a complete Science of Institutions for Greece even.

The time has come, then, particularly in America, for the citizen to become conscious of his Institutions. He must know them in order to preserve them. The Institutional Sentiment is no longer to remain in blissful ignorance of itself, but is to become self-aware, that it may develop rationally and continuously, not fitfully and gropingly. The coming age belongs to it, and it cannot be left to be a Feeling only, but must rise to a knowledge of its destiny.

Of Social Institutions we may count five great ones, connected, overlapping in places, yet each with its distinct process. These are Family, Society, State, which comprise the secular Institution, to which must be added the religious and the educative Institution (see our *Social Institutions* Introduction, *et passim*).

3. *The Universal Institutional Sentiment.*— There always has been and still is a Sentiment which aspires for and even seeks to actualize the Universal Institution. If we go far back, perhaps the Family would show itself the one primordial Institution, the original institutional germ out of which other Institutions have

evolved. In Asia we have the Theocracy which united the two Institutions, political and religious very closely, making them two sides of one Whole. On the other hand in developed Greece the political Institution was of paramount interest, and the same may be said of Rome. But the Middle Ages had the tendency to invert the institutional situation, and to put the Church over the State. In the modern world the State has the stress over the Church, and Civilization seems to advance mainly on political lines. In the latest form of government, that of the United States, the religious Institution is entirely separated from the political, and is left to take care of itself in its own way.

The result is we see reversions to Asiatic forms, in which both secular and religious authority is again united in one Institution and even in one person (Mormonism, Salvation Army, Dowieism, etc.). Some of these phases have even collided with existent political authority in the prosecution of their plans. But all strive to restore and represent that unity of Institutions which began man's institutional existence.

Will there be an institutional Federal Union? That lies far in the future, beyond even the union of Religions — and the latter is not yet by any means a fact. Still such a Sentiment exists and at times manifests itself. Here, however, its existence can only be indicated.

In the preceding account the reader will observe that I have not so much been engaged in the act of Willing as in thinking about it and setting forth its order and meaning. What is that which arranges and defines the foregoing Practical Sentiment? Not itself certainly; the Will is not self-ordering and self-defining; in it the Ego does not turn back upon itself and contemplate its own working. The Will goes forth, moves out of itself, acts; properly in itself it is not the self-returning stage of the Ego. Thus I have been employing throughout this whole exposition of Will the Intellect, the self-seeing and self-knowing activity of the Ego. I cannot understand Practical Sentiment without resorting to my Theoretic faculty.

Moreover this self-knowledge is likewise at first in the form of Feeling. The All as Ego must be self-knowing, and it imparts this trait to its child, the individual Ego. Hence there rises the Feeling of Knowledge as the necessary complement of the Feeling of Freedom. In fact the Will, taken by itself with its movement persistently outward, would nullify the Ego; the Will alone would in its doing become self-undoing. Experience has told us in many ways that Freedom in its excess is not only destructive but self-destructive. This goes back to the very nature of the Will, when it is separated from Intellect. Psychologically I must see that it is but a part, the second stage of the total Ego, and that it demands the completion of itself in the third stage, which makes it truly whole even as a part.

Accordingly we have reached an original, elemental Feeling of Knowledge, of the Ego as self-returning, which is in its turn to be ordered and made the source of a new kind of Absolute Feeling.

SECTION THIRD — THEORETIC SENTIMENT.

We are now to consider the third and last stage of Absolute Feeling, or of Sentiment, which is called Theoretic, since it both leads to and springs from Intellect (*Theoria*, vision, contemplation, intellection). Already we have treated of Feeling and Will as the ground of Absolute Feeling, under the heads of Religious and Practical Sentiments. The All-Ego which has the process of Feeling, Will, and Intellect is imparted to the human Ego in Consciousness, which thus has the same process of Feeling, Will, and Intellect for its own, but is implicit, potential, or as an ideal end which it always feels and seeks to make real. This primordial Feeling of the All-Ego in the individual Ego is the substrate or protoplasmic material out of which grows Absolute Feeling in its three forms. The first Feeling of the All-Ego, my creator, in me is my Consciousness, which we have already considered as elemental (p. 132). Now it is this original, elemental Feeling common to all Egos which the Genius proceeds to form, and it is these new forms of the All-Ego which call forth properly Absolute Feeling, or the Feeling of the Absolute, in the Finite Ego. At present we are to set forth this Absolute Feeling from the side of Intellect.

If in Will I feel the Universe to be free and self-determined, this being stamped upon me in my creation: in Intellect I feel the Universe to be knowing, yea, self-knowing, this also being stamped upon me in my creation. As I must be free within, so I must know within, like the Universe which created me after its own pattern, universal.

The Universe must not only be seeing but be self-seeing, as there is nothing outside of it to see or to be seen. All knowledge or Intellect is a kind of seeing and ultimately a self-seeing, a seeing of the Self in everything, which is indeed a product of the innermost Self. In the highest sense I must be Self-knowing, not only subjectively but objectively; as long as I know merely the outside, and not the Self in the outside, my knowing is inadequate and finite.

Accordingly Man, as created by the All-knowing One, must feel that he too can know; you can know the All, though this be but a Feeling. It is, however, that primordial Feeling of knowledge in Intellect, which correlates with the Feeling of God in Religion, and with the Feeling of Freedom in Will.

Out of this primordial Feeling of Knowledge common to all Egos as conscious, the Genius rises up and forms anew for the knowing Self the creative All-Ego and its process. He is to formulate and to organize the All-knowing All, the self-knowing Universe, the All-Ego for the finite, human, recipient mass of Egos, to the end that they too may participate in divine knowledge, may know the ordered Absolute. Already every recipient Ego has the Feeling of such knowledge, but not the knowledge formed, expressed, organized. This is, or has been in the World's History, the work of the Genius, the divinely gifted man with his powers of re-creating the All.

Intellect, though in a process with Feeling and Will, has its own inner process or Psychosis, and this too is derived from the All-Ego (Pampsychosis). Intellect takes three main forms, Sense-perception, Representation, and Thought. A theoretic relation as distinct from the practical is indicated by all three; they are ways of seeing the object, or better, of knowing it, of making it a part of my own Ego. When, however, this object is the Universe as Ego, or the All-knowing All, which has created my Intellect, I reach out to know the source of my knowing and manifest my primordial Feeling for knowledge. I seek to know not only myself but the All-Self in All. Such is, then, my deepest aspiration for knowledge, stirring within me not simply to know something but to know the creative source of my knowing, the Universe as knowledge, the All-knowing All.

Intellect, then, our theoretic faculty, will know or see (in the wide sense) the All-knowing All in three ways, or under three forms of itself, Sense-perception, Representation, and Thought. I, receiving this All by observation or knowledge, may sense it, may image it, or may think it. Moreover, the All-knowing All, or self-knowing Universe comes to me already formed for and appealing to my Senses, my Imagination, or my Thought. · As before stated, it comes prepared by the Genius, and rouses my Absolute Feeling as Theoretic Sentiment, which is not simply the Feeling of the ordered Absolute, but of the ordered Absolute as seen and known. Thus the primordial, elemental, immediate Feeling of knowledge rises to an Absolute Feeling, here the Feeling of the Absolute all-knowing (omniscient) as organized.

Such an organization or formulation of the

all-knowing All for the recipient Ego may be called Art in its most extended Sense. Hence we shall have Sense-Arts (Presentative), Image-Arts (Representative), and Thought-Arts (Noetic, Alethic). Such is the side of the recipient Ego. And yet we must remember that the All-Ego is likewise Intellect and has Sense-Perception, Representation, and Thought. Hence we may deem the All-knowing All to manifest himself as All-sensing All, All-representing All, All-thinking All. Thus the Sense-Arts seek to bring to man's senses the All-sensing (seeing) All (Aesthetic); the Image Arts seek to bring to man's imagination the All-representing All (Poetic); the Thought-Arts seek to bring to man's thinking the All-thinking All (Philosophic.)

In Theoretic Sentiment, we shall again see the following stages:—

(I.) The Process of it in general;
(II.) Theoretic Sentiment particularized;
(III.) The same universalized.

We may here state that the *content* of the present sphere (Theoretic Sentiment) we have more fully set forth in another work. Hence we shall only make a brief recapitulation, though the field is vast and important, embracing Art, Poetry, and Philosophy. In the case before us, however, we can simply touch upon the Sentiment which is roused by these subjects and organize it into a system which corresponds to the divisions employed in the work referred to (see *Social Institutions*, Chapter Third of the Educative Institution, pp. 521–615, embracing the Sense-Arts, the Image-Arts, and the Thought-Arts).

I. THE PROCESS OF THEORETIC SENTIMENT.— There is the primordial Feeling of the All-Ego, which we found in Consciousness already as self-knowing. This Feeling is common to all Egos, and upon its presence in man Art relies for power. Now it is this All-Ego or the Universe as Self which is to be ordered and thus made newly existent in the world. Thus we may say, in general, that God has to be re-made in order to be an object of Theoretic Sentiment. The general process of the latter is as follows.

1. *The Theoretic Genius.*—Such is the general name of the creative man in the present sphere, he who is able to reproduce the process of the universal Self in some theoretic form—sensuous, imaginative, philosophic. Examples are the Painter, the Poet, the Thinker. The Theoretic Genius projects into a new reality the form of the divinely creative Ego, which he feels along with the mass of men. But such a Feeling works in him genetically, that is, as Genius, driving him to organize what he feels in forms that all may appropriate, and thereby share in the Highest.

2. *The Theoretic Order.* — So we may name what is organized in the present sphere, which thus is lifted out of its uncertain subjective state into an actual existent object perpetually working in the world. Our knowledge of the Universal or of the Universe as Ego is in this way made definite, formulated, is endowed with reality, which in turn becomes the prolific source of manifold Feelings now truly absolute, as in Art, Poetry, and Science.

3. *The Recipients.* — These are the great end of the present sphere, the people who are to be elevated into participating in the knowledge of the All-Ego through the work of the Genius. Art, Poetry, Science are to impart their treasures to every man that he too may feel and see God. Some may reach Him through His actual presence as in Sculpture; others prefer to grasp Him through the inner image called up by the poet; still others attain Him through imageless thought.

The Ego has also a Gift, that of Evolution whereby it must always be rising out of its limits, be limit-transcending. Thus the Gift of Genius has its corresponding Gift to work upon in every Ego.

II. THEORETIC SENTIMENT PARTICULARIZED.— In giving the preceding account of the general Process of Absolute Sentiment, we have been compelled repeatedly to allude to its particular forms. The Genius is also particularized, he is specially sculptor, or painter, or poet, or philosopher. He has power usually over only one kind of form, he sets forth the Universe through color, or sound, or perchance through abstract speech, each of which forms, however, becomes a new source of Feeling of the absolute kind.

1. *Aesthetic.* — The Fine Arts proper, or the Sense-Arts, stimulate the activity of Absolute Feeling which is called aesthetic, since it comes directly through the Senses. The Genius as artist projects the process of the All-Ego into forms which are taken up through Sense-perception, specially through Sight and Hearing.

Aesthetic Sentiment is still further divided according to the Arts which may be its source, or according to the Presentative Arts. These are the Somatic Arts, Architecture, and Music, each of which in its own way brings home to the Feeling of the recipient the divinely creative Self, and thereby stirs in him the aesthetic Sentiment. (For further elaboration of these Arts, see our *Social Institutions*, pp. 547–577.)

Art particularly represents the form of the All-sensing All to the senses of the recipient. Through the form of Zeus you see the All-seeing All, without the finite eye, however, which is simply indicated. Artistic objects are finite, but they stimulate, not merely external sensuous vision, but the vision of the All, else they are not artistic. In Telesthesis the Ego could see and feel at a distance, through the medium of the Over-Self; but the All-Self becomes visible in Art, for instance in a statue of the God.

2. *Poetic.* — With the inner Image Poetic Sentiment properly deals, hence it is stirred also by the Image-Arts, which in general are known as Literature. The word spoken and written now becomes the vehicle of rousing the Feeling which springs from the All organized. This organization can be far more perfectly represented in speech than by the foregoing Sense-Arts. Hence the mightest and most influential expression of the ordered Absolute is in the Great Books, the Bibles of the World, both sacred and secular. To be sure Poetic Sentiment is exceedingly varied, it may be roused by the little lyric as well as by the great epic or drama.

The word spoken and written, when truly poetic, becomes the bearer of the Pampsychosis to the Ego, stirring the latter to take up and assimilate the former. The Mythus, Folk-lore, even the Novel have this function in various degrees.

3. *Alethic.* — The Universe as Ego now seeks a new expression, not in the forms of Sense, nor of the Image, but of Thought. What is universal drives forward to utter itself in a form corresponding to its character, namely universal. Speech becomes, therefore, abstract, being abstracted

from its sensuous and imaginative determinations. Such an utterance is universal, that is, true; Truth is not only universal, but must be told universally, must be put into an universal form. Here, then, rises a new art with its peculiar expression and its peculiar Sentiment, which we may call alethic (from Truth) or noetic (from Thought).

Alethic Art splits up into three main divisions, those of Natural Science, History, and Philosophy. These have been and still are the great, trainers of man in the pursuit of Truth as such in the form of abstract Thought. Hence in the present sphere we note the following subordinate Sentiments, each of which springs from and goes toward the Absolute ordered. There is first *the Scientific Sentiment* (or Feeling) whose object or content is the Truth of Nature as expressed in the categories of Natural Science. Second comes *the Historic Sentiment*, which has as its source the Truth underlying human deeds and events Third is *the Philosophic Sentiment*, for Philosophy, or the Universe of Thought organized as Thought, begets a strong Sentiment in its devotees, as time has shown and still shows. Thus the Absolute as such, through its own congruent philosophical form, has stirred the Feeling of the Absolute. That is, Absolute Feeling or Sentiment has attained the Feeling of the Absolute in the latter's own native shape.

Alethic Sentiment has thus had as its content Science, History, and Philosophy, which are the ordering of Nature, Man (in action) and God (or the Absolute). These three stages — Nature, Man, and God — form the complete process of the Universe as the Grand Totality which we have often called the Pampsychosis, which is also to have its Feeling or Sentiment, distinct from any hitherto set forth.

But now appears the limitation of the present sphere. The Thought-form of the All-Ego is declared to be universal. And yet it shows itself as particular over against the Image-form and the Sense-form. Thus the Alethic Sentiment comes to feel that it is not universal, and yet must make itself such, in order to be adequate to its content, the All-Ego.

III. THEORETIC SENTIMENT UNIVERSALIZED.— Philosophy or the Pure Thought of the Universe has unfolded the process of Nature, Man, and the Absolute (or God), and therein given the organized content of Alethic Sentiment. But Thought finds itself to be only one stage of the greater cycle of Intellect, which embraces also Sense-perception and Representation. Hence Theoretic Sentiment must rise beyond the narrower sphere of Alethic Sentiment, or the Sentiment of Philosophy, into the complete movement of the Intellect, and therein start to become psychical, having the triple process of the Intellect explicitly for its content. Here begins, then, the Feeling, not of Philosophy, but of Psychology, and a new order of Sentiment opens.

1. *The Sentiment of the Pampsychosis — its Rise.* — The Feeling of the All-Ego ordered as psychical has now dawned, this psychical order manifesting itself in the theoretic sphere of the Intellect. But even Intellect finds itself limited; the theoretic sphere has its bounds in the Practical and the Religious. In other words Intellect shows itself but a part of a greater process which includes Will and Feeling in order to be complete psychically. Thus even Intellect is not universal, but has to make itself such by taking up into itself its two correlative stages. My Intellect in order to know itself as truly universal, must go back and see itself united in one process with Will and Feeling. Thus it has universalized itself by making itself psychological, formulating the Ego as Feeling, Will, and Intellect.

This is what we call the Psychosis in its simple concrete form, the naked movement of the Ego as such. But this is not the end; the psychical process is not merely mine, or individual; if it be universal it must be the process of the Universe. Not merely that of all Egos, but that of the All itself; it cannot be simply subjective, but must be objective too, universal. Thus rises before us an All-Ego often noted hitherto, with its Feeling, Will, and Intellect, which we may more specially consider as All-feeling All, All-willing All, All-knowing All. This is distinctively the Pampsychosis.

Moreover it has its primordial Feeling in the individual Ego correlative with the primordial Feeling of Religion, of Freedom, and of Knowledge. But the new Feeling is that of the process of them all, of the Pampsychosis itself.

2. *The Sentiment of the Pampsychosis organized.*— The original Feeling of the triune process of the Universe as Feeling, Will, and Intellect is next to be put into order, that is, into its own pampsychical order. This is the work of the Genius, the creative spirit who rises out of the common Feeling (here pampsychical), and establishes his system, doing something similar to what the Genius did also in Religion, Institutions, Art, and Philosophy. Such new ordering of the All-Ego psychically through and through gives rise to the new science — Psychology. The Feeling of the Absolute organized is finally to come to the individual, not through Feeling, Will, and Intellect singly ordered (as hitherto), but in their complete psychical round. This in turn calls forth the pampsychical Sentiment proper, alethic in a new sense, the Feeling of the truth of Psychology.

The present Sentiment, therefore, demands

that the Universe be ordered not as an abstract idea (as in Philosophy), not simply as an image (as in Poetry), not simply as a sensuous object (as in Art), but as all three and their process. And this is not enough: the present Sentiment demands that the Universe be ordered not simply as Intellect (All-knowing All, omniscience), not simply as Will (All-willing All, omnipotence), not simply as Feeling (All-feeling All, omnisentience), but as all three and their process.

Such we may deem the Pampsychosis organized psychically in its primal stages. This triple impress is what is stamped upon every created thing by the creative All-Ego which thus imparts itself in manifold grades from lowest to highest.

3. *Sentiment of the Pampsychosis — the Recipient.* — In the other fields of Absolute Feeling we have had to speak of the many recipient Egos, the mass, the people, who are to receive and appropriate, and then feel the ordering of the creative man, the Genius, the special favorite of the Universe, being endowed with its universal genetic power.

Nothing would seem, therefore, to be more absolute, more autocratic than Genius, being the only born ruler of men, associating them by his Divine Gift. The recipient mass of Egos is to accept directly at first his message, his organization; in Asia the Genius is deemed the God Himself or next to the God as Prophet, Revealer. In Europe the Genius is essentially aristocratic, divinely gifted by birth, yet human and appealing to humanity; he is Genius through the Grace of God. But this Divine Right of Genius is likewise to be transformed in the Occident, along with other Divine Rights; not lost or thrown away by any means, but renewed and reconstructed.

The Recipient Ego is undoubtedly to receive and to assimilate still what the Genius creatively orders in every field; but it must also be made a part of the process. I am to recreate what creates me, and am myself to become a stage in such creation. I, the Recipient, am not to be left out of my own supreme process, I am to be explicitly present. The Genius is to make me, in his formulation of the All-Ego, a sharer, a co-worker in creating the Universe, without whom indeed it could not be completely created. Thus I am not only to reproduce the Pampsychosis within, but am to include myself in such reproduction. My Sentiment becomes pampsychical when I, as Recipient Ego, feel the process of the All, and feel myself to be a necessary inherent element of that process. Herein the worth of the individual has dawned.

Such is or may be the gift of the Genius to the Recipient Ego. But the latter is to advance one step higher: he is himself to become Genius.

That is, the Genius is finally to impart himself, his creativity, to every Ego of the mass, who is to receive not so much the product of Genius, as the very Genius itself. We say that it is the ultimate function of Genius (as far as we can at present see) to make each Ego what it is; it must endow every man with itself, namely Genius. The Many are not merely to participate, but to create.

It is evident that the Recipient Ego in this last stage of the Pampsychosis, has returned to the Genius and taken him up into itself, becoming the total process of the All-Ego within itself, establishing its own order in the full freedom of the spirit. Every Ego has some such Sentiment or perchance Pre-Sentiment of the Pampsychosis fulfilled or to be fulfilled.

The outcome of the total movement of Feeling is, therefore, the pampsychical Sentiment. The Ego feels not only the creative power of the Universe, but that it can and must recreate this creative power which indeed creates it. And not only feel and will and think this power, but also formulate it and impart it to others; therein the Ego brings forth the new science, Psychology, the science of itself and of the Self as All. In Psychology every man is to be at last his own Genius, and make his own Universe as psychical, including himself as a creative part thereof.

Observations on Absolute Feeling. The reader is not to forget that the words *practical* and *theoretical* are here employed in a wider sense than in ordinary usage. The practical man is commonly understood to mean him who is ready and skillful in adapting means to ends, quick to act in emergencies. Here it pertains to the Will in its whole sphere, Will being the practical activity of man. On the other hand theoretical activity in the present connection means that of the Intellect as a whole, though in common speech it often means some scheme or thought which is impractical, that is, cannot be realized, and hence of small account. The two words are, therefore, the adjectives of Will and Intellect — a usage derived from Greek Philosophy and well known in modern philosophical writers.

1. It is perhaps easier to grasp practical Feeling or the primal Feeling of Freedom, which we may observe in the lowest animal, than either religious or theoretic Feeling. To this fact more than to any other we may ascribe the prevalence of the doctrine which asserts the primacy of the Will, or of practical Feeling. That there is no such primacy of Will as against Feeling and Intellect, or any similar primacy of Feeling or of Intellect in themselves, we have elsewhere tried to show. (See *Prolegomena.*) The true primacy is that of the process

itself which includes all three — Feeling, Will, Intellect. And yet there is a priority of order in this process, which priority belongs to Feeling, as is manifest in the formula just given. This order is also what determines the successive stages of Absolute Feeling as above set forth — religious, practical, and theoretical.

We can, then, without much difficulty, identify in ourselves the Feeling of Freedom (practical); with a somewhat greater effort we can find within us the Feeling of Knowledge (theoretic); we are certainly aware we can do and can know. But in religious Feeling something harder to understand appears: there may be a Feeling of Feeling, the Ego feels that it feels (not simply feels that it wills and knows). Can we discover in our emotional experience anything that corresponds to such a statement? An inner condition of mine is when I feel myself feeling God. There is this self-reference in the feeling Ego which does not rise to self-knowing (see preceding pp. 58, 65). So the Ego, the individual, feels itself feeling the All-Ego or God. Moreover the latter is felt in its process. I may say, therefore, that I feel myself feeling God's Feeling (or Presence), God's Will (to which I yield), and God's Knowing (which too I must know in a measure).

2. These subjective states which we call religious Feelings ramify endlessly and become

very subtle and intricate. Still they in their manifold labyrinths reach back to the simple Feeling of the all-creative Self, the first God-consciousness, the primal Feeling of Religion. Now this primal Feeling is the raw material out of which is organized Absolute Feeling in all its forms. It is the plastic substance which the Genius works in and organizes, as has been repeatedly set forth in the preceding exposition.

But let us take up our " raw material " again and see it unfolding, as it is expressed in the formula: I feel myself feeling God or the All-Ego. Here, then, are two Egos, each necessarily with its process of Feeling, Will, and Intellect. That is, my individual Ego on the one side with its threefold nature is stirred to its primordial Feeling by the universal Ego which also has a threefold nature on the other side. Then the statement will run more fully: I (as Feeling, Will, and Intellect) feel myself feeling God (as Feeling, Will and Intellect).

Still more fully the foregoing statement may be developed into the following propositions:—

(*a*) I feel primordially the All-Ego (God) as Feeling stimulating my Feeling. The raw material (Feeling of God) of Religion organized.

(*b*) I feel primordially the All-Ego as Will stimulating my Will. The raw material (Feeling of Freedom) of the moral and institutional worlds.

(c) I feel primordially the All-Ego as Intellect stimulating my Intellect. The raw material (Feeling of Knowledge) of the artistic, poetic and philosophic realms.

The common element emphasized in these propositions is the All-Ego, which we call also conscious in the wide sense of the word, the original protoplasm of all mind. The protoplasmic Ego is Consciousness.

3. Now this primordial unorganized Feeling of the All-Ego in the individual Ego must next be organized in objective forms, around which and through which new Feeling arises. This new Feeling is that of the Absolute or of the All-Ego realized, objectified, formulated — the sphere of Absolute Feeling or Sentiment. The three kinds of Sentiment we may recapitulate once more, and add some points.

(a) The Sentiment of God as distinct from the primordial Feeling of Him. The two may become antagonistic.

(b) The Sentiment of Freedom as distinct from the primordial Feeling of it. The two may become antagonistic.

(c) The Sentiment of Knowledge as distinct from the primordial Feeling of it. The two may become antagonistic.

In this tabular form we seek to bring out the fact that the original, elemental, primordial Feeling of God, of Freedom, and of Knowledge may become hostile, in fact is sure to become hostile to the organized Feeling or Sentiment of the same three — God, Freedom, Knowledge, though this second as Sentiment has its source in that first as Feeling.

Let us illustrate. There is always an attempt to go back out of organized Religion to that original, spontaneous well-head of Feeling which is often called emotional Religion. And let it be added there is a continual need of it, of this return out of formal established Religion to its primordial protoplasmic Feeling whence it sprang, for it is not created once for all but should be perpetually re-created. When, however, the two get to fighting each other (as we see often in Revivals), it is a combat between parent and child. The same struggle we observe between Freedom organized in institutions and the elemental Freedom of the Ego, which in its wrath has been often seen in history to turn against and destroy the institutional world, which is its own product and guarantee. But just now the strongest example is the feud between knowledge organized and knowledge spontaneously expressing itself in the way of immediate experience. Even in the seats of learning where, one might think, organized knowledge ought to be at home and be transmitted to the future, it is very often disparaged and ridiculed with many pretentious airs of superiority. And yet the original elemental Feeling of Knowledge should be kept alive and at work, as the creative energy antecedent to all organized science and indispensable to the same. The point is, however, not to set the two against each other, but to unite them together in a common process of which both are necessary stages. And what is true in this last case is true in the other cases. The two kinds of Religion, the two kinds of Freedom and the two kinds of Knowledge expressing themselves respectively in two kinds of Feeling, are not to remain in their dualism, but are to be reconciled in the triune movement of the Psychosis.

4. It is an old idea that Fear is the source of Religion, though we find this same idea in some recent books on Psychology written by preachers of the Gospel. *Timor fecit Deos*, said the ancient Epicurean. Rather it is the God that produces the Fear than the Fear that produces the God. For the God-consciousness must be primordial, existent before there can be any terror of Him. You must first feel God ere you can feel any Fear of Him. An animal may fear the storm, but this calls up in it no God to be afraid of and to be appeased with offerings. The Feeling of God must, therefore, pre-exist, and set to work all kinds of God-making and of religious organization. The same is true of Herbert Spencer's famous source of religion,

the worship of ancestors. This worship cannot appear till the aforesaid Feeling of God, which is born in and with Consciousness itself, renders such worship possible. All other so-called causes of Religion pre-suppose this primordial Feeling.

5. The conflict in the conception of God (that between His Transcendence and His Immanence, p. 326), has always given and is still giving much trouble to Theology and even to Philosophy. Among the philosophers who have grappled with it, the most famous is Kant, who, in his Second Book of the Transcendental Dialectic of the *Critique of Pure Reason*, develops what he deems the contradiction in the idea of God. Without going into details, we may say that Kant's whole argument rests upon two meanings which he unconsciously puts into the conception of God, who, therefore, is laden from the start with two opposite predications. On the one hand God as creator of the World and Man is transcendent, being separate from both; on the other hand God as the All, the Universe (*Omnitudo realitatis*), is within it, immanent. Thus Kant pre-supposes a Double God, whose contradiction he has no great difficulty in finding. (In like manner he presupposes a Double World in his Antinomies, and even a Double Ego in his Paralogisms.) Kant's negative conclusion is that

the conception of God contradicts itself, and hence is delusive.

And yet both these ideas, Transcendence and Immanence, have made themselves tremendously valid in the history of man's spiritual nature. Still further, every thinking person, who occupies his mind with these ideas, gives validity to both. Properly both belong to the individual Ego seeking to grasp and formulate the Universe. Still they are not to be held in opposition to each other, but are to be seen as parts or stages of the one All-Ego (the Pampsychosis), whose third part or stage is the Return out of the World through Man back to God. Thus we behold the triple form of God, World, and Man linked together into the one process of the Universe.

6. We may say another word about the Pampsychosis, which has so often risen up in the background of our thought and encompassed the whole of it, being the great Totality or the All itself. We have seen it determining the supreme forms of our three kinds of Sentiment, religious, practical, theoretic. It reveals itself as the ultimate source of our Feeling of God, of Freedom, and of Knowledge. It may be said that the three basic forms of the Ego — Feeling, Will, and Intellect — seek to attain the Pampsychosis and to manifest it, each of them doing this separately and in its own way.

But the true pampsychical Sentiment is not

reached except through the organization of these three forms — Feeling, Will, and Intellect — into one process through Psychology. It is, therefore, supremely the psychological Sentiment, as distinct from the philosophic, aesthetic, or religious Sentiments, each of which is limited to the one form of the Ego. In Religion we gave to the process of the Norm — God, Nature, and Man — the name of Pampsychosis or the All-Ego, which, however, must be further unfolded, since this All-Ego is likewise the total process of Feeling, Will, and Intellect, in each stage and in the whole of the Norm.

Psychology is in its deepest sense the science of the Pampsychosis, the Self divine, human, and even physical. The old Norm — God, Nature, Man — is quite abstract and internally separated, till it be psychically united both in its parts and in its totality through the triune act of Feeling, Will, and Intellect, which form the process of the All-Ego and constitute the theme of Psychology. The Universe itself is primarily psychical; but when it gets truly organized into a science, then it is psychological.

The highest attainment in the entire realm of Feeling, the culmination and transfiguration of the emotional man, is the pampsychical Sentiment. This not only feels the triune process of the Universe organized, and makes itself harmonious with the same, but rises to feeling itself creative of that process which created it and imparted to it the supreme gift of creativity. Such is the felt return of the individual or recipient Ego into unity with the All-Ego, in whose creative power every man and not simply the Genius, is ultimately destined to share. Even now we all may feel or rather fore-feel such a consummation aproaching from afar. Thereby we may be said to participate in the pampsychical Sentiment.

7. When the Pampsychosis puts its creative stamp upon the Ego, we have Consciousness, which seems to be at the present time the great problem exercising psychologists. In the preceding exposition of Feeling as a whole, we have had a good deal to do with it, in various relations and even under various names. We have called it the All-feeling Ego (third stage of Elemental Feeling) when it is taken as originating from the All; more commonly we name it the Psychosis when we grasp it as the movement of the Ego in and of itself, as having a volitional element; also it is the protoplasmic Ego in its primordial process. Consciousness suggests all these meanings, and more: it hints the intellectual element in Feeling, the self-reference which becomes self-cognition, or self-knowing, for Feeling must have also an intellectual element lurking in its process. Strictly Consciousness is not Self-consciousness, which

has within itself a second separation and return; this is Consciousness dividing within and getting conscious of itself, or the Ego conscious of being conscious as distinct from the non-Ego.

It must be confessed that Consciousness is not an easy term to handle. In its wide usage it embraces the two extremes, the Unconscious and the Self-conscious, as well as its own narrower meaning. Here is a brief table of it: —

Consciousness (general).
- (1) the Unconscious
- (2) the Conscious (special)
- (3) the Self-conscious.

There is no doubt that these three or rather four meanings have a tendency to run together and to produce confusion. We probably have not escaped the trouble which lies deep: so let the reader be warned. But to avoid in part at least, the ambiguities of the word we have used the compounds *sub-conscious* and *supra-conscious*, and even *pre-conscious* (see the section on *All-Feeling*). Still underneath all these variations there lies the one fact: the process of the All-Ego in the individual Ego, which thus may be regarded as in a perpetual round of self-creation within itself. It is a Whole which is continuously self-dividing and self-returning, all of which takes place through its own inner self-activity. This self-activity taken by itself we may consider as the element of Will in Consciousness, which has also the element of Intellect in its Self-cognition. For the All-Ego must know itself, since there is nothing outside of it to know or to be known, and this trait of self-knowing it imparts to the individual Ego, more particularly in the form of Intellect. But the All-Ego has no non-Ego strictly, Nature being really a part of its total process: whereas the individual Ego has the non-Ego as its stimulus to knowledge and self-knowledge. Thus Consciousness has, more or less implicitly, Feeling, Will, and Intellect, which constitute the imprint upon it of the All-Ego (Pampsychosis).

8. But with this last statement a new and deeper difficulty begins to raise its head, if it has not already made itself felt in the inquiring mind. Consciousness is represented as God-made, yet it is also evolved out of antecedent stages. Which is, then, its true source, from above or from below? It seems to come from opposite directions, having not only an evolution but also a devolution, an ascent as well as a descent. Must it arise in one way or the other, or are both ways possible, indeed necessary?

When Evolution mounting upward from Nature reaches Consciousness, there appears a vast gap in the succession, nay a direct wheeling about and inversion of the scientific order. Very puzzled is the scientist when he comes to this jumping-off place. We may take the illustrious Du Bois-Reymond as an example. Says he: "A bridge cannot be built into the realm of Consciousness" out of the realm of Nature through any manipulation of the molecules of the brain. And yet the Ego does make the passage. But how the thing is done, *ignoramus et ignorabinus*. Thus Consciousness is the eternal " world-riddle." Even the first act of Sensation can never be scientifically explained, still less can Consciousness, since it is the explicit turning around and contradiction of Nature's measured and measurable movement in Space and Time.

Coming back to Evolution, we see that the self-creative All has created an Ego which is likewise self-creative, and is a stage in the total process of that self-creative All. Such a created Ego is a necessity of the Universe, which otherwise would not be itself, not having reproduced its own very creativity which is truly its essence. Still this creative Ego is not the Universe, not the All-process in its round as *creating*, but is *created*, separated, externalized in the world, and hence moves through its own external stages towards its source, the All-Ego. So the individual Ego through its very creation as creative, must evolve, must be perpetually transcending limits; it is created as creating and so must be incessantly evolving. Behind Evolution there is an Evolution of Evolution; Evolution is itself created evolving.

Possibly it may be more simple and easy if we

say that the descent from above and the ascent from below are but two stages of a circular movement which goes forth and then comes back. Consciousness as evolving from previous lower forms is the pivot of the return out of Nature which is successive and evolutionary through Man back to the creative All-Ego from which it (Consciousness) sprang. Thus we behold the cycle of God, Nature, and Man as the completed process of both ascent and descent, of evolution and devolution. From this view-point our two directions — which gave us our first trouble — Consciousness coming from above and also from below — are seen to be two phases of one process, two segments of one circle. They through their inner opposition force us to rise to the conception of the total process of the Universe (Pampsychosis) in order to behold them as members of one harmonious Whole.

Nor must we forget that Consciousness contains internally or ideally the process of the Universe, whereby it becomes truly a stage or member of the Universe. Such is the fact which will be repeated in the remotest ramifications of the realm of Consciousness: each of its activities, however small, has the total process of it through which this minutest conscious activity bears the impress of the All-conscious One, and is connected thereby with Universe. Moreover, such a connection is to be explicitly set forth in the science of Psychology, through the interlinking of the Psychosis, which joins together the widest sweeps as well as the smallest acts of mentation.

9. The view of Genius which has been set forth in the foregoing pages (pp. 129, 298, etc.) is on all essential points quite the contrary to that of a well-known alienist and psychiatrist, Prof. Cesare Lombroso, of Turin, Italy, whose books have gone over the world and produced numerous admiring disciples. Particularly his work on *The Man of Genius* has found a considerable echo among civilized peoples, specially appealing to those who seem to be in a state of protest against civilization.

As a sort of prelude we may take one sentence out of many similar ones: "The great progressive movements of nations, in politics and religion, have *often* been brought about or at least determined by insane or half-insane persons" (*The Man of Genius*, C. 4, Eng. Trans.). We have italicized the word *often* in the preceding citation, in order to indicate a characteristic of Lombroso's writing. He is a circumspect man, and has the habit of modifying by some little word his universal propositions even when he intends them to leave the impression of being universal. So he really expects his reader to forget that small intruder *often*, which pops up briefly its unwelcome head, in the above sentence.

In this way the reader will have *often* to take some measure of Lombroso himself measuring Genius.

There are two pre-eminent religious heroes of Europe, Luther and Christ. Both of them, according to Lombroso, were insane or were decidedly tinged with insanity. The one was the founder of the Reformation, the other was the founder of Christianity itself. Both show the symptoms of a common disease called *megalomania*, or the delusion of being great men. Veritably a mighty delusion on their part as time has shown. One reader at least begins to think to himself on hearing this diagnosis: What is the matter with Prof. Lombroso? Has he not a touch of megalomania in delivering such a judgment garnished though it be with various scientific proofs so-called?

Concerning Christ the opinion of Renan, that good Christian, is cited. "The title of the son of David, the first which Jesus Christ accepted, was a fraud" which, even if innocent, indicated insane delusion. A much deeper phase of insanity was that be deemed himself the son of God, and finally to be God. For this sort of madness, found to-day in many insane asylums, a special name has been invented, Theomania or God-madness. "His Father had given him all power; nature obeyed him; he could forgive sins; he was superior to David,

Abraham, and all the prophets — a greater than Jonah is here." Surely a case of an acute form of megalomania, rising to Theomania — such must be the scientific inference. (*Op. cit.*, p. 45.)

But this is not all. Christ manifests another symptom of insanity, to which Lombroso gives the technical name of emotional anæsthesia (p. 63). Genius shows an abnormal indifference to all the tender relations of life, to parents, children, wife, benefactor. Says the author: "I have noted among all (Geniuses) a strange apathy for everything which does not concern them; as though plunged in the hypnotic condition, they did not perceive the troubles of others or even the most pressing needs of those who were dearest to them;" though at times they might get tender, this tenderness was soon burnt out, like a lit straw. Whereat Lombroso gives a list of such people among whom is Christ. For listen to some of the latter's brutal menaces: I bring not peace but a sword; I come to produce division between father and son, mother and daughter; my disciple is to hate his parents and family, etc. (p. 63). Such is the Prince of Peace, originator of Christian civilization, a man clearly afflicted with emotional anæsthesia, literally a feeling which does not feel. Is it not to be inferred that all Europe, idealizing and worshiping such a madman, is insane and has been so for quite two thousand years at least?

At this point we begin to touch the unconscious undercurrent which flows through Lombroso's book, and is the secret determining character of it from beginning to end. It is a keen though indirect critique of Europe and its civilization as embodied and promulgated in its greatest men. These are scientifically examined, classified, and pronounced madmen by the expert alienist, to be fit only for the madhouse, each having some "lesion of the brain," with a few exceptions which seem, however, to be only seeming. And as in this matter we have to study Dr. Lombroso himself, for certainly he invites it; we must record the fact that he is of Hebrew descent according to biographical notices of him. He is the Oriental settled in a strange land institutionally, whose culture and language he has acquired in a high degree, but who still feels himself an alien possibly after thousands of years of ancestral residence, and who proceeds to subject the whole European civilization at its most creative point, namely in its Great Men, to a fiercely destructive and damnatory Last Judgment. Thus Lombroso becomes a part of that marvelous Jewish phenomenon which has caused and still causes so much speculation. Here let the reflection be added that this Oriental criticism of Europe is a very old thing; it may be traced in ancient Greek writers; it appears with emphatic outlines in Herodotus, the Father of History, who gives the Persian and Egyptian damnation of Helen and the Trojan War. In the Hellenistic period it could be heard everywhere in the Macedonian and Roman Empires; we may mark it in Philo, the illustrious Jew of Alexandria, and specially in the Neo-Platonic Philosophy which was founded and formulated by Orientals (by the Egyptians Ammonius Saccas and Plotinus), and was specially propagated by Semites (the Syrians Iamblichus and Porphyry). Though Neo-Platonism claims to be a restoration of Greek Philosophy, a little study soon shows it to be quite the opposite, to be really the dissolution of the Greek and indeed of the whole European world. (See *Ancient European Philosophy*, pp. 591-9.)

Here it must be affirmed that Lombroso has brought to the surface a very important fact in the character of Christ, who was certainly one of the most self-assertive men that ever lived. The sacerdotal view puts all stress upon Christ's humility; as a kind of corrective we may look at the other side of him, and contemplate the lofty declarations of his divinity. But he was not insane in so regarding himself; on the contrary that may be cited as a supreme proof of his sanity, which all succeeding history has verified, unless of course history itself has gone wholly wrong, particularly in Europe, and God himself has made a mistake. Christ undoubtedly believed in his own Genius, had to do so in order to fulfill his mission. Some such faith may be predicated of the whole class of Geniuses. Many a poor fellow may think that he is God, or that God is in his belly, and may have to be sent to the asylum for the insane on account of megalomania. But such people do not found Christianities, produce Reformations, and change the entire spiritual character of the world. Otherwise we have to think all Europe crazy, and that I, just I, am the sane man. Who has the attack of megalomania in that case?

Certainly the religious Genius, the founder of a Religion, Prophet, Lawgiver, Reformer, has played a very important part in the development of man, uniting his tribe, his nation, perchance his race in a common inner faith as well as in an external ceremonial. It must be granted that he is an exceedingly unusual man, one who holds some communion with the governing principle of the world not attainable or intelligible to the ordinary run of people. But it does not bring us very far by calling him madman or impostor. Already we have tried to set forth his positive function and to give him his place in the movement of humanity.

When Lombroso takes up the secular Genius there is even severer treatment. The great conquerors, statesmen, as well as the poets and literary men, are in a state of "moral insanity, that loss of the moral sense, common to all men of Genius, whether sane or insane" (p. 337). Napoleon and Caesar (Lombroso's namesake) are overhauled and shown to have had epilepsy, which is a sign of insanity: "the creative power of Genius may be a form of degenerative psychosis belonging to the family of epileptic affections" (p. 336). Note the abuse of our word *psychosis*. But that is a small matter compared to the statement that "the creative power of Genius" is a degeneration, a malady, really insanity. The Genius whom we see at every important turn of the World's History directing the destiny of nations, is simply having an epileptic fit, the poor crazy fellow! Socrates, the most original teacher of morals of all time, was a degenerate, afflicted with moral insanity.

It is evident that Lombroso has a keen eye for all the human weaknesses, caprices, finite elements which are unfailingly bound up with Genius; but he has no eye at all for its mighty world-historical significance. Let him study Julius Caesar as portrayed by Plutarch or, what would be far better, by Shakespeare, who brings out in a very striking way both sides of the Genius — Caesar the epileptic, the weak mortal individual, and also Caesar the universal man of his age, the bearer of the new order, the spirit that lives after death. By the way it is a curious fact that Lombroso spares Shakespeare, probably the greatest Genius of modern Europe, who, therefore, ought to be the insanest specimen of all. Moreover Shakespeare shows the chief signs of a " degenerative psychosis " upon which Lombroso places so much stress, namely his habit of depicting insane people, of using big words, his tremendous explosions of passion, not to speak of his " emotional anaesthesia" manifested in his staying away so long from his family at Stratford.

The insanity, or at least the degeneracy of the literary and artistic Genius, is a theme that has been specially wrought out in a book called *Degeneration* by Max Nordau, Lombroso's fervid disciple, often with a bitterness of criticism which defeats its own end, even when just. In another book Nordau distinguished himself by a furious attack on the " conventional lies " of civilized society, certainly a fruitful theme. In a different sphere, that of the socio-economic Order, the works of Lassalle and Marx may be deemed an Oriental criticism of European civilization, suggesting a parallelism with the viewpoint of Lombroso and Nordau.

Now we hold that a criticism of Europe as a whole is a legitimate theme. But if given from the Orient, out of which Europe sprang, it is likely, amid all its excellences, to end negatively. A positive world-critique of Europe must naturally come from the other direction, from the Occident, which is an evolution out of Europe, as Europe is an evolution out of the Orient. It is the next higher stage, in the development of civilization, which is to criticise and to explain the antecedent stage.

In like manner the criticism of Genius should show its positive place and work in the supreme Order of History, though its negative, individual side need not be overlooked. No man is a hero to his valet, says the adage, since the valet sees only wherein the hero is like to or perchance weaker than other men. Still the hero exists in spite of his valet. And the Genuis also, we cannot help believing will continue to appear and to do his work in the world, without being shut up in an insane asylum under the charge of an expert alienist, who " knows better."

10. On looking back at the total movement of Feeling, the student can find illustrated the various points which were set forth in the *Prolegomena*. He will note the working of the Psychosis and its method of interconnecting all the divisions of the science with the entirety of the same. And the hope may be permitted that he will reflect on the pedagogical trend of the foregoing way of considering Psychology. This

book on the Feeling with its somewhat extensive and intricate organization is intended to stamp upon the student the decided impress of the cyclical procedure of education, which was suggested long ago by the old Greeks, though not elaborated. In training the human mind, the fundamental native process of that mind should be followed, and the Psychosis in one form or other should become the driving wheel of Pedagogy, as it is of Psychology.

But now this realm of Feeling, with its turning inward from without, is to be turned outward from within — whereat a wholly new realm of the Ego begins to appear — that of Will, the second great stage of psychological science.